ROME AND THE WESTERN GREEKS
350 BC–AD 200

ROME AND THE WESTERN GREEKS
350 BC–AD 200

Conquest and acculturation in
southern Italy

Kathryn Lomas

London and New York

First published 1993
by Routledge
11 New Fetter Lane, London EC4P 4EE

Simultaneously published in the USA and Canada
by Routledge
29 West 35th Street, New York, NY 10001

Typeset in 10 on 12 point Garamond by
Computerset, Harmondsworth, Middlesex
Printed in Great Britain by
T.J. Press (Padstow) Ltd, Padstow, Cornwall

British Library Cataloguing in Publication Data
A catalogue record for this book is available from the British Library

Library of Congress Cataloging in Publication Data
Lomas, Kathryn
Rome and the Western Greeks, 350 BC–AD 200: conquest and acculturation
in Southern Italy/Kathryn Lomas.
p. cm.
Includes bibliographical references and index.
1. Magna Graecia (Italy)–History. 2. Rome–History–Republic, 510-30 BC 3.
Rome–History–Empire, 30 BC–284 AD 4. Rome–Relations–Italy–Magna
Graecia. 5. Magna Graecia (Italy)–Relations–Rome. 6. Acculturation–Italy–
History. I. Title.
DG55.M3L66   1993
937–dc20   92-40807

ISBN 0-415-05022-7

Contents

CONTENTS

Illustrations

Preface

Studies of Magna Graecia and its constituent cities have multiplied rapidly over the past twenty years. The vast amount of excavation in the region has greatly increased the evidence at our disposal, and surveys have added immeasurably to our understanding of the economy and society of southern Italy. Despite this, it is a region which remains relatively little known in the English-speaking world. In particular, the later history of Magna Graecia – the Hellenistic and Roman periods – have not received the attention they deserve, despite posing some fascinating historical problems.

This book originated as a Ph.D. thesis for the University of Newcastle-upon-Tyne, which aimed to explore selected problems connected with the Roman conquest of the South and the post-conquest processes of assimilation. In the evolution from thesis into book, I have widened the scope of the discussion in order to place some of the more specific issues into a broader context, and to consider the conquest of the South as a case study of Roman treatment of a particular region. Given the enormous range of archaeological material now at our disposal, this cannot hope to be a complete synthesis of all available data, but I hope that it will contribute to the debate on the history of Magna Graecia.

I would like to thank the British School at Rome for its generous support of the doctoral research project on which this book is based. I would also like to thank the supervisor of the original thesis, Mr J.J. Paterson, and also Dr T.J. Cornell, Prof. M.H. Crawford, Prof. J.G.F. Powell, Prof. B.B. Sheftopn and Dr A.J.S. Spawforth for their help and advice at various stages of preparation.

Plate 1 appears by permission of the Greek Museum, University of Newcastle-upon-Tyne, and Plates 6–12 by courtesy of the Trustees of the British Museum. All other maps and photographs are the author's own.

Abbreviations

The majority of abbreviations used in this volume follow the conventions of the relevant volume of *L'Année Philologique*.

AE	*L'Année Épigraphique*
AAAN	*Atti di Reale Accademia di Archeologia, Lettere e Belle Arti di Napoli*
ABSA	*Annual of the British School at Athens*
AC	*Archeologia Classica*
ACMG	*Atti di Convegno sulla Studi della Magna Grecia*
AION	*Annali dell'Istituto Universitario Orientale di Napoli. Dipartimento di Studi del Mondo Classico e del Mediterraneo Antico. Sezione di Archeologia e storia antica*
AJP	*American Journal of Philology*
Ant. Journ.	*Antiquaries Journal*
ARAN	See *AAAN* (alternative convention)
Arch. Anz.	*Archäologischer Anzeiger*
ARID	*Analecta Romana Instituti Damici*
ASCL	*Archivio Storico per la Calabria e la Lucania*
ASMG	*Atti e Memorie della Società Magna Grecia*
Atti Accad. Patav.	*Memorie dell'Accademia Patavina, Classe di Scienze Morali, Lettere e Arti*
BCH	*Bulletin de Correspondance Héllenique*
CIL	*Corpus Inscriptionum Latinarum*
CP	*Classical Philology*
CQ	*Classical Quarterly*
CS	*Critica Storica*
DdA	*Dialoghi di Archeologia*

ABBREVIATIONS

EE	*Ephemeris Epigraphica*
FD	*Fouille de Delphes*
HSCP	*Harvard Studies in Classical Philology*
IDel.	*Inscriptions de Délos*
IG	*Inscriptiones Graecae*
IGRR	Cagnat, R. (1906–27) *Inscriptiones Graecae ad Res Romanas Pertinentes*
ILLRP	*Inscriptiones Latinae Liberae Rei Publicae*
ILP	Mello, M. and Voza, G. (1968) *Le Iscrizioni Latine di Paestum*, Naples
ILS	*Inscriptiones Latinae Selectae*
J. Phil.	*Journal of Philology*
JRS	*Journal of Roman Studies*
MAL	*Monumenta Antichi dell'Accademia dei Lincei*
MAMA	*Monumenta Asiae Minoris Antiqua*
MDAI(R)	*Mitteilung des Deutschen Archäologischen Instituts, Römische Abteilung*
MEFR	*Mélanges d'Archéologie et d'Histoire de l'École Française de Rome*
Mem. Linc.	*Memorie della Classe di Scienze Morali, Storiche e Filologiche dell'Academia Nazionale dei Lincei*
MG	*Magna Grecia*
NSc	*Notizie degli Scavi di Antichità. Atti dell'Accademia dei Lincei*
Num. Chron.	*Numismatic Chronicle*
OGIS	*Orientis Graecae Inscriptiones Selectae*
PBSR	*Papers of the British School at Rome*
PCPS	*Proceedings of the Cambridge Philological Society*
PdP	*La Parola del Passato*
PECS	Stillwell, R., Macdowell, W.L. and McAllister, M. (1976) *Princeton Encyclopedia of Classical Sites*, Princeton
QS	*Quaderni di Storia*
RAAN	*Rendiconti dell'Accademia di Archeologia, Lettere e Belle Arti di Napoli*
RE	Pauly–Wissowa, *Realencyclopädie der Classischen Altertumswissenschaft*
Rend. Ist. Lomb.	*Rendiconti dell'Istituto Lombardo, Classe di Lettere, Scienze Morali e Storiche*
Rend. Linc.	*Rendiconti della Classe di Scienze Morali, Storiche e Filologiche dell'Academia Nazionale dei Lincei*

RFIC	*Rivista di Filologia e d'Istruzione Classica*
RIGI	*Rivista Indo-Greco-Italica*
RSA	*Rivista Storica dell'Antichità*
RSI	*Rivista Storica Italiana*
SEG	*Supplementum Epigraphicum Graecum*
SGDI	*Sammlung der Griechischen Dialekt-Inschriften*
SR	*Studi Romani*
Syll.³	*Sylloge Inscriptionum Graecarum*, 3rd edn
TAPA	*Transactions of the American Philological Association*

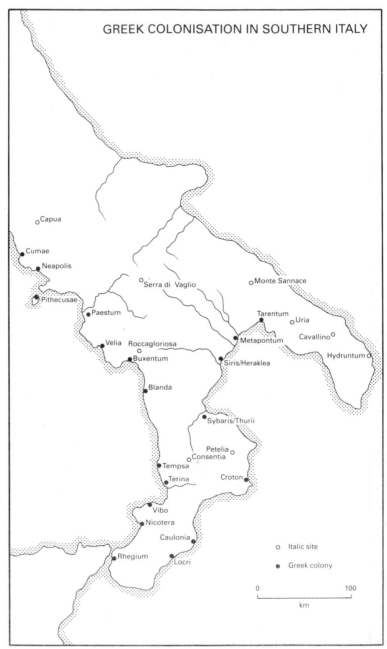

GREEK COLONISATION IN SOUTHERN ITALY

○Capua

●Cumae

Neapolis

○Serra di Vaglio

○Monte Sannace

Pithecusae

Paestum

Tarentum

○Uria

Cavallino○

Velia Roccagloriosa○

Metapontum

Buxentum

Siris/Heraklea

Hydruntum○

Blanda

Sybaris/Thurii

Petelia

Consentia○ ○

Tempsa

Terina

Croton

Vibo

Nicotera

Caulonia

Rhegium

Locri

○ Italic site

● Greek colony

0   100

km

Map 1 Greek colonisation in southern Italy

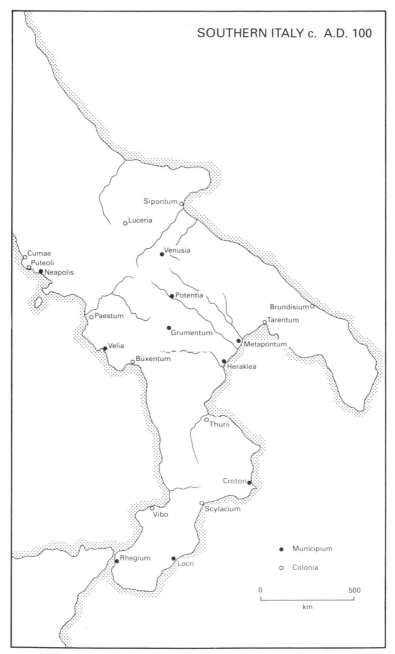

SOUTHERN ITALY c. A.D. 100

Sipontum ○
○ Luceria
Cumae ○
Puteoli ○
● Neapolis
● Venusia
○ Paestum
● Potentia
Brundisium ○
Velia ●
● Grumentum
Tarentum ○
Buxentum ○
● Metapontum
● Heraklea
○ Thurii
Croton ●
Vibo ○
○ Scylacium
Rhegium ●
● Locri

● Municipium
○ Colonia

0 ⟷ 500
km

Map 2 Southern Italy *c.* AD 100

xiii

Introduction

*. . . magnamque Graeciam, quae nunc quidem
deleta est, tum florebat . . .*[1]

This fundamental contrast, articulated by Cicero in the first century BC, represents the dominant view of the region known as Magna Graecia in the years after the Roman conquest – a region once stupendously wealthy, even decadently so, now shorn of its past glories and largely deserted. It is an image perpetuated not only by ancient authors but also in many modern perceptions of the region. The apparent poverty and depopulation of the region of southern Italy known as the Mezzogiorno in more recent times may have unconsciously reinforced the dismal images of Magna Graecia preserved for us in Roman and Greek literature alike during the Roman Empire. Since Late Antiquity, the majority of cities which were Greek foundations have indeed been abandoned, preserved only as picturesque ruins, if at all.[2] Those which continued as urban centres – Naples, Taranto, Reggio – were far distant from the new centres of power in Italy. It seems, though, that these images of desolation from both the ancient world and from more recent times have coloured our perceptions of Magna Graecia too much. Over the last thirty years, there has been a tremendous, and ever increasing, volume of archaeological evidence from both survey and excavation in the Mezzogiorno which is forcing a radical reassessment of many aspects of its history, including the history of Magna Graecia. Slowly but surely, the 'dark ages' of the Greek colonies, following their conquest by Rome in the third century BC, are emerging into the light. It is becoming clear that the history of Magna Graecia was not simply one of frenetic overachievement followed by decline and desolation, but that many of the Greek cities continued to flourish under Roman rule and played an important role in the development of Roman Italy.

1

Despite the comparative lack of evidence, Roman relations with Magna Graecia and the post-conquest development of the Greek South is an extremely diverse topic, but one which provides important insights into the nature of Roman expansion within Italy, and that complex of processes of acculturation which is frequently termed Romanisation. The great differences between the Greek communities of the South and the other peoples encountered by Rome during the conquest of Italy serve to illuminate the adaptability of Rome in dealing with the other areas, and also to underline the importance of regional factors in the development of Italy under Roman rule.

The history of the Roman expansion in Italy, and the gradual absorption of Roman influences and way of life by the Italian communities, is extremely diverse in the number and variety of factors which must be taken into consideration. Experiences differed widely from region to region, according to the reactions to Rome's presence by the indigenous population, the economy of the region, its political and administrative organisation, level of urbanisation, and a number of other factors. In the central and southern Apennines, for instance, the resistance put up by the Samnites to Roman expansion meant that the region was subject to a series of punitive settlements imposed by Rome and to a high degree of Roman control and interference. Land confiscation opened the way to influxes of new population; the predominantly non-urban organisation of the region led to central pressure towards urbanisation, breaking up the existing socio-economic structures; Roman municipal organisation replaced the Oscan non-urban administrative arrangements based on villages (*pagi*).

In contrast, Campania was urbanised on the lines of the Greek city-state, or *polis*, well before the Roman conquest. Diplomatic relations with Rome were mixed, but not uniformly hostile. With the exception of the aftermath of the Punic Wars, when reprisals for disloyalty during Hannibal's invasion included the introduction of direct rule by Rome, there was remarkably little interference in the life of the Campanian cities.[3]

It is dangerous, therefore, to generalise about the Romanisation of Italy. Despite Finley's strictures on the subject of local histories ('In the end, I believe that the history of *individual* ancient towns is a *cul-de-sac*, given the limits of the available (and potential) documentation . . .'), the study of individual cities, or in this case a group of related cities, must surely be valid in such a case, where the broader issues within a subject can only be approached adequately from the basis of detailed studies of individual areas.[4] The conquest and Romanisation of Magna Graecia

2

must be approached as a case study, by which a single region of Italy, albeit a large and diverse one, can be examined with a view to providing some detailed information about the ways in which it responded to the political and cultural expansion of Rome.[5]

Magna Graecia is of particular interest precisely because of its difference from other regions of Italy encountered by Rome. It was economically, politically and geographically diverse, stretching from Campania to southern Apulia, and united only by the fact that all the Greek colonies were coastal in location. It was non-Italian in culture, language and political structure, possessing a well-established Greek urban tradition. As such, it approximates only to Etruria, among other areas of Italy, and posed unique problems for Rome. Falling under Roman influence during a particularly fraught period of south Italian history, which was characterised by bouts of intense conflict between Greeks and Oscans with all its attendant disruptions to the life of the region, Magna Graecia posed many practical problems. The group of Oscan-speaking peoples, including the Lucanians, Bruttians, Samnites and Campanians, who occupied the majority of southern Italy, were aggressively expansionist for most of the fourth century BC and posed a major threat to both Greeks and Romans. Alliances between Greeks and Greeks, Greeks and Oscans, and Greeks and Romans were unstable and impermanent. Further to this, the political life of many cities was bedevilled by *stasis* and instability, a situation which was reflected in the shifting patterns of alliances and diplomatic contacts. Within Rome itself, there were ambivalent attitudes to expansion in the South. The ever-present Samnite threat tied down much of Rome's manpower in central Italy and there were intermittent hostilities in Etruria, Gallic raids, and political tensions within Rome to contend with, all factors which drew attention away from the South. It was not, however, the practical difficulties which made Magna Graecia so unique in Roman experience. Other regions had put up much greater resistance to Rome and were much more difficult to control. The factor which makes for such uniqueness is the cultural difference, the Greekness of the region, and its physical and cultural location.

By the end of the second century BC, the conquest of southern Italy, Sicily and the eastern Mediterranean had brought Rome into close contact with the Hellenistic world and with Greek culture. By the beginning of the first century, Hellenism was becoming increasingly acceptable amongst the Roman élite. Over the next fifty years, Greek culture became a central part of the education and life of the Roman upper classes, and played an important role in shaping the intellectual life of the late republic and early empire.[6] In this sense, Hellenism (and, by extension, the Greeks) occupied a unique and privileged position in the Roman world view. At the same time, there was also a deep ambivalence towards all things Greek. Reaction to the Hellenism of second-century aristocrats such as Scipio and his circle of associates in some quarters was one of horror that a Roman general should behave in such a manner. Hellenising behaviour was stigmatised as unroman, scandalous, and almost treasonable.[7] Even at a later date, when Hellenism had become much more acceptable for wealthy and educated Romans, there was still a residual sense that contemporary Greeks, in particular those of Asiatic origin, were degenerate descendants of the fifth-century Greeks whose literature, intellectual achievements and material culture were so much admired. Nevertheless, Hellenism played a central role in the life of the élite and those who aspired to join that élite. Unlike most of the other local cultures of Italy and the provinces, it retained a high profile throughout the Late Republic and Empire.

The interest in Hellenism among the Roman élite placed Magna Graecia in a position of considerable importance. Although other areas of Italy, notably Etruria and parts of Lucania, Apulia and Bruttium, were Hellenised to some degree, the region was unique in being the only direct Greek settlement on the Italian mainland. Prior to the Roman conquest, it was the point from which Greek influence was diffused throughout southern Italy, a process which is reflected in the adoption of the Greek alphabet and language, Greek architecture and fortifications, and Greek material goods. Nor was the process only one way. Many of the Italiote cities (i.e. Greek cities of Italy, as opposed to Italian ones, or to the Greeks of the rest of the Greek world) show signs of having absorbed Oscan and Messapian features. At a later date, Magna Graecia was on the periphery both of the Greek world and of Roman Italy, but it was the point at which these very different worlds overlapped, culturally and geographically. As such, it was an important point of diffusion of Hellenism in Italy, from the early contacts between Greeks and Italians in southern Italy to the influx of Greek influence into Roman Italy.[8] This was not a simple process, however. As conquests in the eastern Mediterranean brought Rome into increasingly close contact with the Hellenistic world, Greek influence was disseminated by direct contact with the Greek East to a much greater degree. The colonies of southern Italy, some of them discredited by their enmity towards Rome, were no longer the primary source of Greek influence in Italy. Nevertheless, they retained an important role in the Hellenisation of Rome and Italy. A large number of traders operating between Italy and the Aegean were of South Italian origin, both Greek and Oscan. Cultural contacts still operated, with writers, scholars and athletes from the Eastern Empire gravitating towards Magna Graecia, drawn by the opportunities for patronage afforded by working in Italy. During the Empire, patronage by emperors with philhellenic sympathies as well as by the Italian and Roman élites provided much increased encouragement for the survival of Hellenism in Magna Graecia, giving a graphic illustration of the continuing importance of the Hellenism of southern Italy, both to the Roman élite and to the civic identity of the Italiote cities.

This peripheral, yet curiously pivotal, role played by Magna Graecia in relation to both Greek and Roman history may go some way to explain why relatively few attempts have been made to write a history of the region in its own right. Apart from Ciaceri's monumental *Storia della Magna Grecia* published between 1926 and 1930, there has been a notable lack of works of synthesis on the region as a whole, despite the many valuable studies of individual cities and aspects of the development of the region. Because of its peripheral position, Magna Graecia does not fit naturally into a history of either the Greek or the Roman world. Unlike other regions of Italy, there are enough literary sources to allow a very bare account of the history of the region, but not enough to allow for a full-scale chronological account of events and personalities, such as can be written for Rome or for Athens. In a recent work, Pallottino has pointed out the inherent fallacy of assuming that a history of non-Roman Italy cannot be written, simply because such a work must inevitably concentrate on cultural, political and socio-economic structures, an *histoire des mentalités* rather than an *histoire des événements*, a narrative of events.[9] Pallottino's arguments for the construction of a history of Italy rather than of Rome refer principally to the period prior to 270 BC, but the same arguments could equally well be applied to the Italy of the Later Republic and Early Empire, and in particular to an area such as Magna Graecia, with its great diversity of evidence.

It is all too easy to create a very 'Romano-centric' view of history, but this need not necessarily be the case. While emphasis on the Roman point of view is to some extent inescapable, given the nature of the sources available, this can be counteracted by considering events in their local, Italian context, and by using all the evidence at the historian's disposal – archaeological, epigraphic, numismatic and linguistic, as well as literary – to build up a complete profile of a region and its interactions with Rome. The complex cultural, linguistic and political character of southern Italy provides a good illustration of the need to consider the interaction between Rome and Italy on both a regional and an Italian basis, giving due weight to local considerations. Throughout the period 350–90 BC, the Greek cities of southern Italy appear to have maintained a distinct local identity and to have been influenced very largely, in their response to events, by local factors.

ACCULTURATION IN MAGNA GRAECIA: ROMANISATION AND HELLENISATION

One problem in the study of Magna Graecia which must be confronted is that of terminology. The concept of Romanisation, or acculturation, is one which is central to any regional study or analysis of relations with Rome, and which requires discussion and definition. However, terms such as 'Romanisation' and 'Hellenisation' are rightly viewed as ill-defined and unsatisfactory in their implication that cultural influences are always transmitted in one direction only, from a dominant to a subordinate culture.[10] This is a distortion of the nature of cultural change and interaction, since it is very rare that these are simple one-way processes. In the case of interactions between Roman and Greek culture, the processes are very complex and far from being uni-directional.[11] In southern Italy, there is the additional complication that there was already a considerable degree of interaction between Oscan, Messapian and Greek culture before the region ever came under Roman control. This factor poses a terminological problem in that 'accultura-tion' merely describes a process and does not allow the user to define the various ethnic elements – Greek, Oscan, Messapian or Roman – which may be present in any given cultural transaction. For present purposes, the terms 'Hellenism' and 'Romanisation' will be used, on the under-standing that these are not mutually exclusive terms. In a recent work, Bowersock has made a powerful case for the use of 'Hellenism' rather than 'Hellenisation' in that it preserves the concept of a set of cultural ideas and artefacts which can be transmitted as a whole or in part and adapted in various ways, without the implication of dominance or cultural imperialism.[12] Romanisation is a rather more problematic term to define, since Rome was in fact politically dominant and this undoubt-edly affected the process of cultural transmission. What is certain is that Romanisation cannot be regarded as a simple linear process operating at the same rate and in the same manner at all levels of society.[13] As a loose definition, the process could be described as the transmission of a characteristically Roman set of cultural attributes and assumptions, assuming that the speed and mode of transmission and the nature of their reception varies according to the nature of the recipient and the social and economic level at which the transmission operates at any given moment.

It is clear from studies of various regions of Italy that Romanisation cannot be regarded as synonymous with the political unification which was the consequence of the extension of the citizenship in 90/89 BC. It is even doubtful whether the process can be regarded as complete by the Augustan period in southern Italy, although there is evidence for the gradual abandonment of local cults and shrines, local dialects and other local customs.[14] Clearly, the dissemination of Roman influence must have been facilitated by the political unification, and the need for administrative coherence undoubtedly led to a greater degree of uniformity in municipal government, but even here considerable variations remained. In this and other fields, the traditions of the different areas of Italy, their political and social organisation, distance from Rome, language and numerous other factors had a profound effect on the means and the rate by which Roman culture was assimilated. Even within the area under consideration, the communities studied are very diverse, with only a very general linguistic and cultural unity. This can be seen in the vast differences in their treatment by Rome, and their responses to it, from the early and complete assimilation of Cumae and Paestum, to the long continuity of Greek language and culture at Naples and Rhegium.

The converse of this is also true, namely that Roman attitudes to Italian communities varied widely, and were in themselves a factor which influenced acculturation. It seems likely that the degree of uniformity enforced by Rome, both in diplomatic contacts before the Social War and in municipal administration after 89 BC, can be over-emphasised. There is evidence that the nature of relations with Rome before the extension of the franchise had considerable impact on later assimilation of Roman influences. For instance, Cumae, which had a large number of Italian inhabitants and acquired *civitas sine suffragio* at an early date, and Paestum which was also Italicised and had colonial status, are both communities which show a high degree of Romanisation in their social structure and civic life. There are also other instances in which cities were drawn into contact with Rome by reason of Roman influence. Cumae is known to have benefited from Augustus's interest in the cult of Apollo and the Sibyl, while Naples gained a considerable amount of imperial patronage as a result of official interest in the Greek games. All three cities have a very different cultural and ethnic profile, despite their common Greek origins, and the varied nature of their

7

interactions with Rome illustrates very clearly the multifarious nature of the processes known as acculturation.

THE EMERGENCE OF A REGIONAL IDENTITY

Another central question which must be discussed is that of the concept of Magna Graecia, or *Megale Hellas*, and what it signified in the ancient world. Definitions of what areas of Italy and/or Sicily constituted Magna Graecia are almost as numerous as the authors who use the term. The region which is known to modern historians as Magna Graecia is a large area, stretching from Cumae to Tarentum but occupying only a restricted strip of territory along the coast for most of this distance. It contained a disparate collection of cities with differing social and political structures, different economic interests and different networks of alliances both in Greece and in Italy. Not unnaturally, there were many possibilities for conflict, and interstate warfare was common in the history of pre-Roman Magna Graecia, but there were also signs that they had some perception of common Greekness which made them distinct from their Italian neighbours. The strength of this perception of common heritage and community of interest, relative to the opposing pressure to Italicise and come to terms with the other inhabitants of Italy, including the Romans, is something which played an important part in shaping the history of the region.

As a term used to describe the Western Greek colonies, *Megale Hellas* first appears in the sources at a late date, and also lacks any defined meaning.[15] References are also surprisingly few in number. Among those ancient authors who use it, there is little consensus as to which areas actually constitute Magna Graecia. It was sometimes equated with the notion of *Italia*, but could also refer to more specific portions of southern Italy, principally to all or part of the coastal areas colonised by the Greeks.

The chronology of *Megale Hellas* is inexact in the extreme. It first occurs in the sixth century, although the exact date and interpretation are open to question. The earliest appearances of Magna Graecia in Greek literature are in Pindar and Euripides,[16] dating it to at least the fifth century BC, and possibly earlier. These instances, however, seem to imply a wider and more general meaning than that which is customary among later authors. It clearly embraces the whole of the Greek world, and does not define any particular part of it. The first appearance of *Megale Hellas* as an exclusively Italian entity is comparatively late. A fragment of Timaeus preserved by a scholiast on Plato's Phaedrus makes reference to *Megale Hellas*, which suggests that it had acquired its exclusively Italian connotations by the fourth century, but this passage is problematic and it is not at all certain that Timaeus actually used the phrase *Megale Hellas*.[17] The first absolutely unambiguous appearance of Magna Graecia in an Italian context is in Polybios, writing in the second century BC, but with reference to the sixth century.[18] He describes the exile of the Pythagoreans from many of the Greek colonies and the subsequent formation of the Italiote League, saying that the region of Italy in which these events took place was known as *Megale Hellas*. Roman authors have a tendency to be more specific still. Pliny implies that Magna Graecia was the region between Locri and Tarentum, a definition which is followed broadly by Silius Italicus, Ptolemy and Pseudo-Scymnus. Servius' commentary on the Aeneid suggests that it stretched from Cumae to Tarentum, as does Seneca. Strabo is less specific, but implies that Magna Graecia stretched from Paestum to Tarentum, but included Sicily.[19]

So far, the general trend seems to be the inverse of the development of the concept of *Italia*, originally only a small part of Calabria, but later comprising the whole of peninsular Italy.[20] Whereas *Italia* grew in size and scope in the later sources, Magna Graecia shrank, or perhaps became more strictly defined. In the earliest sources, Magna Graecia is the Greek world as a whole. By the fourth century, it has come to mean the Greeks of Italy, and by the Roman period it is being defined increasingly specifically with reference to particular areas of southern Italy. In both these instances, political, cultural and ethnic identities are constructed with reference to changing circumstances, both internal and external, and are being constantly redefined.

One of the problems raised by this brief survey of the evidence is the position of Sicily. Of the surviving sources, only Strabo includes it as part of Magna Graecia, and modern opinion is deeply divided over whether it was truly part of Magna Graecia or not. Momigliano has argued that Sicily was indeed part of the earlier definition of Magna Graecia but was later excluded as part of the process of narrowing down and specifying more exactly the definition of the region.[21] We know, on his own admission, that Strabo made extensive use of the work of the Sicilian writer Antiochus, and may also have used the works of Timaeus, also a Sicilian, a fact which may go some way to explain the amount of space devoted by Strabo to the island.[22] However, most ancient authors made some use of earlier authorities and this cannot be regarded as decisive. The debate about whether Sicily was part of Magna Graecia is ultimately not resolvable, but it is true to say that the exclusion of Sicily from most definitions of Magna Graecia at some stage between the fourth and first centuries BC is consistent with the other evidence for the progressive definition of the region.

Another group of references, however, proposes a different view of Magna Graecia. Pompeius Trogus makes the startling assertion that the Greeks occupied *'non partem sed universam ferme Italiam'* ('not just part, but almost all of Italy'), thereby equating Magna Graecia with the whole of Italy.[23] This same theme is picked up in Latin literature, and relates to the notion that Rome was itself a Greek *polis*.[24] It contrasts sharply with the trend towards a more stringent definition, in which *Italia* clearly encapsulates the notion of Magna Graecia.

Clearly there are two strands to the ancient sources for Magna Graecia, but they are not necessarily irreconcilable. The first, and more pervasive of the two, may be in part a product of more extensive exploration of Italy and an increasing understanding of the geography of the South, but it may also have a wider significance. Magna Graecia was a region which had shown considerable hostility to Rome and was not fully subdued until 200 BC, if then. The process of narrowing the definition of Magna Graecia can potentially be seen as a process of reduction or belittlement, hinted at by Pliny's scornful assertion that the Greeks were demonstrating their boastful and vainglorious nature by calling such a small area Great Greece.[25] This would certainly be consistent with other sources for the history of Magna Graecia, which are uniformly hostile and derogatory towards the Italiotes, stressing their perceived combination of weakness, arrogance and decadent behaviour. On the other hand, the increasing pervasiveness and accept-ability of Greek culture amongst the Roman élite during the Late Republic and Early Empire meant that the idea of a Greek Italy, and Rome as a Greek *polis*, had its attractions, particularly if that Hellenism could be related to a heroic age and thus distanced from the less desirable characteristics attributed to contemporary Greeks.

Several attempts have been made to trace a single origin for the idea of Magna Graecia. Calderone and Musti have argued persuasively that since the most extensive use of the term is found in those sources which relate to Pythagoreanism, either directly or through their use of earlier authorities,[26] the recognition of Magna Graecia as an area with geo-graphical and cultural unity may be attributable to the Pythagoreans, and have come into use during the fourth century.[27] The importance of the role played by the Pythagoreans in shaping the political and intellectual history of southern Italy means that their world-view was undoubtedly influential in the development of a concept of Magna

10

Graecia, but many other influences and contributory factors were also at work. Napoli's suggestion that recognition of Magna Graecia was a late development which post-dated the Roman conquest raises some interesting questions but rather oversimplifies the issue and fails to take into account the earlier Greek evidence.[28] The apparent trend towards narrower and more specific definitions in the later sources does indeed suggest that the Roman conquest in some way changed perceptions of the region, but there was certainly some sense of regional identity before the third and second centuries BC, even if, as seems likely, it was less clearly developed. What seems to emerge from a brief survey of the evidence is a gradual chronological progression towards a specific definition and sense of regional identity which was influenced by a number of different factors.

Aside from chronological problems, the question which naturally raises itself concerns the 'greatness' of Magna Graecia. In what sense was it Magna (or *Megale*)? The very phrase, with its stress on the greatness of Great Greece, invites a comparison and poses the question, greater than what?[29] The early usages of *Megale Hellas* are clearly in a territorial sense to draw the distinction between the Greek world as a whole, and Greece as a geographical unit. Later, the meaning is less clear. Cicero claims that it acquired the name because of its great wealth and opulent material culture,[30] and there are also hints that it may be a reference to the reputation for intellectual pre-eminence fostered by the Pythagoreans. It is possibly this theme which later became debased as the *topos* of Italiote luxury and decadence. The implied comparison is with the Greek cities of the Aegean, but this was later turned against the Italiotes, who were satirised by Pliny for claiming that such a small region was Great Greece.[31]

There seems, then, to be a major change in the scope and interpretation of the name Magna Graecia which represents a broad chronological development and which reflects changes in political consciousness and sense of identity. One of the problems in studying this region is that we have no reliable first-hand evidence from Magna Graecia and thus very little idea of the extent to which the Italiotes themselves had a sense of communal regional identity. There are many examples of strife between the Greek cities and the region is a very diverse one, but the existence of the Italiote League argues that there was some sense of common Greek identity among the Italiotes from the sixth century onwards. Later, however, things became more complicated as the distinction between Greeks and Italians blurred and still more so when Roman administrative patterns and Roman culture became a feature of Italian life. As early as the fourth century BC, it becomes obvious that there was considerable contact and cultural diffusion between Greeks and Italians, despite the fact that they continued to fight each other on a regular basis. There is considerable archaeological evidence for the growing Hellenisation of some areas of Bruttium, Lucania and Apulia, for the tendency of some Italians, during the fourth century, to adopt an urban organisation based on the Greek *polis*, and for the absorption of Italians into some Greek cities.[32]

Later, from the second century BC onwards, there was increasingly strong Roman influence in southern Italy, coupled with a growing interest in Hellenism on the part of the Roman élite, which culminated in the imperial endorsement of Greek culture by some of the more philhellenic emperors. One of the effects of this was the generation of renewed interest in the Greek past of southern Italy. There is abundant literary evidence, much of it of imperial date, of Greek foundation myths, mainly concerning Herakles or Homeric heroes, which became attached to Italian cities. According to Vergil, the Bruttian city of Petelia was founded by Philoctetes. Other Homeric founders include Antenor in the Veneto and Diomedes in Apulia. Jason is cited in connection with the sanctuary of Argive Hera near Paestum, and Odysseus and his companions are commemorated in a number of Calabrian cities.[33] These appear as early as the fourth century BC, but are given a high profile by later authors, a fact which mirrors a similar emphasis on Greek heroic foundation myths in the Eastern Empire. In both southern Italy and the Eastern Empire, Greek priesthoods, festivals, magistracies and the trappings of civic life were revived or given greater prominence. Greek inscriptions have been found at Naples, Rhegium, and Velia, recording Greek festivals and ceremonies. Literary sources also demonstrate the continuing importance of Hellenism, particularly on the Bay of Naples, and the crucial role of the Roman élite in encouraging this revival.[34]

The changes in the shifting perceptions of Magna Graecia, and the added prominence given to them, are closely related to these changes in the cultural and political climate of Italy. As already noted, the increasing narrowness of the term is consistent with the general tone of the Roman sources on Magna Graecia, and also with the administrative regionalisation of Italy imposed by Augustus. At the same time, the privileged position of Hellenism in Roman Italy provided the impetus for an increasing interest in the Greek history of southern Italy and in the creation of a specifically Greek regional identity. This change is also a reflection of an increasingly Italicised world view. The Greeks notoriously did not have a strong sense of national identity in anything other than a broad cultural sense. They maintained a sense of the distinction between Greeks and barbarians,[35] based mainly on linguistic and cultural differences, but they did not have a sense of Greece as a political unit. As noted by Finley, their political loyalties were restricted to the *polis* and the *ethnos*.[36] In Italy, however, there were a number of ethnically distinct units – Latins, Oscans, Etruscans, Greeks, Messapians etc. – which had their own unique identities as both cultural and political units. The metamorphosis of Magna Graecia from a loosely defined phrase denoting the entire Greek world to a limited and precise area is a direct reflection of Roman or Italian perceptions of regional and ethnic boundaries.

THE SOURCE MATERIAL

Any attempt to reconstruct a history of Magna Graecia is bedevilled by a major and fundamental problem, namely the inadequate nature of the written sources. Such sources as there are for the history of the Italiotes survive principally as scattered comments and fragments rather than as coherent narrative. This body of evidence for the Hellenistic and Roman periods presents a problem, for a number of reasons. First, these sources are, for the most part, considerably later in date than the period which they describe. There are comments about the contemporary state of Magna Graecia in some sources of Roman date, but there are no contemporary accounts of the earlier history of the area. Some fragments and quotations from earlier authors survive – principally Timaeus, although there are also extant fragments of Antiochus, Philistus, Theopompus and other Italiote historians – and attempts have been made to reconstruct the content of their work, but few firm conclusions can be drawn.[37] Second, and more importantly, the sources are all, almost without exception, written from the standpoint of support for Roman power, of a period in which the majority of the Italiote cities were in opposition to Rome. This clearly raises the problem of anti-Italiote bias, particularly those sources which deal with the period of conquest and conflict. This body of material, while retaining some historical value, essentially illustrates ambivalence of Roman attitudes towards the Greeks and crystallises these into literary stereotypes, rather than reflecting historical reality. When contrasted with non-literary forms of evidence, it can be shown that a quite different, and much more positive, history of Roman relations with Magna Graecia can be constructed.

The image of Magna Graecia presented in the later sources owes more to the stereotypes and commonplaces used to express Roman views of the Greeks as a whole than to any true reflection of the Hellenistic history of southern Italy. Methodologically, it is necessary to collate and analyse those comments by ancient authors which can be construed as constituting a series of stereotypes, before any attempt at historical reconstruction can take place. Briefly, the most important *topoi* which are found in the sources include charges of decadence, luxuriousness, indolence and drunkenness on the part of the Italiotes in general, and the Tarentines in particular; decline and depopulation of the area after 270 BC; untrustworthiness and lack of loyalty to Rome; and political instability.

The most persistent and best-documented source tradition is that of *tryphe*.[38] This embraces a large number of interrelated aspects covering the general area of luxurious living, material self-indulgence and moral decline, all features which were attributed to the Italiotes in general and to the Tarentines in particular. The various attributes and activities which fall into this category are stigmatised by many of the moralising Roman and Greek authors of the Late Republic and Empire, and are used to explain the decline of Italiote power. The accusations of *tryphe* are also used as a means of establishing Tarentum as the offending party in accounts of Roman wars in the South, and deflecting any possible accusation of Roman aggression. Accounts of the outbreak of the Pyrrhic War are rich in allegations of drunken frivolity at Tarentum, cited to account for many decisions from the original attack on the Roman fleet to the final unseemly rebuff of the Roman ambassadors.[39] The attribution of an image of wealth and luxury to the Italiotes first occurs with reference to Sybaris,[40] a connection which still persists in modern times. The implication is that *luxuria* and *tryphe* imply *hubris* and moral decline and are therefore integrally connected with the downfall of the city. The same theme is found applied to Tarentum. Plato compares Tarentine drinking habits with the abstemiousness of the Spartans, the founders of Tarentum.[41] Polybios alludes to insolence in dealing with Roman ambassadors in 282/1 BC and *eudaimonia* as a factor in the start of the Pyrrhic War but makes little moral comment on Tarentine actions.[42] In contrast, later accounts of the third century stress the more sensational aspects of Tarentine behaviour.[43] Another *topos* which overlaps with the general theme of moral decline is that of the unwarlike, if not positively cowardly, nature of the Italiotes. The theme of their softness and unwarlike nature is sometimes advanced to explain the defeat of the Italiotes in 270 and their military setbacks against the

14

Italians in the years preceding this.[44] There is surprisingly little evidence of this in the Greek sources, and there is a curious tension between the role of the Tarentines as aggressors and their feebleness when faced with the Roman response, which may be intended to convey the *levitas* of the Tarentine character. Lack of military prowess is also stressed by Livy, and in later literature the same theme is reflected in references to Tarentum as *mollis* and *imbellis*.[45]

The theme of lost greatness and the physical and economic decline of the Italiote cities is stressed by many Roman authors. Although the South undoubtedly did undergo a period of decline after the second Punic War, these themes persist in the literary tradition long after they must have ceased to be true. Significantly, none of the references to decline dates from the immediate post-war period, a time of economic recession for most of southern Italy. Authors of the first century AD, however, frequently refer to Italiote cities as being deserted,[46] in the face of solid epigraphical and archaeological evidence to the contrary, or at best as quiet backwaters. For instance, Cumae is named as being deserted, but inscriptions reveal that it was a flourishing city, the administrative centre for Baiae and Bauli and with a large shifting population of Roman notables.[47] This image of decline was not merely satirical exaggeration, but was deeply rooted in Roman literature. The same theme also occurs with reference to the entire region, which Cicero describes as entirely deserted.[48] There is an implied comparison between the past importance of the area and its present condition, and also an implicit connection between physical and economic decline and moral decline.

The *topos* of political instability occurs in the sources for both 280 and 215–208 BC. Many authors, both Greek and Roman, accept the view, which may be attributable ultimately to Timaeus, that Tarentum entered its period of decline as a result of abandoning moderate democracy in favour of a more radical form.[49] This led to political instability and degeneration, manifesting itself in reliance on foreign military power. In relation to later wars, Livy adopts it as an explanation for the conduct of anti-Roman Greek and Italian cities after 216 BC.[50] Almost all secessions to Hannibal are seen in terms of *stasis* between pro-Roman and anti-Roman parties. These are identified with the aristocratic and democratic factions respectively. This is an undoubted simplification of the facts, but it cannot be dismissed as merely a reworking of Timaeus and fourth-century politics. *Stasis* in moments of crisis is a well-documented phenomenon in the Greek world. The attribution of the democrats and *levissimi* to the pro-Carthaginian cause and the *optimates* to that of Rome must, however, be inaccurate, and seems to owe more to the patterns of Late Republican politics at Rome than to Greek politics of the third century.

The pattern which emerges is that the theme of luxuriousness and decadence was attached to the Greek cities of the South, but not to those of Campania. Similarly, the theme of softness and cowardice appears mainly in connection with Tarentum, as does that of demagoguery and political disorder. Both of these are elaborated in Roman literature. In contrast to this, the *topos* of an area in a state of economic and demographic decline is one which is not found in the earlier Greek sources, or what we can reconstruct of them, but appears most strongly in the Late Republic and becomes a standard rhetorical and literary commonplace. The more positive qualities attributed to Magna Graecia – its peacefulness, the opportunity to lead a cultured life, the connections with philosophy and literature – are much less prominent, although one suspects that they also gradually became literary clichés, and most often refer to the Bay of Naples, the part of Magna Graecia most frequented by the Roman elite.[51]

The origin of these *topoi* lies partly in the historiographic tradition of the fourth century BC, but they were undoubtedly strengthened by Roman prejudices towards the Greeks in particular and outsiders in general. The tradition of *tryphe*, characterised by a cyclical progression of achievement followed by a period of decline and degeneration (*eudaimonia* → *hubris* → *tryphe*), is traceable to the fourth century, to Timaeus and the historians influenced by him.[52] These included many Roman authors, and the popularity of Timaeus' work in Rome is beyond doubt. Nor can it be denied that his anti-Italiote bias was likely to find favour amongst Romans,[53] but his views were not unchallenged. In particular, Polybios explicitly declares himself opposed to Timaeus' views and his methods as a historian.[54] Although Timaeus' role in shaping the historical tradition must be recognised, he cannot be blamed for all hostile *topoi* connected with Magna Graecia. There is a strongly ambivalent tradition towards all Greeks in Roman history and literature, of which the perjorative references to the Italiotes are only a part. The charge of *luxuria* occurs in Roman literature as an attribute of Greeks, in particular those of Asia. Similarly, *topoi* concerning the Greeks, in Roman literature include volubility, arrogance, deceit and lack of faith, luxuriousness, *ineptia*, *impudentia*, cowardice and lack of military prowess, *levitas*. Even a fairly cursory glance at the literary references to Magna Graecia will indicate that they describe the Italiotes very much in the terms listed above.[55] The charges of *levitas*, idleness and decadence levelled against the Greeks of Italy must be seen in terms of the ambivalent Roman attitude to Greeks in general, and in terms of the nature of contemporary thought as well as in the context of the Timaean historical tradition.

The very nature of the source material indicates that there are serious problems in attempting a straightforward history of Magna Graecia. Aside from the inevitable pro-Roman bias and the anachronisms encountered in dealing with later source material, there is also the problem of 'otherness' – the Roman ambivalence to outside influences and a tendency to view the Italiotes through the distorting lense of their notions about Greeks and the Greek world at large. The purpose of this book is not to try to provide such a history, or to provide a comprehensive guide to the vast quantities of archaeological data, but to attempt a more thematic treatment of the Roman conquest of Magna Graecia and the life of the region in the post-conquest period. Pallottino's assertion that it is possible to write a history of Italy, as opposed to a history of Rome, is surely true for archaic Italy, but it may also be true for the period after the Roman conquest.[56] While it is not possible to ignore the all-embracing presence of Rome in post-conquest southern Italy, it may nevertheless be possible to reconstruct a history for Magna Graecia under Roman rule. It is becoming increasingly clear from archaeological and epigraphic evidence that Magna Graecia did not disappear into oblivion after the Roman conquest but remained a region with a strong sense of local identity and a flourishing cultural life, which is as deserving of study as the earlier periods of Italiote history and which sheds valuable light on relations with Rome and the processes of acculturation.

1

The Geography and Early Settlement
of Magna Graecia

The importance of the physical geography of Italy in moulding the
development and political integration of the peninsula cannot be
overestimated. Its central position in the Mediterranean facilitates
communications and trade with both West and East, and its shape,
being much longer than wide, ensures that peninsular Italy covers a
broad spectrum of climatic and geological conditions. All of these
factors have significant bearing on the economic and political development of communities and also on the ways in which they interact.[1] Even
within the area of this study, the coastal region from the Bay of
Naples to Taranto, there is a wide range of climate, vegetation and
physical landforms which had a major impact on the siting and development of cities, their interaction, and their wider network of
communications. However, it must be stressed that although an appre-
ciation of the geography of southern Italy is vital to our understanding
of its historical development, it is not an unchanging factor. Climatic
fluctuations affect local economies and habitation patterns, and landforms can change significantly over a relatively short period of time, due
to the effects of erosion and siltation. Survey work in Apulia using
geological core sampling techniques has revealed that the ancient
coastline was considerably further inland than the modern one in many
places, and that a number of rivers have changed course.[2] Extensive
coastal erosion or deposition of this type can potentially have a drastic
effect on local economies of coastal cities such as those of Magna
Graecia.[3]

The Greek cities were essentially maritime settlements, occupying
areas of coastal plain. These plains are not continuous, however, but are
broken, particularly in Calabria, by mountainous terrain. Many settlements are restricted to a fairly narrow strip of low-lying ground
separating the mountains of the hinterland from the sea. In this respect,

the Greek cities of Italy experienced similar restrictions on territorial growth, communications and transport to those of mainland Greece. A further consequence of the mountainous nature of the region is that local conditions of soil, climate and vegetation can vary considerably from one area to another, giving rise to a wide spectrum of conditions within Magna Graecia.[4]

Modern Campania is an economically depressed area, but in Antiquity it was regarded as being one of the most important regions of Italy, noted for its wealth, the diversity of its agricultural produce and the number and importance of its urban centres.[5] The major determining features of the topography are the intense volcanic activity of the area and its poor drainage, with numerous waterways and lagoons. Drainage schemes and canal-building were pursued both by the Romans and more recently,[6] while siltation was a problem from a very early date. Volcanic activity was also a problem. Vesuvius is situated close to Naples and although there is no certain evidence for the number and dates of its eruptions, other than that of AD 79 which buried Pompeii and Herculaneum, it was active on several occasions.[7] The frequency of earthquakes is attested both in literary sources and by an inscription found at Naples which records repairs to buildings damaged by earthquakes.[8] On the northern side of the Bay of Naples, the area known as the Campi Flegrei (Phlegraean Fields), which lies between Naples and Misenum, is characterised by hot springs, seismic activity and bradyseism, that is, the rapid rising and falling of localised areas of land in response to movements of the earth's crust. This has been most pronounced at Puteoli, but seismic activity is common over all of the Campi Flegrei.[9] The volcanic hot springs at Baiae and Bauli formed the basis of their prosperity as spa towns in the Roman period, and volcanic activity around Lake Acherusia, which lies a short distance inland from Cumae, led to the belief that it was an entrance to Hades.[10] As well as these regular fluctuations, the whole of southern Italy was, and still is, prone to earthquakes.

To the south of the Bay of Naples, the terrain is similar: coastal plain with poor natural drainage but with enough layers of volcanic soil to render the land fertile, limited by the mountains of the interior. The Greek cities of northern Lucania, Paestum and Velia, both have severely restricted territories.[11] Further south, the coastal plain narrows considerably and is broken by points where the mountains descend to the sea. Unlike Campania and Apulia, Calabria is almost entirely mountainous, forming a major barrier to overland trade and communications. In Antiquity it was heavily wooded and was a source of timber and pitch, but it has since been subject to extensive deforestation.[12] Most of this region was unsuitable for agriculture and could only be used for forestry and pasturage, although there is evidence of both Italic settlement and Roman colonisation in the Tanagro valley. A number of small Greek cities were founded on the west coast of Calabria but only Rhegium and Vibo survived in any significant form into the Hellenistic and Roman periods, the rest having succumbed to the inhospitable terrain and to encroachment by native Italians. Rhegium and Vibo occupied a narrow strip of flat ground on the 'toe' of Italy and both relied on the sea for their economic survival. Of the two, Vibo had more cultivable land, sufficient to support a group of Roman colonists who were added to the Greek city in 194 BC.[13] Rhegium is more restricted, occupying a very steep site which commands the shortest sea crossing to Sicily.

The Greek settlements on the south coast were among the most famous in the ancient world, and were noted for their fabulous wealth.[14] All had ample room for expansion, occupying fertile plains, and all had access to the sea. The combination of these two factors led to the development of cities with large territories and strong agricultural economies. Tarentum, the only Greek city in Apulia, occupied a strategic site dominating an excellent natural harbour, but was situated on a flat coastal plain with few natural defences on the landward side. It possessed considerable territory but much of the city's wealth came from commerce, fishing and textile production.[15] In point of fact, the size of many of the Greek colonies in the West, both in Italy and in Sicily, was larger than most others in the ancient world. Ampolo estimates city areas of 510 ha for Tarentum, 141 ha for Metapontum and 281 ha for Croton.[16] While these represent the entire walled area of the city, which was not necessarily the same as the populated area, such enclosures argue that the Italiote cities housed large populations.

PRE-COLONIAL CONTACTS

Although Tarentum was the only fully fledged Greek colony in southeast Italy, there is an increasing amount of evidence for Greek contacts with other parts of Apulia and the Adriatic coast. As already mentioned, there is a high concentration of Mycenaean material in the Sallentine peninsula, and excavations recently undertaken in this region have unearthed substantial quantities of later Greek material. In particular, there are signs of a Greek presence at Otranto (ancient Hydruntum), and at Gallipoli (ancient Callipolis). There is also a tradition in ancient literature which attributes Greek origins to many settlements in the

Sallentine peninsula. Although it seems unlikely that any of these were Greek colonies, since the Messapian elements are dominant, the whole area was Hellenised and recent research has revealed the extent to which south-east Italy was an important point of contact between Greece, Illyria and Italy.[17] The high density of Messapian settlements may have limited the opportunities for Greek colonisation but the coastal cities of the Sallentine peninsula were situated on trade routes whose importance has only recently been recognised.

The earliest Greek colonies in the West were founded in the eighth and seventh centuries BC. Their appearance raises a number of questions about the nature of earlier Greek contacts with the West and the factors which prompted the transition from sporadic contact to the establishment of permanent settlements in Italy and Sicily. There is a tradition in ancient literature which dates the majority of the colonial foundations to the late eighth or early seventh centuries BC, and much recent research has been devoted to attempts to correlate this tradition with the ever-increasing archaeological data for the pre-colonial and colonial phases of Ischia, Cumae and some of the Sicilian colonies. In general terms, the archaeological and literary evidence agree remarkably well, with evidence on many sites for settlement during the late eighth century BC, but the exact nature of early contact and the processes of colonisation remain uncertain.

There is an increasing amount of evidence that contacts between Greece and Italy pre-dated the colonisation phase, and that the colonial foundations of the eighth century BC were not an entirely new phenomenon, but took place against a background of long-standing Greek contact with southern Italy, possibly with a break in continuity between the Mycenaean contacts and the pre-colonial phase of the ninth century. Mycenaean goods have come to light at a number of prehistoric sites, principally in Apulia and Calabria – at Porto Cesareo, Coppa Nevigata, Torre Castellucia and others – although there are more sporadic finds in Campania and central Italy as well.[18] All of these sites are on or near the coast and not surprisingly there is little sign of any Mycenaean presence further inland. The majority of Mycenaean goods can be dated to Late Helladic IIIB and IIIC although earlier material (IIIA) has been found at Scoglio del Tonno on the Bay of Naples, one of the best documented of this group of sites.[19] At most sites, Mycenaean finds are associated with Italic material of the Late Bronze Age – pottery and fibulae of Protovillanovan and Subapennine types or with pottery of Iapygian protogeometric style. Pottery forms the largest proportion of the Greek material, but some weapons and metal goods have been found. Mycenaean objects are generally only found in small quantities, a fact which, together with the restricted distribution of finds, the small number of types of object and the co-existence of Mycenaean finds with Italic assemblages, suggests that the relationship was one of contacts based on trade or gift exchange rather than on Mycenaean settlement on any substantial scale.[20] It is worth noting that some of the foundation myths of colonies in the West imply earlier contacts, which are in some cases consistent with archaeological evidence of Mycenaean contacts.[21] The immediate pre-colonisation phase, and the dates of the earliest colonies, however, are obscured by dating problems associated with the Middle Geometric II pottery found in the earliest levels at Cumae and Naxos.[22]

The reasons for the Greek colonisation which took place in the Mediterranean during the eighth century BC have been widely debated, and there are still no conclusive answers to this problem. One explanation centres on land shortages and demographic growth in Greece which, it is suggested, led smaller and less prosperous cities to offload their surplus population by establishing colonies elsewhere.[23] This model has been challenged on the basis of detailed archaeological exploration of sites with a strong Greek presence, notably Pithecusae in the West and Al Mina in Syria.[24] The presence of earlier Greek material at many colonial sites has also contributed to the development of a model in which trade was the determining factor and in which trading contacts both preceded and dictated the site of colonial foundations. However, there are problems with this model. Pithecusae, where the economic activity seems to have been metalworking using ores imported from Etruria, failed to develop into a colony of significant size, and Al Mina is now recognised as a Phoenician city rather than a Greek colony.

Indeed, it is unlikely that all colonial foundations can be attributed to a single cause. Given the disparity in the circumstances of the colonies and of their founding cities, it is more plausible to regard colonisation as the product of a number of factors. Herring has argued persuasively that conceptualisation of early colonisation in terms of the structures of the city-state is incorrect, projecting the decision-making processes of the fifth century on to a proto-urban society. Instead, he suggests that it should be seen as part of the evolution of the *polis*, involving some degree of fission as the population expands and socio-political organisation becomes more complex, and that emphasis on land or trade were

Table 1 Greek colonisation in Italy

City	Founded by	Foundation date BC
Pithecusae	Euboean	c. 770
Cumae (Kyme)	Pithecusan	c. 725
Rhegium (Rhegion)	Chalcidian (Zankle) and Messenian	c. 720
Sybaris	Achaean	c. 720
Croton	Achaean	c. 710
Tarentum (Taras)	Spartan	c. 710–700
Metapontum	Achaean	c. 700
Palaepolis/Neapolis	Cumaean/Syracusan/Athenian	c. 700–600
Caulonia	Crotoniate	c. 700–675
Laos	Sybarite	c. 700–600
Tempsa (Temesa)	Crotoniate	c. 700–600
Terina	Crotoniate	c. 700–600
Poseidonia (Paestum)	Sybarite	c. 700–675
Locri	Locrian (Gk)	c. 675
Siris	Colophonian	650
Vibo (Hipponion)	Locrian (It)	625–600
Nicotera	Locrian (?)	c. 600
Medma	Locrian (It)	c. 600
Elea (Velia)	Phocaean	c. 535
Buxentum (Pyxus)	Rhegine	c. 471
Thurii	Athenian/Pan-Hellenic	444/3
Heraklea	Tarentine	433

the results of a particular choice of location rather than a cause of foundation.[25]

The chronological span of colonisation in the West must also be borne in mind. The colonisation phase in the eighth century during which Aegean cities founded colonies in the West was only the first stage of an ongoing process. Many Italiote cities (see Table 1) were the product of secondary colonisation by the Greeks in Italy, and there was a second phase of colonisation from Greece with the foundation of Thurii in 444/3 BC. In these circumstances, it is very unlikely that motives for colonisation remained constant. Whereas the earlier foundations may have been the result of stresses within the kinship-based society of the developing *poleis*, later colonisation was frequently a response to specific political needs. Thurii, a pan-Hellenic foundation but with a large number of Athenian colonists, filled the vacuum left by the destruction of Sybaris and consolidated Athenian interests in the West. The Tarentine colony of Heraklea, founded in 433 BC on the site of the earlier city of Siris which had been destroyed during the sixth century, provided a counterweight to Thurii and protected Tarentine interests.[26] This later phase of colonisation was also motivated by the balance of power within Greece, where rivalry between Athens and Sparta was escalating. The foundation of Thurii was in part an Athenian move to obtain a base in the West and to curb the power of the Doric cities there, and was countered with the foundation of Heraklea by the Spartan colony of Tarentum.[27] Thus even a cursory glance at the evidence provides a strong indication that the Greek colonies of Italy were, from the very first, a diverse group of cities, some growing out of the evolution of the city-state, others founded in response to the political pressures of the fifth century. This lack of coherence and common purpose among the Italiotes remained a major factor in shaping the development of southern Italy and was later an important determinant in the history of their relations with Rome.

THE PRE-GREEK INHABITANTS OF MAGNA GRAECIA

So far, much has been said of the Greeks and their surroundings, but very little of the indigenous inhabitants of southern Italy. Since the Greek colonies clearly did not exist in a vacuum, some consideration must be given to the nature of their Italian neighbours and to the relations between Greeks and Italians prior to 350 BC. Apart from the basic requirement to consider the Greeks in context and not in isolation, the theme of Graeco-Italian conflict is one of great importance in shaping the later history of Magna Graecia. During the fourth and third centuries BC, even after the conquest of the South by Rome, local conflicts or alliances between Greek cities or between Greeks and Italians were major factors in shaping the reactions of Italiote cities towards the larger issues of the day.[28] In the modern era of mass media and rapid access to information, the global significance of an issue may be readily apparent, and it is all too easy to forget that without the means to disseminate information widely and rapidly, much of the ancient world must have taken its decisions on a rather different basis. Given that the ancient sources, mostly written with the benefit of hindsight, concentrate on large-scale struggles and global issues – Rome against Hannibal, Rome against the Samnites – it is very tempting to forget that these local alliances or enmities were very much more immediate for the people of Magna Graecia, and thus more influential in determining their actions. Given that perceptions were limited by this lack of information, it is not surprising that the somewhat fraught relations between Greeks and Italians remained a major force in the history of the Italiote cities.

The inhabitants of Iron Age Italy encountered by the early Greek colonists are known principally from archaeological research. Literary references are sparse and confused, naming Ausonians, Oenotrians, Chones, Opici and Iapygians as the main Italic groups, but with little consensus as to who they were or where they lived, and an overriding enthusiasm for concocting Greek heroic genealogies and foundation legends to explain their presence.[29] The tradition of mythical Greek foundations, often attributed to Homeric heroes, has an early date in Greek literature, and finds its way into Roman literature, via Timaeus and Cato, by the second century BC. Archaeologically, the most easily identifiable of these groups are the Iapygians, who inhabited southern Apulia and the Sallentine peninsula, and were still a definable ethnic group in the historical period.[30] These people, together with the Daunians and Messapians, who also inhabited south-east Italy, were distinct from other Italian peoples in that they had a marked cultural and linguistic affinity with the Illyrians of the Dalmatian coast.[31] Unlike the Chones, Oenotrians, Opici and Ausones, they remained a recognisable cultural group, but many of the other groups mentioned in ancient sources remain very elusive. Some scholars have identified the Ausones with the Aurunci[32] who inhabited northern Campania in the fourth and third centuries, but who may originally have controlled a larger area. *Opikoi* seems to have been used as a generic term for all indigenous Italians by Greek writers, although it came to be used as a Greek translation of the Latin *Osci*, and the other terms listed also appear to have been generic terms for the non-Greek inhabitants of southern Italy.[33]

In archaeological terms, the Early Iron Age (*c.* 900–700 BC), which approximately coincides in southern Italy with the first period of colonisation, appears to have been a period of demographic expansion and growing economic prosperity. All areas show an increase in numbers of settlements, but this is particularly marked in Calabria and Basilicata, where Bronze Age settlement density had been low.[34] There are also signs of a difference in settlement types. In Apulia, the majority of settlements are situated on the plain, while in Calabria, many sites occupy high ground and make use of natural defences.[35] Most sites excavated seem to have been large villages, some containing the large 'megaron' huts which were characteristic of the Late Bronze Age. These communities may have been formed, at least in part, by synoecism of smaller units, a process which would have required some sophistication of social and economic organisation. Most notably, there is a great increase in settlement size between the late seventh and fourth centuries. Centres such as Gravina, Cavallino, Serra di Vaglio and Monte Sannace expand rapidly, and abandonment of smaller settlements argues for a greater centralisation of population.[36] To a large extent, the study of the social and political organisation of the Italians is hampered by the fact that most of the evidence is from cemeteries rather than habitation sites. However, examination of the grave goods and the topography of cemeteries indicates a considerable degree of social stratification. The majority of burials are inhumations with grave goods, principally pottery and metal objects. Most cemeteries contain a number of conspicuously rich burials, many characterised by the presence of weapons and by physical separation from the other graves, which has led to suggestions that the Iron Age élite was a warrior aristocracy, possibly feudal in nature.[37] Excavations at Sala Consilina have given some support to this view, revealing groups of burials which form distinct clusters of poorer graves surrounding a single wealthy one.[38] However, the evidence is not conclusive, and the nature of the élite must remain a matter for speculation.

Literary sources give little help on this point, but references to rule by kings among the Iapygians in the fifth century may provide some support for the archaeological evidence for a stratified society.[39] This type of social stratification is illustrated even more sharply by the princely burials of the sixth century – at Pontecagnano and Fondo Artaiaco in Campania and Palestrina and Castel di Decima in Latium – which contain rich grave goods and show close similarities to rich graves in Etruria.[40] Unfortunately, little is known of the political organisation of the region. The centres of habitation may have been independent political units, or part of a more complex structure with a central as well as local power structure, as is implied by the evidence for a king of the Iapygians. However, this is too imprecise to be conclusive.

In addition to social stratification, there is evidence of growing technical and economic sophistication. Impasto pottery is gradually displaced by painted pottery manufactured initially in Apulia.[41] A widespread network of trade and exchange is demonstrated by the occurrence of Villanovan and Latin pottery, Phoenician material, Illyrian goods and Greek goods of both pre-colonial and colonial date, as well as by the diffusion of southern goods, particularly pottery, throughout other areas of Italy. Daunian imports are found in Picenum and Campania, and Phoenician goods occur in burials at Francavilla Marittima.[42] Iron Age society was clearly thriving, with a sophisticated economic and social organisation and a wide range of external contacts.

However, the extent to which it was urbanised at this time is open to debate. Despite the growth in size of communities and the sophistication of their social and economic organisation, they seem closer to proto-urban rather than fully urbanised communities. Most units were small by comparison with the Greek colonies – large villages rather than cities in size and lacking monumental architecture or any obvious sign of social or economic zoning. The process of synoecism may have been a response to the arrival of the Greeks, although not, apparently, in imitation.[43] In Apulia, settlements were already large and developing a complex structure at the time of the first colonies. Most settlements included a large walled area which enclosed a smaller area, or areas, of habitation, together with cemeteries and cultivated land. The layout is quite distinct from that of the Greek *polis*. Whether fully urbanised or not, these settlements were developing independently as urban units in a different tradition from that of the Greek colonists.[44] Thus the arrival of the Greeks created a dual tradition of urban development in southern Italy which had a profound influence on the later development of the region.

THE GREEK COLONISATION

The initial impact of the Greek colonies on the native Italians varies greatly according to area, but there is little doubt that the colonisation was aggressive. For example, in Apulia, where most of the existing Iapygian communities appear relatively unchanged during the eighth and seventh centuries, those in close proximity to Tarentum disappear at the time of the colonisation.[45]

Similarly, in Calabria and Basilicata, many of the Italic settlements in the hinterland of the colonies disappear, frequently with evidence implying a violent destruction. A number of new settlements appear but many of these are Greek, or at any rate extensively Hellenised, and in several instances incorporate Greek sanctuaries. In the hinterland of Sybaris, Torre del Mordillo was destroyed by fire, while Francavilla Marittima seems to have become entirely Greek and home to a Greek sanctuary of Athena.[46] A similar pattern can be seen in the territory of Metapontum, where the Italic sites of Cozzo Presepe and L'Incoronata disappear, as in the vicinity of most other colonies.[47] A number of reasons have been advanced for this phenomenon, but the most likely explanation is a twofold one. The initial need to secure the colonies and their surrounding territories may well have involved some aggression on the part of the Greeks and it is probable that much of the native population was forced to migrate to more readily defensible sites further inland. La Genière identifies changes in the Valle di Diano which are consistent with an influx of new population. It also seems likely that there was some degree of absorption of Italians into the new colonies.[48]

In Campania, the Italic response to the arrival of the Greeks was different again. Here, there is no sign of disruption of the indigenous Italic population. The inland settlements, which already showed signs of contact with the Villanovan centres of Etruria at the time of the colonisation, develop into fully urbanised centres with signs of strong Etruscan influence during the seventh century.[49] Some of these, notably Capua, Nola and Suessula, show continuous occupation from the eighth century, but the area also shows signs of an increasing number of settlements, with the foundation of Nuceria, Abella, Acerrae and others, all of which show signs of Hellenisation but not to the same overwhelming degree as many of the Italic sites in Calabria. However, the traffic was not all one-way. There are a number of possible Greek foundations in Campania which rapidly became Italicised. Pompeii, Herculaneum and Puteoli may fall into this category, and also possibly Surrentum.[50] By c. 650 BC there was another major influence in Campania besides that of the Greeks. The Etruscan interest in Campania which had been manifest even in the eighth century intensified at this time, probably resulting in new cities in Campania, and reflected in the later traditions concerning the foundation of Capua and Nola.[51] Archaeologically, this political domination is reflected in the large numbers of Etruscan goods, principally pottery, metal objects and terracottas, found in many areas of Campania. Contact between Greeks, Etruscans and Campanians appears to have been extensive, reflected in Etruscan imports at Cumae and Greek, or Greek-influenced objects found at other Campanian sites.

Despite the evidence for economic interaction between Greeks and Italians, and the probability that some Italians were absorbed into Greek communities, the relationship was clearly one of considerable hostility for much of the time. Modern scholars have been inclined to adopt one of two interpretations. Either the Greeks expanded aggressively, forcing the Italians to flee, or alternatively they sought to dominate the Italians economically and culturally.[52] However, there is no inherent contradiction between these two views. Both Greeks and Italians were diverse groups, and it is entirely possible that a Greek city could be at war with one group of Italians while still maintaining trading relations with others.[53] Similarly, the same group of Italians could be at odds with some Greeks but on friendly terms with others. It is also possible that Greek goods did not come direct from Greeks but were circulated through intermediate groups. The existence of evidence for networks of trade and exchange between Greeks and Italians does not necessarily preclude hostilities and aggressive expansion.

GREEK EXPANSION

Greek power in the South grew steadily during the seventh and sixth centuries, which was a period of expansion for many cities. Croton, Sybaris and Metapontum all controlled large territories, indicating expansion inland during the seventh century. However, most Italiote cities continued to regard themselves as part of the Aegean world and may have had little interest in Italy beyond the maintainance of their own security.[54] Cultural contacts are reflected in dedications at pan-Hellenic sanctuaries and participation in festivals. The cities of Magna Graecia were noted for their athletic prowess, resulting in many victories at the Olympics and other pan-Hellenic games.[55] Magna Graecia had also become an intellectual centre for the Greek world. A strong Pythagorean tradition developed at Croton, Metapontum and Rhegium, and some attempt was made by the ruling oligarchies to govern these cities according to Pythagorean precepts. An Eleatic philosophical school developed at Velia under the leadership of Zeno. The region was also noted for its law-codes and law-givers, of whom the earliest was Zaleucus.[56]

On the other hand, disunity amongst the Greeks was apparent from an early date. Siris was destroyed by an alliance of Rhegium, Metapontum and Sybaris, probably c. 550–530 BC, and Sybaris itself fell to Croton in 510. The end of the sixth century and the beginning of the fifth was a period of widespread political upheaval in southern Italy, marked by the ejection of the Pythagorean factions in many cities and a movement towards more democratic forms of government. In Campania, Cumae was at the height of its power but was engaged in intermittent conflict with the Etruscans. The Cumaeans won notable land victories against the Etruscans near Cumae in 524 and at Aricia in 505, led by the tyrant Aristodemos. Relations with Rome seem to have been amicable, and Roman tradition records regular supplies of grain from Cumae in times of shortage, even after the ejection of the Etruscanising regime of Tarquin, who eventually went into exile at Cumae.[57]

During the fifth century, relations between Greeks and Italians seem to have declined. In Apulia, Tarentum was engaged in intermittent warfare with the Iapygians. The city of Karbina was savagely sacked at some point during the 470s. The Tarentine successes were clearly felt to have been of major significance, since they were commemorated by two large victory monuments at Delphi. However, there was a major reverse in 473 BC, when a joint force of Rhegines and Tarentines was crushingly defeated by the Iapygians.[58] Also in 474, Cumae formed an alliance with Hieron of Syracuse to defeat an Etruscan fleet, an event which marked the final breakup of Etruscan power in Campania, but which also signalled the decline of Cumaean power and the rise of Syracuse to prominence.[59]

It is clear that the cities of Magna Graecia were suffering from encroachments from other Greeks, as well as pressure from the Italians, during the fifth century. The power of Syracuse was expanding and continued to become more intrusive throughout the fifth century, culminating in the capture of Locri, Rhegium, Caulonia and Croton by Dionysios I in the 390s.[60] Athenian interest in the West was also growing. In 444/3, Thurii was founded on the site of Sybaris, nominally as a pan-Hellenic venture, but with a very strong Athenian presence. The foundation of Heraklea in 433 by Tarentum, itself a colony of Athens' enemy, Sparta, may have been an assertion of Tarentine power in response to this, as well as to Italic aggression.[61] A more direct Athenian interest is demonstrated by the visit of the Athenian admiral Diotimos to Naples, with a squadron of ships. The date and purpose of this visit, recorded by Timaeus and echoed by Lycophron, is much disputed.[62] The most obvious context, the Athenian expedition against Syracuse in 415, is too late to fit the numismatic evidence for the adoption of Athenian coin types. Of the other possible dates put forward, c. 470 and c. 450, the latter looks more plausible, although numismatic data could support either. However, a date sometime in the 450s is fairly close to the date of the foundation of Thurii and thus falls into a period when Athens was known to have had interests in the West.[63]

The visit seems to have been connected with the foundation of Neapolis. An earlier city, Palaepolis, had been founded on the Bay of Naples in the seventh century, initially by Cumae, but with some Syracusan settlers.[64] Neapolis is recorded by the sources as a later foundation, occupying a site very close to Palaepolis but remaining a separate city until 327 BC, when the two were merged as Neapolis. The evidence for this is extremely confused, and is further muddled by a small number of references to a still earlier settlement called Parthenope.[65] Archaeological finds at Pizzofalcone in modern Naples confirm that there was an early settlement on the site, and literary sources broadly agree that there was a Cumaean colony with later additions by Syracuse and Athens, which eventually became the city of Neapolis, but the details remain confused. Livy's account of the war with Rome in 327/6 BC suggests that the city was already a single political entity but occupied two physically separate locations until encouraged to merge after the war.[66] It may be stretching the already slender evidence for the foundation of Neapolis to say that it was an entirely Athenian colony, but there was certainly a strong Athenian interest in its foundation, possibly as a counterbalance to the power of Syracuse, a co-founder of Palaepolis and an ally of Cumae.

The importance of contacts in the West for the Greeks of the Aegean is illustrated by the events of 415/14, when the Athenian expeditionary fleet against Syracuse landed in Italy. Most of the Italiote cities followed the lead of their founding cities in their reactions to the Athenians. Tarentum, as a colony of Sparta, refused to admit the Athenians to the harbour and the city, although there were no overt hostilities. Other Doric cities allowed harbour facilities to the fleet but refused to admit Athenians within their walls. Only Chalcidian Rhegium provided assistance.[67] In the light of this, Athenian anxiety to maintain a permanent presence through the foundation of Thurii and the addition of Athenian colonists to Neapolis is comprehensible.

Despite the divisions between the Italiotes which dominated the history of the Greeks in the West, there was an attempt to create some degree of unity. This took the form of a league of Greek cities, known to modern scholars as the Italiote League, which was probably founded during the period of Crotoniate pre-eminence at the end of the sixth century. Its organisation was modelled on that of the Achaean League, and entailed a central treasury, a central meeting place, and regular meetings of member states.[68] Unfortunately, no details are known of the decision-making mechanisms of the League, the arrangements for levying and command of forces, or the initial purpose of the League. However, the location of the treasury and meeting place at the Crotoniate sanctuary of Hera Lacinia is a strong indication that Croton was regarded as *hegemon* in the early years of the League's existence.

The membership of the League fluctuated, developing from a core of Achaean cities and probably excluding Tarentum and the cities of Campania and northern Lucania. Later, it became much larger, and included most Italiote cities, with the exception of those conquered by the Italians during the course of the fifth century, since Tarentum, Heraklea and Thurii are mentioned by the sources as members of the League. There was also a change of leadership, which reflected the changing balance of power among the Greeks. Crotoniate wealth and influence gradually declined during the fifth century, while that of Tarentum grew steadily after a period of recovery following the disaster of 473.

The League was dissolved by Dionysios I during the Syracusan occupation of Croton in 391/0 BC, but was later revived under the leadership of Tarentum. The treasury and meeting place were transferred from Croton to the sanctuary of Demeter at Heraklea. Polybios gives no hint of a revival, but there is strong circumstantial evidence.[69] The primary purpose of the League was almost certainly to defend Greek interests against the Italians, who were in an aggressively expansionist phase for much of the fifth century. It did not preclude other alliances between Italiotes, or indeed other hostilities. It may also have allowed for bilateral agreements between Greeks and Italians. Certainly, the history of the Italiotes shows such disunity of interests that it is difficult to believe that any effective unity of purpose was possible other than on the most basic issues of common security.

In the middle years of the fifth century, a further factor emerged which was to have a profound effect on the political and cultural shape of southern Italy, and was largely to be responsible for bringing the South to the notice of Rome. The Oscan-speaking Sabellians who originated in Samnium began to migrate during this period into Campania, northern Apulia, Lucania and Bruttium.[70] Many ancient writers fail to differentiate between them, referring to them all as *Opikoi*, but it is clear that the migrants rapidly fragmented into separate entities, sharing a common language and cultural attributes, but with separate political identities.[71] The disintegration of the Etruscan hegemony in Campania and the decline of Cumaean power left a vacuum which facilitated the take-over of the area by the vigorous and aggressive Oscans. Capua fell to the invaders in 423 BC, Cumae in 421, Poseidonia (renamed Paestum) in 410, Terina in 395 and Laos in 390. Thurii was allegedly attacked by Lucanians as early as 433.[72]

From the date assigned by Diodorus for the formation of a Campanian people in 438/7, the aggressive phase of the expansion took place very rapidly, although this is clearly the date of a political event marking the culmination of a process of ethnic and cultural transformation. It was apparently facilitated by the presence of a large number of Oscans who had migrated to Campania during the preceding years as part of a gradual and peaceful settlement of the area.[73] The cause of the transition from peaceful infiltration to violent conquest is not known, but whatever it was, it may have been a localised phenomenon. Cumae, Capua and the smaller cities of Terina and Laos were sacked, and a large part of the Greek population of Cumae was massacred or driven out.

In contrast, Naples maintained a peaceful relationship with her Oscan inhabitants. Oscans were admitted to the citizenship, and Strabo records that they forced the Greeks to share political control of the city with them, indicating that they were a reasonably strong force within the city.[74] However, Naples remained substantially a Greek city, and the lack of Oscan impact on the culture and language suggests a process of gradual acculturation and absorption of the Italic elements by the Greeks. This is a feature which is found in other Italiote cities in the fourth and third centuries, as demonstrated by the occurrence of Italic names in the epigraphy of Greek cities, and is an indication that the integration of Italic elements was not restricted to the early phases of Italiote history.[75]

Paestum is a rather more problematic case, since the literary sources and archaeological evidence are at odds with each other. A fragment of Aristoxenos describes the subjugation of the Greek population and the suppression of Greek culture and religion, and implies a violent conquest of the city by the Lucanians. The predominantly Oscan culture of Paestum after 410 provides some support for this, but the lack of a destruction layer on the site casts doubt on Aristoxenos' implication that there the Greek population met a violent end.[76]

The violent circumstances of the Oscan expansion in some areas of the South does not imply that southern Italy entered a period of decline at the end of the fifth century. On the contrary, many cities of Campania entered on a period of great prosperity. Capua, in particular, gained a reputation for great wealth and power.[77] At Cumae and Paestum, however, a combination of political and geological factors seems fundamentally to have changed the economy of these cities. The gradual silting of the harbours and the fact that the Oscans originated inland and had no maritime tradition effectively directed both cities towards a land-based economy and away from maritime interests. The cities captured by the Oscans adopted Oscan culture and language.[78] Politically, the Graeco-Etruscan type of city-state continued to be the basic unit, but with modifications to the internal political process, replacing the existing mechanisms of government with the Oscan system of magistrates, possibly annual and elective, of which the chief was the *Meddix*.[79]

In northern Apulia, there was a tendency towards the development of fully urban communities. The Lucanians and Bruttians, however, were organised on less urbanised lines. There were fewer urban centres in Calabria and Basilicata – with the exception of the Greek cities – than was the case in Campania, and the tendency seems to have been towards a federal structure of smaller, proto-urban communities, with a small number of larger settlements which are sometimes referred to by the sources as *poleis* or *urbes*.[80] Despite the state of intermittent warfare which existed between Greeks and Oscans, trade and other exchanges between them persisted, as they had done between the Greeks and Italians during the sixth century. Greek goods are found on Oscan sites, and native pottery production adopted Greek techniques, particularly in Apulia. Greek weapons and armour are found, sometimes inscribed with Italian names, and Greek building techniques were diffused, often with adaptations which suggest an Italian architect rather than a Greek one.[81] Thus a dual process seems to have been in operation, whereby the Oscans imposed their own culture and language on conquered areas, but continued to be open to diffusion of Greek material goods and cultural influences.[82]

For the Italiote cities which remained under Greek control, the fourth century was a time of constant pressure from a number of sources. In the 390s the Greeks of Calabria fell victim to Syracusan expansion. Dionysios I invaded Italy and captured Locri, Croton, Rhegium and Caulonia, inflicting considerable loss of manpower and economic disruption. They remained garrisoned by his troops as part of a Syracusan empire for a period of twelve years before managing to eject the invaders.[83] This had the effect of significantly shifting the balance of power within the Italiote League. Tarentum, which had rapidly recovered from the disasters of the 470s, was now possibly the wealthiest and physically largest city in Italy, and also managed to escape the attentions of Syracuse. The capture of Croton left the Italiote League without a *hegemon*, and it is probably at this point that Tarentum assumed leadership of the League and transferred the treasury to Heraklea.

The direction of Tarentine policy in this period must be largely speculation since there is little evidence, but some conjectures can be made. The leading figure, and one of the few identifiable personalities in Italiote history, was Archytas,[84] a Pythagorean philosopher and mathematician who dominated Tarentine politics until his death sometime in the 350s BC. Few details of his career are known. He held the office of *strategos* – the major magistracy at Tarentum by this date – seven times, but the dates are not known and it is uncertain whether his years of office were consecutive or not. Many of the anecdotes about Archytas concern his philosophical beliefs and his friendship with Plato. His political supremacy can be dated approximately by reference to Plato's visits to

Syracuse as tutor to the future Dionysios II. Unfortunately, the dates of these visits are also uncertain, but have been recently assigned to 388/7 and 367/6.[85] Archytas was responsible for forcing Dionysios to release Plato from house arrest during his second visit, and this incident may give a clue to Tarentine policy in the early fourth century.

The influence of Archytas at Syracuse and the freedom of Tarentum from any attack by Dionysios point towards the possibility of a Tarentine treaty with Syracuse.[86] This would have had the effect of freeing Tarentum to deal with Italian incursions and to consolidate its hegemony of the Italiote League while leaving Syracuse to control the cities of Rhegium and Locri, which were strategically vital to communications between Italy and Sicily, thus effectively defining the Tarentine and Syracusan spheres of influence. It does not seem reasonable, however, to use this as evidence that Archytas was a puppet ruler on behalf of Syracuse. Many of the arguments in favour of this view rest on unsatisfactory assumptions about the nature of the Tarentine constitution. Aristotle defines it as a moderate democracy, but little is known abouts its workings. Thus it does not support the argument that Archytas' seven *strategia* overrode the constitution and are therefore evidence that he was imposed by an internal faction or external pressure. There is no evidence that Archytas' multiple *strategia* were unconstitutional (although such a long run of offices must have been exceptional) or that there was no provision for iteration of offices in time of crisis.[87]

Whatever the exact details of Archytas' career, his period of prominence certainly coincided with the height of Tarentine power in Italy. Economically, the city was flourishing, with a thriving export trade in wine, dyes, textiles, pottery, terracottas and metalwork to other areas of Italy and the Greek world. This is attested both by archaeological evidence and by the *topoi* of the wealth and luxurious lifestyle of the Tarentines which are found in later literature but which seem to stem from fourth-century sources. In military terms, the Tarentine cavalry was noted for its prowess, and Archytas' victories over the Italians are an indication of the efficiency of the army, but the main source of both military and economic power was maritime.

Elsewhere, some of the cities which had fallen to the Oscans failed to revive, but others began to recover. Cumae and Paestum remained relatively prosperous, although they now fell outside the political and cultural orbit of the other Greeks. Naples began to expand its power at this date, but Velia seems to have remained a relative backwater, despite being strong enough to withstand Oscan attacks. The Greeks of Bruttium had suffered, in many cases, from the attentions of Dionysios

I, and were in a period of recovery from the effects of the war and the occupation by Syracusan troops. Although the impoverishment of Magna Graecia, which is such a favourite theme with ancient authors, refers to a later period and may be exaggerated, it does seem true to say that the cities of Croton, Metapontum and Rhegium were considerably less powerful economically than during the sixth and fifth centuries, and were politically overshadowed by the growing power of Tarentum and Syracuse. Externally, the restlessness of the Lucanians and Bruttians continued to be a problem, although the Greeks of Campania lived on rather better terms with their Oscan neighbours, possibly as a result of the greater economic success and more settled and urbanised organisation of the Campanians.

Within the Greek community, the Italiote League may have included most of the remaining Greek cities (although evidence is scarce) and was firmly under the domination of Tarentum. Most cities maintained trading and diplomatic contacts with the Aegean world – although the extent of these is poorly documented – and with central Italy, including Rome. Thus Magna Graecia c. 350 BC, despite the pressures on the Greeks, was a strategically and economically significant area of Italy, holding an intermediate position between eastern and western Mediterranean, and thus occupying a unique position in both Greek and Italian terms.

2

Roman Conquest: Magna Graecia 350–270 BC

The death of Archytas of Tarentum at some unspecified date during the 350s BC is noted by many sources as the turning point which marked the start of the moral and political decline of Magna Graecia. After this date, the Greeks, corrupted by excessive wealth, abandoned moderate government in favour of radical democracy which led to *stasis* and social breakdown, and in foreign policy committed the supreme folly of opposition to the growing power of Rome. The historiographical implications of this have already been discussed in the Introduction, but will be considered again in the course of this chapter in the light of the events of the fourth and third centuries. However simplistic the ancient view may be as an historical analysis, its prevalence makes the death of Archytas a useful starting point for a study of Hellenistic and Roman Magna Graecia and also for a discussion of relations with Rome, since it marks the beginning of the expansion of Roman interests in Campania and southern Italy.

The period from 350 to 270 BC is therefore of importance for our understanding both of the history of Magna Graecia and of the processes of Roman expansion. It is also of interest in that a number of features become apparent at this time which continue to be significant factors in Roman relations with the Greeks. The internal *stasis* in many cities, which Livy identifies as endemic by 218–200 BC, first becomes apparent in the fourth century.[1] The question of whether it was a symptom of weakness and degeneration and a cause of the problems faced by the Italiotes, as Livy and others suggest, or a product of the pressures on these states, is something that will be discussed further in the context of the Punic wars.[2] The continuing rivalries between the Greeks and their Italian neighbours are vital to our understanding of Italiote history, despite the advent of Rome as a new and important factor. Indeed, the striking thing about the history of the fourth and third centuries BC is the extent to which local concerns continued to be paramount to the Italiotes, even during periods of wide-ranging conflict such as the Pyrrhic and Punic Wars. From the standpoint of Magna Graecia, Rome was very distant for all but the most northerly cities – Naples, Cumae, etc. – and Roman power cannot have been a very major concern in comparison with the far more pressing threat to security posed by Lucanian and Bruttian raids. This is not to deny that states in ancient Italy did not have any wider perspective on the world, but the importance of more immediate concerns must not be forgotten. Ancient authors, and some modern ones, writing with the benefit of hindsight, find many Italiote reactions to Rome inconsistent and ill-advised. Charges of weakness, indecision, arrogance and foolhardiness abound in the pro-Roman accounts written centuries after the events described, and in full knowledge of the later extent of Roman power.[3] However, many of these actions become more comprehensible when considered in the context of southern Italy, and from the standpoint that for the Italiotes, the important issues were those of maintaining security on a regional level and maintaining their position in relation to the other Greeks and Italians.

A further problem for the historian of the fourth century is the role of the Italiote League,[4] and the extent to which League actions and interests can be differentiated from those of its member states. Given that it was quite possible for enmities and alliances to exist between League members which were in no way connected with the activities of the League, it becomes difficult to extrapolate League policy from the actions of any particular city. These difficulties are especially acute in the case of Tarentum. The overwhelming extent to which ancient sources focused on Tarentum as the main protagonist in southern Italy means that the history of Magna Graecia at this period must, to a large extent, be the history of Tarentum. Since Tarentum was the *hegemon* of the Italiote League by the fourth century, the question which must inevitably be asked is to what extent Tarentine actions can be distinguished from League actions. The answer is that they cannot, with any degree of reliability, except in the rare cases where the sources give explicit information on this point or where a large number of Greek cities can be seen to be working in collaboration, as with the anti-Roman coalition of 280 BC.[5] Thus the assumption that Tarentine policy always equalled League policy will be avoided except where there is evidence to the contrary.

After the death of Archytas, the Greeks in Calabria and Apulia found themselves under increasing military pressure from their immediate neighbours. Apart from Tarentum, which maintained good relations with Syracuse, many of the cities of Calabria had suffered greatly from the depredations of Dionysios I and Dionysios II, considerably weakening them in terms of both economic and military strength. Tarentum, too, was overstretched, although still at the height of its power and wealth. In 356 BC, Terina had been sacked by the Bruttians, and Metapontum and Heraklea by the Messapians.[6] The newly formed Bruttian League was an ominous sign of growing strength, political coherence and military co-ordination in Calabria.[7] The solution adopted by the Italiotes to this problem of containment was to invite Greek or Macedonian generals to operate in Italy as semi-independent *condottieri*, with a broad mandate and some financial backing from the Italiote League. These generals used largely mercenary armies with some assistance from Greek (mainly Tarentine) levies.[8] This is the subject of considerable disapproval by most ancient authors. It is frequently cited as an indication of Tarentine decadence, and of the weakness of the city.[9] Certainly it was a problematic solution, since there was no effective means of making these *condottieri* accountable for their actions and relations between Tarentum and its generals were frequently strained.[10] Thus it is difficult to determine to what extent the policies pursued by Cleonymus, Alexander and others were those favoured by the Italiote League and by Tarentum. The likelihood is that their actions were not an indication of official policy, and it is possible that they were not operating as agents of the League or of Tarentum, but as independent agents to distract and harass the Oscan tribes of the interior. Certainly the campaigns of Cleonymus – who formed an alliance with the Messapians, attacked Metapontum, and departed after a dispute with Tarentum – do not show much respect for either Tarentine or League policy.[11]

The military success of the *condottieri* was very mixed, as far as we can ascertain from the few surviving sources. Their presence also created a large number of political difficulties which seem severely to have strained the patience of some members of the Italiote League. Even the basis on which these generals operated is uncertain. Although most of the ancient sources explicitly say that the Tarentines were responsible for inviting external help, it is more likely that the decisions were taken, at least nominally, under the aegis of the Italiote League.[12] However, since Tarentum was effectively the League *hegemon*, it is an easy confusion to make, and the Tarentines do seem to be the prime movers on many occasions. More importantly, it also served the purposes of the anti-Tarentine historians who are our only surviving sources, since it enabled the perpetuation of the *topos* that the Tarentines were degenerate and unwarlike, too lazy or cowardly to fight their own battles. The later dissatisfaction with Tarentine actions expressed by other League members was generated by Tarentine domination of League policy rather than by unilateral action. If Tarentum had requested assistance and had paid for it as an independent action, there would not have been a case for complaint, as there was in the 280s, that Tarentum was failing to give adequate protection to the other Greeks.[13]

There is no doubt, however, that Tarentum was the main political force in southern Italy. The choice of generals reflects Tarentine connections – with Sparta, Sicily and Epirus – and includes a number of the more exotic characters of Hellenistic history. Apart from the larger-than-life Pyrrhus (the last and most significant of these *condottieri*), they include Archidamus, Cleonymus and Acrotatus (all scions of the Spartan royal houses), Alexander of Epirus, and Agathocles, (the exiled tyrant of Syracuse). All commanded armies which were largely mercenary, with some Italiote assistance, and operated more or less as free agents within the general terms of the need to harass the Messapians, Bruttians and Lucanians. Indeed, there were moments when Tarentum found the actions of these generals embarrassingly at odds with its own policies. Many showed an inconvenient tendency to be side-tracked by the possibility of richer pickings in Sicily, but looked at objectively, these *condottieri* were not by any means unsuccessful.[14]

The earliest of these was Archidamus of Sparta. The dates of his campaigns are disputed, but he may have arrived in Italy between 344 and 342 BC. Very little is known of his campaigns, but he seems to have enjoyed some success against the Messapians before his death in battle at Manduria in 340 BC.[15] An alternative source tradition, probably deriving from Theopompus, names his enemies as the Lucanians, but this may be a confusion with Alexander of Epirus who arrived in Italy sometime around 333 BC. He proved to be a very effective general, with a run of victories against the Lucanians which very nearly extended Greek-dominated territory as far as southern Campania.[16] In Apulia, he defeated a coalition of Messapians, Daunians and Peucetians, and drove the Messapians out of Metapontum and Heraklea. On the Tyrrhenian coast, he also took a number of the Italiote cities which had fallen to the Lucanians and Bruttians including, briefly, Paestum.[17] This proved to be the limit of his operations. By moving into Campania, he had entered into territory contested by both Rome and the Samnites. He attempted to safeguard his position against the Samnites by making a treaty with Rome, then marched back into Calabria, where he captured Consentia, the chief city of the Bruttian League.[18] Strabo alleges strained political relations with Tarentum which somewhat marred these achievements, and his plan to move the headquarters of the Italiote League from Heraklea, a Tarentine colony, to Thurii may reflect a wish to establish a strong base independent of Tarentum.[19] However, this is the only reference to political problems, and it may be part of the general anti-Tarentine tradition in the sources. Livy's evidence that Heraklea had been captured by the Lucanians suggests that there was a good strategic reason behind the move. Whatever the reason, this proved to be a transient change. Alexander was killed in a skirmish with the Lucanians near Pandosia in 330 BC and Tarentum promptly reinstated Heraklea as the meeting place of the League.[20]

The later *condottieri* were rather less effective, and mostly more concerned with affairs in Sicily than Italy. Agathocles of Syracuse made several interventions in Italy, but with little lasting impact, although he seems to have made himself rather unpopular.[21] In 315/4, Tarentum once again developed an interest in Sicilian affairs, this time in opposition to Syracuse. Acrotatos, son of King Cleomenes of Sparta, mounted an expedition against Agathocles, using Tarentum as a base and supported by the Tarentine fleet.[22] The background to this is hard to disentangle, but from a Tarentine point of view, it seems to be an attempt to guard against the establishment of a strong regime in Syracuse. Agathocles had already shown an unwelcome degree of interest in Italy, and there was the precedent of Dionysios I as an example of the effects of Syracusan ambitions. In 303/2, Acrotatos' brother, Cleonymus, also mounted an expedition to the West, but this time with Italy as its main focus.[23] The Lucanians were once again proving troublesome and he mounted a campaign against them in alliance with Tarentum and the Messapians. Eventually, however, he entered into alliance with the Lucanians and turned his attention to Metapontum, demanding a fine of 200 female hostages and 600 talents of silver from the ruling élite. This proved to be extremely unpopular among the Italiotes and Cleonymus departed, with some rancour, in 301 BC, having provided a startling example of the extent to which alliances could be formed which cut across both ethnic divisions and long-term political structures.[24]

Agathocles, the tyrant of Syracuse, made two expeditions to Italy, both of which took place during periods of exile. The first of these, which seems to have occurred around 315 BC, is very poorly documented. The second, which took place in 300 BC, involved campaigns in Calabria and an apparent attempt to build up a power base using the cities of Croton, Locri and Vibo. In this, he differs markedly from other *condottieri*, who focused their attention on south-east Italy or the Lucanians. His presence in Calabria, an area which had close connections with Sicily, suggests a fundamentally different policy, with an emphasis on building support for his interests in Sicily.[25]

Overall, then, the various mercenary generals were a mixed bag in their effectiveness. Alexander was certainly the most successful in military terms, although he did not have time to consolidate and most territorial gains were lost after his death in 330 BC. Others were rather less so. Undoubtedly the most interesting character and the most important of them, however, was Pyrrhus, who will be discussed below.

What the history of the late fourth century illustrates more than anything is the opportunist nature of most of these interventions. It also highlights the rapidly changing character of diplomatic contacts. Alliances were not necessarily based on a model of Greeks versus Italians, but frequently involved coalitions of Greeks, Messapians, and sometimes others, against enemies who could include both Italians and other Greeks. In general, the Tarentines, Messapians and Peucetians seem to have been allied more often than not after 340 BC. The Lucanians and Bruttians were hostile, more often than not, although there were short periods of alliance with the Tarentine power block. The Samnites, despite their powerful position, seem to have been peripheral to the Italiotes until very late in the fourth century.

The first evidence of conflict between Rome and the Greeks took place in 327/6 BC, in the context of the second Samnite War, although there is evidence of contact with southern Italy from a much earlier period. Cumae sent grain to relieve famines at Rome in the sixth century, and the Sibylline books and the cults of Demeter/Ceres and Venus Erycina reached Rome from the Western Greeks.[26] As for so much of the fourth century, we are reliant on fragmentary and inadequate source material, but the war with Naples is unusual in that two accounts, those of Livy and Dionysios of Halicarnassus, survive in a fairly full, although not complete, form.[27] They differ on points of detail and interpretation, but a broad outline of events can be reconstructed fairly readily. Both present lengthy accounts of the debate preceding the outbreak of war, with a distinctly anti-Oscan flavour.

The background to the war was the Roman anxiety to secure control of northern Campania and to extend Roman control into the Volturnus valley. The Campanians, meanwhile, were increasingly inclined to support the Samnites, unsurprisingly in view of the ethnic connections and the blatant Roman encroachment on the Capuan sphere of influence.[28] Although Livy is inclined to pin the blame for the Neapolitan war on the Samnites, who allegedly subverted a city which was more naturally inclined to support Rome,[29] it is clear that Naples was moving against Rome quite independently of external influence. The actual *casus belli* was a series of raids made by Naples on Roman settlers in the Ager Falernus in 326 BC. Roman protests against this were rejected and war was declared.[30] Naples promptly received support in the form of Campanian troops sent from Nola, and a promise of assistance from Tarentum.[31]

The campaign itself was short and sharp, and was concluded in the following year as a result of *stasis* in Naples rather than by military action. The Roman commander Q. Publilius Philo opened operations with raids on Neapolitan territory and a march on the city. He set up camp between the settlements of Palaepolis and Neapolis, thus severing communications between the two parts of the city.[32] This effectively produced a stalemate. Naples was not easy to besiege since its harbour allowed it to be supplied by sea, but it was hampered by lack of communication between the two parts of the city, and by internal instability. The expected reinforcements from Tarentum (or more probably the Italiote League) failed to arrive, and the Nolan troops within the city made themselves unpopular in some quarters.[33] Early in 326 BC, a group of disaffected Neapolitans, led by the Greek Charilaus and the Oscan Nympsius, staged a *coup* and opened the city gates to the Roman forces. The city, under its new pro-Roman regime, was rewarded for its timely change of heart by a treaty of exceptionally favourable terms.[34] Unfortunately, no details of this document have been preserved, but it went down as a byword in Roman history, being referred to by both Livy and Cicero as a *foedus aequissimum*.

Although Livy and Dionysios differ on details,[35] there are few fundamental incompatibilities. The common features are that there was a political division within Naples, and that pressure was brought to bear both by Tarentum and by the Campanians to support the Samnites against Rome. This combination of internal *stasis* and pressure emanating from relations with neighbouring Italians is a feature of Italiote history which can be traced in the events of the second Punic War and later. Dionysios gives the more detailed account of the negotiations between Naples and the Samnites.[36] He also adds the detail that the Samnites offered to restore Cumae to the Greeks, thereby gaining the support of the Cumaeans who had migrated to Naples in 421. Frederiksen suggests, plausibly, that the central portion of the account, which gives details of the negotiations with the Samnite ambassadors, is probably drawn from a Greek source, while the later portions of the account follow the same source as Livy. Dionysios' version is noticeably less anti-Greek, although it ultimately favours the Roman point of view and, unlike Livy, places less emphasis on the the division between 'good' aristocrats and 'bad' democrats.

One point which emerges from both versions is that Tarentum clearly had an alliance with Naples,[37] and it seems likely that Naples was a member of the Italiote League.[38] It is possible that geographical isolation from the rest of the League made it difficult for Tarentum to supply the assistance promised, a failure which is interpreted as an example of Tarentine bad faith but which may rather reflect a reluctance to become involved in a distant conflict, not an explicitly broken promise. The League as a whole, and Tarentum in particular, may have been unwilling to declare support for the Samnites. They were a powerful group whose interests potentially collided with those of Tarentum, and the League had much to gain by a war which would keep their forces engaged elsewhere. There is no evidence that Tarentum was concerned about Roman expansion at this date, or had any reason to favour an anti-Roman policy. Only a few years earlier, Alexander of Epirus had fought against the Samnites and concluded some form of treaty or *amicitia* with Rome. The early development of Tarentine hostility to Rome is clearly part of the anti-Tarentine tradition in the sources.

The political divisions, as described by both Dionysios and Livy,[39] do not fit a simple pattern of Greek community versus Oscans. The leaders of the *coup* which led to the surrender of the city to Rome were Charilaus, a Greek, and Nympsius, an Oscan – an indication that it was organised by a faction drawn from both groups. There is a strong likelihood that in this case, the Livian identification of the aristocratic faction as supporters of Rome is correct,[40] although this pattern does not always hold good for other cities or at other periods of history. There were long-established contacts between the Campanian and Roman élites.[41] The leaders of the revolt against the Samnites are described as *principes civitatis*,[42] which implies that they were of the élite, but not necessarily holders of public office. It has been suggested, plausibly, that the revolt may have been instigated largely by the class which provided the cavalry,[43] which confirms the largely aristocratic nature of the pro-Roman party.

Overall, the significance of the agreement between Rome and Naples was that it brought southern Italy firmly into the Roman orbit. The treaty with Naples consolidated Roman interests in Campania and detached the most northerly outpost of the Italiote League. Perhaps more importantly, the network of Roman alliances in Lucania and northern Apulia, initially designed to isolate the Samnites, signalled growing encroachment on the Tarentine sphere of influence.

In northern Lucania, the earliest signs of Roman interest begin in the 290s. Paestum and Velia may have already had contacts with Rome, but with virtually no evidence to go on, it is difficult to judge how extensive these were. Paestum, like Cumae, was extensively Oscanised. Literary evidence suggests that the Lucanian takeover was violent, and that the Greeks were oppressed, being unable openly to retain their Greek identity.[44] However, there is no archaeological evidence for a destruction phase, and there are many signs of continuing Hellenism.[45] Oscanisation was a less harsh and abrupt process than literature would have us believe. The Lucanian domination of the city is not in doubt, however, and it seems likely that Paestum came under Roman control during the conflicts between Rome and the Lucanians in the closing years of the fourth century. Whatever the circumstances, the city received a Latin colony in 273 BC,[46] bringing it into close contact with Rome. Roman interest in the neighbouring city of Velia was more limited. This may simply mean that the Velians remained neutral or friendly to Rome during the closing years of the fourth century. However, by the first decade of the third century, Rome and Velia were at war. Velia supported the Samnites during the third Samnite War, and was conquered by Carvilius in 293 BC.[47]

By the beginning of the third century, Roman contacts in southern Italy were becoming more extensive, but they still stopped short of a direct encroachment on Tarentine interests. The danger in 326 BC lay in a treaty between Rome and the Lucanians. This gave support to a powerful enemy of Tarentum and provided Rome with an excuse to interfere more directly in the South. Livy gives a graphic and detailed account of the stratagem used by the Tarentines to disrupt this alliance, attributing it to Tarentine duplicity.[48] In fact, the prime movers were a group of anti-Roman Lucanians, although they acted with support from the Greeks. They staged a fake assault on a number of aristocratic Lucanian youths who then exhibited their injuries at a Lucanian assembly, claiming that these had been caused by a group of Romans. The Lucanians reacted with righteous indignation and broke their treaty with Rome forthwith. This dramatic tale is clearly part of an anti-Tarentine source tradition, but it reveals a high level of political instability among the Lucanians and a deep ambivalence towards an alliance with Rome. The Greeks may have prodded the anti-Roman factions into action in order to prevent the formation of a potentially troublesome coalition, but there is no evidence of a grand anti-Roman strategy on the part of Tarentum. It is presented as an example of Tarentine hostility to Rome,[49] but it is more likely that it was motivated by a wish to destabilise the Lucanians by setting the pro- and anti-Roman factions against each other to protect the Tarentine sphere of interest and to remove a possible means of support for the Lucanians. Significantly, there is no sign of an alliance between Greeks and Lucanians.

Frederiksen argues that after *c.* 334 BC, Tarentum adopted a firmly pro-Samnite and anti-Roman foreign policy, thereby shocking the rest of the Greeks in Italy and eventually inducing them to look to Rome rather than Tarentum as *hegemon*.[50] One of the allegations made against the pro-Samnite faction in Naples in 326 was that they were behaving in a manner unworthy of Greeks in proposing to make an alliance with the Oscans.[51] However, this may not signify anything more than the general moral disapproval evident in many sources for Italiote history.

In fact, there is evidence that Tarentum had friendly connections with the Samnites earlier in the fourth century. An anecdote told by Cicero points to personal connections between individual members of the Samnite and Tarentine élites, notably Archytas, and there is archaeological evidence of Hellenisation in Samnium.[52] The history of the fourth century does not support the notion of a division between a pro-Samnite and anti-Samnite phase in Tarentine policy. Rather, it resolves into a shifting pattern of short-term alliances and hostilities which frequently cut across ethnic divisions – Tarentines and Messapians against Lucanians; Tarentines, Messapians and Lucanians against Metapontines; Greeks and Peucetians against Samnites and Lucanians. Tarentine or Italiote League support for Naples' brief pro-Samnite initiative was lukewarm, and there is no obvious reason why Tarentum should have wished to see a powerful neighbour strengthened or should have unnecessarily provoked Roman hostility. Since there is evidence of increasing pressure from the Lucanians and Bruttians in the late fourth century,[53] it seems unlikely that Tarentum would wish to provoke an avoidable war.

Equally, the view that Tarentum was trading opposition to Rome and support for the Samnites for Samnite assistance in wars against other Oscans,[54] is not borne out by the evidence. There is no direct evidence for the Samnite assistance, but there are references which suggest that the Samnites may have suffered at the hands of some of the Tarentine-employed *condottieri*.[55] Nor is archaeology much help on this point.

48

Frederiksen's assertion that the addition of Greek fortifications to Lucanian settlements is evidence of direct military assistance to the Samnites in garrisoning Lucania is doubtful. Greek construction techniques were not unusual in fourth-century Calabria and may well owe more to processes of cultural contact and diffusion than to military considerations.[56] In general, Tarentine policy seems to have been aimed at maintaining Tarentine supremacy by means of encouraging divisions and instability among the neighbouring Oscan tribes, rather than adopting a consistent stance over the question of Romano-Samnite conflict.

A similar trend can be observed in 320, when Tarentum attempted to arbitrate between Rome and the Samnites.[57] By this time, the conflict had moved much further towards Tarentine territory, and Rome was showing signs of expansion in Apulia.[58] In the aftermath of the defeat at the Caudine Forks in 321, the focus of operations was switched to northern Apulia, in an attempt to surround the Samnites with hostile territory. Many Daunian cities were favourably disposed towards Rome and a large number of them became allies. The Samnites retaliated by sending a force against the Romans and in 320 the two armies met near Luceria.[59] Before the battle took place, a Tarentine delegation intervened and offered to arbitrate between the two sides, with the inducement that the Tarentine army would fight against the side which refused. Seizing the main chance, the Samnites agreed. The Romans, however, replied in scornful terms that the Tarentines were not strong enough to dictate terms, and in the ensuing battle the Samnites were defeated.

The threat to the Tarentine sphere of influence implied by the Roman presence in Apulia may have inspired this direct action. The intervention in 320 was a Tarentine attempt to take control of the situation and impose an arbitrated settlement, a common diplomatic device in the Hellenistic world.[60] It rather contradicts the view that Tarentine hostility to Rome was unprovoked. Roman interests in Apulia provided a good reason for action, and far from showing a preference for the Samnite cause, as Livy implies, Tarentum attempted to force both sides to negotiate, only joining the Samnites after Rome had finally refused.[61] There is little to support Livy's implication that the Tarentines were blindly and unprovokedly hostile to Rome. Given that the Samnites were historically far more likely to be on bad terms with Tarentum, it was more in the interest of Tarentum to join Rome in curbing Samnite power, than to have a strong immediate neighbour as a result of a Samnite victory.

The negotiations of 320 BC may form the context for the first documented treaty between Rome and Tarentum.[62] This is known from an account of the outbreak of the Pyrrhic War, which indicates the violation, by a Roman commander, of an agreement that the Roman fleet should not sail east of Cape Lacinium.[63] There has been considerable debate concerning the dating of this agreement, which is clearly designed to delimit the respective spheres of interest of Rome and Tarentum. Appian refers to it as being an ancient agreement, 'παλαιῶν τοὺς Ταραντίνους ἀπεμίμνησκε συνθηκῶν . . .', raising the question as to whether an agreement of forty years standing or less could be described in these terms.[64] Appian, writing long after the event, may not have known the date of the original agreement, and his evidence cannot be regarded as a conclusive reason for rejecting any of the proposed dates in the late fourth century. The incident of 320 seems to be the first indication of a direct conflict of interest between the two main powers in Italy, and thus provides a plausible context for an agreement seeking to remove the grounds for possible conflict. However, it is possible that it could be dated to the period following this. There is some evidence for a conflict between Rome and Tarentum in 303/2, as a result of Cleonymus's campaigns in the South.[65] Thus the period between 320 and 302 seems to have been marked by an increasing number of incidents in which Tarentine and Roman spheres of interest coincided. A formal agreement which defined those spheres of interest more precisely could have been negotiated at any stage in this period, but 320 or shortly afterwards seems an appropriate point.

The Pyrrhic War, which began in 280 BC, marks the entry of Rome into permanent contact with Magna Graecia. It also illustrates the importance of political considerations and of local questions in determining relations with immediate neighbours and relations between Rome and the South. The accounts of the war differ in their assessment of the cause, but are not incompatible. The immediate *casus belli* was the breaking of the treaty which stipulated that Roman warships should not enter Tarentine waters. A Roman squadron sailed into the Gulf of Tarentum in 282 BC, apparently on a reconnaissance mission. The Tarentine fleet attacked and sank five out of the ten Roman ships.[66] Despite the fact that this was a clear act of aggression, Rome sent an embassy led by L. Postumius to demand reparations. Not surprisingly, this was rejected by the Tarentine assembly which was swayed, according to the sources, by irresponsible and anti-Roman demagogues who offered gross insults to the Roman ambassadors.[67] In fact, it seems more likely that Tarentum reacted violently because Rome had apparently threatened Tarentine control of the seas, which represented a direct threat to both security and trade, and also because Roman influence was eroding control of the main Tarentine power base, namely the Italiote League. In 285 BC, Thurii, presumably a member of the League, had appealed to Rome rather than Tarentum for assistance in a war against the Lucanians.[68] This had been granted, and a garrison had been established at Thurii, setting a dangerous precedent for Tarentum and leaving a permanent military presence within the Tarentine sphere of influence. This garrison was ejected by Tarentum in 282, and Thurii was forcibly returned to the Italiote League.[69] These two incidents represent a gradual escalation of tension between Rome and Tarentum, which culminated in war.

Neither Rome nor Tarentum was wholeheartedly committed to the war in 280. Shortly after the rejection of Postumius' embassy, elections were held at Tarentum and a moderate pro-Roman, Agis, was elected *strategos autokrator*. He advocated further negotiations with Rome, but held office for only a short time before being deposed in favour of a more anti-Roman leader.[70] The reasons behind this are obscure. Clearly there was political strife in Tarentum, involving groups which divided on pro-Roman and anti-Roman lines. The deep internal divisions which can be seen in operation in many cities, both Greek and non-Greek, in southern Italy are characteristic of the political climate of the third century. Livy, defining them in terms of their effect on the progress of the second Punic War, identifies the anti-Roman party in any given state as composed of demagogues, extremists and unreliable elements, while the pro-Romans are identified as aristocrats and described as *optimates*. The implications of this are described in further detail in Chapter 3, but it is worth noting here that these identifications do not necessarily work, either for 280 or 216–209 BC.[71] The power struggle at Tarentum was a fierce one, whoever the participants. In the end, the anti-Roman faction gained control and forced a number of their opponents to flee the city. They then fell back on the policy of looking to mercenary generals from Greece for assistance, and called on Pyrrhus of Epirus to help.[72]

Pyrrhus, the nephew of Alexander the Great, is one of the more exotic characters of Greek history and one who caught the imagination of many later biographers and historians.[73] He was one of the foremost generals of his day, and the Pyrrhic War occupies an important place in military history as the first confrontation between the Roman legions and the Hellenistic phalanx.[74] He is described by Plutarch as being of fierce and forbidding appearance but of noble character, brave in battle, honourable in his negotiations with the Romans and willing to make generous gestures such as releasing prisoners without ransom. Many anecdotes about Pyrrhus and his chief political advisor, the wise and virtuous Cineas, have passed into literary tradition, but it is very difficult, nevertheless, to piece together a coherent picture of the progress of the war. Even Pyrrhus' motivation is uncertain. He is said to have wished to conquer an empire in the West, but this is a motive attributed to many other generals, including Alexander of Epirus, and must be suspect.[75]

Whatever his motives, he presented a powerful threat to Rome, since he came with a large amount of financial and military support from both Italy and the East. Antiochus of Syria and Ptolemy of Egypt made financial donations to his campaign. Tarentum supplied troops and money, as well as transporting his army of 20,000 troops, 2,000 cavalry and 20 elephants to Italy. In addition, Pyrrhus and the Tarentines between them managed to put together a formidable anti-Roman coalition within Italy by making common cause with the Samnites and some Etruscan cities, forcing Rome to fight what was in effect a fourth Samnite War.[76]

The relations between Rome and other Greek cities in the South at this date are obscure. The garrisoning of Thurii in 285 indicates that Rome was now directly involved in southern Italy. There were several defections from the Italiote League, either before or immediately after Pyrrhus' arrival, although the exact chronology is uncertain. Many sources attribute the appeals for Roman help to distaste for Pyrrhus, but at Rhegium, the Roman garrison may have arrived as early as 282, well before the Tarentine invitation to Pyrrhus.[77] Other cities which elected to join Rome, either in 280 or between 285 and 282, were Croton, Locri and Rhegium.[78] Of these, Locri may have been subject to some degree of political unrest, since the city seems to have changed sides a number of times and clearly felt the need to make a public affirmation of loyalty to Rome after the war by the issue of a coin series with the legend *Pistis*. References to an otherwise unnamed *Basileus*[79] in the archives of the Olympieion are probably an indication of support for Pyrrhus. Rhegium seems to have been the city which suffered most serious damage, since it was taken over by a renegade group of Campanian mercenaries who formed the Roman garrison.[80] The sources present this as a gratuitous act of violence on the part of the Campanians, which was subsequently punished. However, the fact that they continued to act on behalf of Rome and also that Rome appears to have been very slow to put down the insurrection, which was a clear act of mutiny, even after the greater part of the fighting was over, may indicate that the issue was not clear cut. In view of the frequent changes of sides by other Italiote cities, it is likely that the takeover originated as an over-enthusiastic response to a projected change of loyalties on behalf of Rhegium.

Initially, Rome seemed reluctant to fight and anxious to end the war quickly. The consul for 279, G. Fabricius Luscinus, was instructed to devastate the territory of Tarentum but not to join battle, presumably in the hope that Tarentum would choose to make peace.[81] The motivation for this seems to have been anxiety over Rome's existing military commitments in Etruria and Samnium, not to mention the ever-present threat of Gallic raids. The victory over a Samnite/Gallic/Etruscan coalition at Sentinum in 295 BC had somewhat relieved pressure on Rome from the North, but not removed it entirely.[82] Certainly, political opinion at Rome was divided over war with Tarentum. There is no reason to believe, however, that there was a simple division into those who favoured expansion to the North and those who believed that Rome's future lay in domination of southern Italy. Still less is it helpful to correlate these divisions with the balance of power between the old patrician aristocracy and the new nobility of plebeian origin.[83] The most likely motive lay in perceptions of the threat from the Samnites, and of the resurgence of a Samnite-led coalition. In the event, Rome's worst fears were realised after the arrival of Pyrrhus. The Tarentines and Pyrrhus between them managed to put together an alliance of Greeks, Samnites, Umbrians and Etruscans which had the potential to open up a war on two fronts.[84]

The first months of the war were fairly quiet. There was little initial reaction to Fabricius' raids, but within Tarentum there were extensive preparations for war. Pyrrhus immediately put the city on a war footing, banning theatrical performances, introducing universal conscription of men of military age and demanding financial contributions from other citizens. Coins minted at Tarentum at this date carry symbols associated with Pyrrhus, including the spearhead emblem of the Epirote royal house and the eagle and thunderbolt of Zeus.[85] There was also some cultural posturing. Rome had developed the foundation legend of Aeneas in the fourth century, but in 280 Pyrrhus neatly overturned this Hellenising propaganda by the claim that the Epirote royal house was descended from Achilles, and that he was therefore a natural heir of the Homeric Greeks, destined to conquer the descendants of Trojans.[86] The main Roman forces under Aemilius Barbula were concentrated around Venusia to contain the Samnites, while the other consul, Valerius Laevinus, advanced on Pyrrhus, finally encountering him near Heraklea. His army substantially outnumbered that of Pyrrhus, who proposed arbitration of the dispute between the Tarentines and Romans. This may have been as a means of gaining time while he sought reinforcements, but it was also a normal feature of Hellenistic diplomacy, which was not, however, recognised by the Romans until *c.* 200 BC.[87] Laevinus rejected the move, and attacked. Against expectations, the ensuing battle was won by Pyrrhus, and the Romans were forced to retreat to Venusia, but Pyrrhus' losses were very heavy. Nevertheless, the victory was a useful public relations exercise and was commemorated by a dedication at Dodona, at the temples of Athena at Athens and Lindos and at the temple of Zeus at Tarentum.[88]

The Battle of Heraklea was a costly victory in terms of manpower, but it tipped the political balance temporarily in favour of Pyrrhus and his allies. Croton and Locri ejected their Roman garrisons and joined him, along with much of the Oscan population of southern Italy. Rhegium may have attempted to do likewise, but the Campanian garrison sent there by Rome took matters into its own hands, by taking direct control of the city and slaughtering the Greek rulers.[89] The Romans were now very much on the defensive. Pyrrhus and his new allies made a rapid march north into Campania, perhaps to reach Naples, but were forestalled by Laevinus. He then marched on as far as Anagnia, 60 km south of Rome, either with a view to besieging Rome or to making contact with the Etruscans. This very nearly led him into a trap as Rome had just made peace with her main Etruscan enemies and Pyrrhus ran a real risk of being trapped between two Roman armies. His reaction was to retreat to Tarentum and open negotiations with Rome.

This episode is somewhat problematic, as our accounts of the negotiations are heavily weighted with anecdotes about Pyrrhus and Cineas.[90] The main clauses, however, seem to have been a guarantee of freedom and autonomy for the Italiotes, an alliance with Pyrrhus himself, and the return of all land taken from the Samnites, Lucanians and Bruttians by Rome. The strength of Pyrrhus' position in relation to Rome can be gauged by the inclination of the Senate to accept these terms, despite the considerable loss of territory involved and the threat of a strong Tarentine power block in southern Italy, not to mention a Samnite resurgence. The clinching factor which ensured its rejection was the opposition of Appius Claudius Caecus, the builder of the Via Appia and one of the few politicians with a stated interest in Roman expansion to the South.[91]

After the failure of these negotiations, Pyrrhus began to exact money from the Italiote cities to finance another campaign. Tarentine staters of this period are reduced in weight, a feature which suggests financial stress. The archives of the Olympieion at Locri show substantial payments from the temple treasury, probably to Pyrrhus. The sums involved add up to approximately 295 tonnes of silver, with a largest single payment of 2,685 talents.[92] With this reserve of cash, together with contributions from other cities, Pyrrhus raised more troops and in 279 mounted a campaign in Apulia, pushing northwards towards Samnium. His way was blocked by the armies of Sulpicius Saverrio and Decimus Mus, who were based at Venusia, and a further battle was fought at Ausculum. Like the Battle of Heraklea, this was quite literally a 'Pyrrhic victory', in which Pyrrhus sustained losses which made him unable to follow up his advantage and forced him to retreat once again to Tarentum.[93]

At this point, several external factors came into play. In addition to his losses at Ausculum, Pyrrhus was under threat at home. The death of Ptolemy Ceraunos left Macedon in a state of civil war, and consequently left Epirus vulnerable. There was also a considerable amount of unrest among Pyrrhus' Italiote allies, presumably as a result of his financial exactions. The situation was resolved, for Pyrrhus if not for the Italiotes, by an invitation from Syracuse to assist it in a war with Carthage. In addition to allowing him to remove himself from Italy, this had the advantage that Pyrrhus had a legitimate claim to rule Syracuse, as a son-in-law of the tyrant Agathocles, who had died in 289 BC. Accordingly, he declared his son (Agathocles' grandson) tyrant of Syracuse, and departed for Sicily, leaving a garrison at Tarentum.[94]

During 278–276, the Romans gradually made encroachments of the territory controlled by Pyrrhus and his allies. Victories over the Lucanians, Bruttians, Samnites and Greeks are recorded. Croton was taken by Cornelius Rufinus, as was Caulonia, and in 276 Pyrrhus was urgently requested to return.[95] During his crossing back to Italy, he was overtaken by a Carthaginian fleet and suffered major losses. He landed at Locri, which still supported him, and attempted to take Rhegium, but without success. He also caused bad feeling by exacting yet more money from the Locrians and seizing the temple treasure from the temple of Persephone. Support from both Oscans and Greeks seems to have been waning considerably, but Pyrrhus mounted a last campaign, marching north through Lucania.[96] He encountered the army of M' Curius Dentatus at Malventum (later Beneventum), where he suffered a decisive defeat.

Following the Battle of Beneventum in 275, Pyrrhus withdrew to Tarentum and shortly afterwards returned to Epirus, leaving a force of Epirotes under his son, Helenus, and Milo, his second-in-command.

Helenus was ordered back to Macedon in 274/3, although Milo remained for a few months longer. Tarentum continued to hold out against Rome until 272, when it was finally taken.[97]

The post-war settlements between Rome and the Greek cities are very poorly documented, leaving great gaps in our knowledge of the basis for Romano-Greek relations prior to 218 BC. Livy, one of the few surviving authors to mention the end of the war, simply says that Tarentum was taken and that peace was made.[98] Even fewer details are known about other cities, unless the peace with Tarentum stands for a settlement with the whole Italiote League. A few details from the years between 272 and 218 give an indication that the peace terms were not too onerous. The events of the first and second Punic Wars show that the Italiotes retained their military capacity, both in land forces and ships. Military assistance to Rome can be inferred, but most of our evidence for this dates from the second century rather than the third. Likewise, it is impossible to judge how onerous the military burdens imposed by Rome on the Italiote cities were. There has been much debate over the nature of the Greek military role in Roman Italy, which will be discussed further in Chapter 4.

Politically, there are equally few details of settlements. It seems probable to the point of certainty that anti-Roman politicians were exiled and pro-Roman governments installed. At Locri, the new regime went out of its way to make a public statement of loyalty to Rome, issuing a series of coins showing Nike crowning the goddess Roma and bearing the legend *Pistis*, indicating fidelity to Rome.[99] One of the major political problems faced by Rome was that of re-establishing credibility at Rhegium. The city had been garrisoned early in the war by Rome, but the Campanian troops constituting the garrison turned on the city, slaughtering many of the Greek ruling élite. The ringleader, Decius Vibellius, was killed by a Rhegine plot but the city remained under Campanian control until 265 BC, several years after the end of the Pyrrhic War. When Rome finally ejected the rebels, reparations were made to Rhegium and the remaining Campanians were executed, but the incident was not a reassuring one for any city which needed Roman military 'protection'.[100] The fate of the Italiote League is completely unknown. There is no record of it being dissolved, but equally no certain evidence that it survived. However, there are precedents which argue for survival. Both the Samnite and Bruttian Leagues survived Roman expansion for a considerable number of years, although both were eventually disbanded.[101] Given that the pattern of alliances during the second Punic War closely mimics those of the fourth century, it is tempting to infer that the League was still in operation, or at least was revived.[102]

The events of the later fourth century underline nothing so much as the shifting and uncertain nature of the pattern of alliances and hostilities in southern Italy. The material culture proclaims the increasing Hellenisation of the Italians of Apulia and Calabria, with attendant implications of economic and political contacts, at a time when the literary sources describe a series of bitter wars between the Greeks and their neighbours. Clearly, these wars are not the whole story. Nor does war with one group of Italians, be they Lucanian, Bruttian or anything else, imply conflict with all the Oscan peoples of the region. The history of Tarentine relations with the Samnites illustrates very well the diplomatic shifts which took place to accommodate changing conditions. By extension, Greek relations with Rome must also be seen against a background of rapidly changing alliances to accommodate pressure from a variety of different sources. The notion, perpetuated by Livy and other authors, that Tarentum pursued a policy of unrelieved and unprovoked hostility to Rome and friendship for the Samnites is one that is unrealistic in these terms. Rome was not a major factor in the Tarentine world-view until 320 BC, with the opening of a second front against the Samnites in Apulia. Thereafter, the consolidation of the Roman presence in the South, signalled by the founding of colonies at Luceria (314 BC), Venusia (291), Paestum (273) and Beneventum (268) and finally, by direct undermining of Tarentine influence with Greek cities, demonstrated that the Roman threat to Tarentum was one to be taken seriously.

3

The Punic Wars

The immediate aftermath of the Pyrrhic War is characterised by an almost total silence in our sources. References are infrequent, to say the least, leaving a gap in the historical record which covers most of the mid-third century BC. Our only detailed information on relations between Rome and Magna Graecia concerns the period 215–207, the years during which many southern cities, both Greek and Oscan, abandoned their alliance with Rome in favour of Hannibal. For this reason, if for no other, the second Punic War is of vital importance for the study of Roman relations with the Italiotes in that it provides a number of relatively detailed case studies of their attitudes to Rome, their reactions to Hannibal, and the sources of any dissatisfaction with Roman behaviour.

Given that all the extant sources were composed a considerable time after the events and had a strong pro-Roman bias,[1] two important questions must be addressed. To what extent is it possible to distinguish historical facts from the literary commonplaces discussed in the Introduction,[2] and are the incidents described genuinely of the later third century or are they based on Timaean material relating to the Pyrrhic War? As already noted, there is the possibility that the historical tradition had absorbed an anti-Italiote, and particularly anti-Tarentine, bias from fourth-century historians, notably Timaeus. The concept of *tryphe*,[3] which is particularly prominent in Pythagorean historiography, may be traceable in the handling of third-century history by later authors. However, while it seems certain that many of the features found in accounts of Greek relations with Rome had become literary *topoi*,[4] it is by no means certain that these can all be traced back to Timaeus or other fourth-century historians.

Our principal source for the period is Livy, together with fragments of Polybios and Appian, and some isolated comments by a variety of other authors, all of imperial date. Given the heterogeneous nature of this collection of material, it seems unlikely in the extreme that all the incidents described can be dismissed as extrapolation from the events of the fourth century and the Pyrrhic War. Undoubtedly Timaeus influenced the development of Roman historiography,[5] but to ascribe the events recounted by Livy for 215–209 to his history of fourth-century Sicily and Italy is to ignore the condition of the third century. It is true that there are similarities between some Italiote actions of 215–209 and aspects of their behaviour in 280–270, but in most cases these actions are not unlikely, in their third-century context.[6] It is also true that the similarities are resemblances of construction by the author rather than exact repetitions of fact, which further underlines the extent to which our sources are pervaded by anti-Greek sentiment.

The reactions of the Italiotes to the arrival of Hannibal in southern Italy varied greatly, and depended on a number of factors reflecting the differing situations of these cities. His resounding victory at Cannae in 216 BC effectively gave all Roman allies in the South an opportunity to renounce their treaties with Rome. The varied reaction among the Italiotes underscores yet again the diverse nature and interests of this group of states. It also emphasises the impossibility of a single explanation for their behaviour and forces us to examine carefully the motivations which are indicated by the sources.

A chronic lack of political stability is highlighted by Livy as the major factor in provoking defections from Rome.[7] This is something which cannot readily be explained by assuming that it is a reiteration of a Timaean theme. Sources for 350–280 BC hint at possible conflict at Tarentum, but it is not heavily emphasised, and the problem is defined in terms of demagoguery rather than *stasis*.[8] In contrast, Livy offers a scenario which emphasises the suppression of the pro-Roman faction, described as *boni* or *optimates*, by the anti-Roman elements. This simplification of the political divide owes more to the first-century divisions between *optimates* and *populares* than to Timaeus' views on fourth-century democracy.[9] In fact, circumstances are clearly more complex than is suggested by Livy's account, with a less clear correlation between so-called optimate political affiliations and loyalty to Rome.

Another aspect of the defections from Rome is the influence of local alliances and enmities on Greek actions. Italiote relations with the Lucanians, Bruttians and Messapians had been intermittently strained throughout much of the history of the Greek colonies, but there had also been periods of alliance[10]. In many cities, the local issues of relations with the neighbouring Italians seem largely to have overshadowed the wider issues raised by the presence of Hannibal. It seems entirely possible that given the slight nature of Roman contacts with the South in the post-Pyrrhic period, the issue of relations with Rome were a consideration of lesser importance than those with the neighbouring tribes, a factor which Hannibal seems to have recognised and played on.[11] To later sources and modern historians, all working with the benefit of hindsight, it is obvious that the significant conflict was that between Rome and Carthage and their respective allies, but this may not have been as clear to the Greeks in the third century, to whom Rome and Carthage were simply another element in an already complex local situation.

It is notable that the cities which defected most readily to Hannibal, and which supported him for longest, included Tarentum, Thurii, Croton, Locri, and Metapontum, all of which were leading members of the Italiote League in the fourth century. With the exception of Rhegium, the cities which remained loyal to Rome were those of Campania and northern Lucania, which were less closely involved with the Italiote League, as far as is known.[12] This may imply that the core of the revolt centred on the League. Given the lack of evidence for the treaties of 270, it is quite possible that the League was never dissolved. The existence of treaties between Roman allies which were quite independent of Rome is well documented in other areas of Italy, and there are parallels for the survival of local leagues.[13] Nevertheless, an argument *ex silentio* is dubious. The most that can be said with any degree of certainty is that the states which opposed Rome in the 270s were broadly those which joined forces with Hannibal after Cannae, with Tarentum apparently very much in the forefront of this secession.

Whatever the reasons for the defections of the Greek cities, they can hardly be attributed to direct Roman action, since involvement in the area seems to have been very slight in the third century. The settlements after the Pyrrhic War do not seem to have been onerous, with an emphasis on maintaining autonomy rather than on specific treaty obligations. In this, the pattern of diplomatic connections with Magna Graecia resembles the early stages of contact with the Hellenistic world, where relations were non-specific.[14] It is notable that the Italiote Greeks maintained a steady diplomatic presence in the East in the period before the Punic Wars, and may have regarded themselves as primarily part of the Greek world.[15] Most of the Greek cities appear to have remained aloof from the events of the first Punic War. Locri, Tarentum and Velia assisted Rome by supplying ships to transport the Roman army to Sicily in 264 BC,[16] but no other military involvement is known. The Greeks are also omitted from the emergency register of Italian manpower drawn up in 225 BC, despite the fact that they clearly had a significant military capability, as demonstrated by the events of 216–203 BC.[17] There is no reason to suspect bad relations with Rome at this point, although it is notable that at the outset of the second Punic War Tarentum was one of the first cities to be garrisoned, and that hostages were taken from Tarentum and Thurii.[18] This argues that there had been some degree of unrest or disaffection in the South in the period immediately before the war. It is not possible, however, to make assertions which are valid about the whole of Magna Graecia, even at the beginning of the war. There is no evidence that there was any perceptible anti-Roman feeling elsewhere, and the Greek cities of Campania were notable for their loyalty during the war.[19]

Our understanding of the role played by the Italiotes in the second Punic War begins essentially with Hannibal's decisive victory over Rome at Cannae in 216 BC, but this is not to say that the Greeks had not been involved in Roman preparations before this date. Tarentum was garrisoned by Rome in 218, immediately after the outbreak of war, an act which is somewhat ambiguous in its implications. It may have been a routine precaution to safeguard the harbour and communications with the East, as was the case in the 180s.[20] However, there are indications that it may have had greater significance. Tarentum remained a powerful city whose harbour was of vital strategic and commercial importance, and which had also, at some stage in the past, had a treaty with Carthage that may still have been valid.[21] Whether relations with Rome in the years between 270 and 218 had been good or not, the prompt garrisoning of the city indicates that Tarentum was perceived as an actual or potential threat. The taking of Tarentine and Thurian hostages who were still held in Rome in 215 BC gives some support to this.[22] Livy does not give any details as to when hostages were taken, why, and whether hostages were demanded from any cities other than Tarentum and Thurii. However, in the light of the other evidence, 218 seems a plausible date. If this was so, the combination of hostages and a garrison would suggest that there was some serious doubt about the reliability of Tarentum and the extent of the threat which it potentially posed to Rome.

On a more general level, it became very clear soon after Hannibal's arrival in Italy that he recognised the importance of Rome's network of colonies and alliances, and realised that breaking up this network was the key to destroying Roman power. After his initial victories at the Battles of Ticinus and Trebia and the crushing defeat of Flaminius' army at Trasimene in 217, he made a concerted effort to detach Italian support from Rome. Polybios records that he announced his intention to liberate the Italians from Roman oppression and underpinned this by his treatment of prisoners of war.[23] The Italians were well treated and released with minimal ransom, while the Roman captives were treated harshly and difficulties were made about their release. The extent to which this affected the attitude of different groups of allies is unclear, and there was no obvious effect until after Cannae, when many of the allies who revolted were newly conquered and with a history of intense hostility to Rome. The majority of secessions occurred in Oscan areas – in Samnium, northern Apulia, Campania, Bruttium and Lucania.

It has been widely believed that Hannibal's ultimate failure to undermine Roman control of Italy reflects a fundamental misunderstanding of the nature of that control.[24] However, the extent of this failure of understanding may be more apparent than real. His appeals to the allies, as transmitted by our sources, are appeals to throw off the oppressive rule of Rome and regain their liberty. While this pose as a liberator is historically plausible, it is also suspiciously close to the rhetoric of many other generals and politicians in Greek historiography,[25] and for this reason it should not be taken too readily at face value as a statement of Hannibal's understanding of the relations between Rome and her allies. The slogan of *eleutheria tōn Hellenōn* – the freedom of the Greeks – had a long tradition in Greek history, literature and rhetoric. It was also a fairly standard element in the propaganda and political sloganising of the Hellenistic world. The earliest examples occur in 319/18 when Polyperchon made a declaration of the freedom of the Greeks, and in 315 when Antigonos did likewise.[26] It became an increasingly frequent element in Hellenistic diplomacy in the third century and was frequently employed by Philip V, a fact which attracted scathing comment from Polybios.[27] The rhetoric of *eleutheria*, however, is notably absent in Italy. Pyrrhus used the rhetoric of liberation, and *libertas* was restored to Rhegium in 270 and Locri in 204, but it was not usual in the Roman world.[28] The invocation of *eleutheria* by both Pyrrhus and Hannibal seems to imply the deliberate use of the conventions of the Hellenistic world, rather than a misunderstanding of the nature of Rome's alliance structure.

Nor was this strategy entirely unsuccessful. There were a substantial number of defections from Rome after the crushing defeat at Cannae in 216. After this date, Hannibal did indeed gain a substantial amount of Italian support, principally from the Greeks and the Oscan-speaking peoples of southern and central Italy, and among the Celts of Cisalpine Gaul.[29] His failure lay not so much in not gaining Italian support in the first place, but in failing to hold it in the later stages of the war. Even without the rhetoric of liberation, Hannibal held readily understandable attractions for the groups which revolted. All these groups were among the most recently conquered and least assimilated of Rome's allies. The Oscan tribes, in particular, had a long history of opposition to Rome. Indeed, the Samnites had been serious rivals to Rome for domination of Italy and an opportunity to proclaim their independence once again would have been welcome. As far as the Greeks went, they had put up a considerable resistance to Rome in the 270s and were not, as far as we know, particularly assimilated into the Roman system. If Hannibal did indeed couch his appeal to the Italians in terms of liberation and freedom, it is likely to have had a particular appeal for the Greeks.

In the immediate aftermath of Cannae, the Roman war effort was in considerable disarray, leaving Hannibal free to consolidate his hold on southern Italy and Campania. During this period, he received a considerable amount of support from some Italians, although this was very regional. However, it is not true, as Livy and others state, that there was a mass defection of Greek and Oscan cities immediately after the battle. It is clear that the Greeks, by and large, only seceded after a period of deliberation, often involving political changes.[30] While there is evidence that Campanians, Bruttians, Lucanians, some Apulians and the majority of Samnites changed sides in 216/15, the Greek cities which seceded did not do so until 214/13.

After Cannae, Hannibal made another of his fast marches, crossing into Campania, where he gained valuable support from some cities of the region, most notably from Capua.[31] The Roman forces were based at Casilinum, and Rome also retained the loyalty of Nola, despite much wavering and the presence of a strong pro-Carthaginian faction. Hannibal's principal objective at this point was to obtain access to a harbour in Campania to allow easier communication with Carthage. With this in mind, he launched a series of attacks on Naples but with little effect.[32] Elsewhere, he was more successful, taking Acerrae, Nuceria and Casilinum, and forcing Petelia – Rome's only remaining ally in Bruttium – into surrender.

After failing to capture Naples, Hannibal turned his attention to Cumae. In 215 BC, he attempted to persuade it to secede, then made several attacks, still with the aim of obtaining a port in Campania.[33] He also tried to reattach Cumae to the main group of Campanian cities, many of which supported him.[34] Leading Cumaeans were invited to attend a festival at Hamae under safe conduct, with the aim of trapping them and forcing them to join the rebellion against Rome. However, the Cumaean delegation was saved by a timely intervention on the part of Gracchus, the Roman commander. As a *civis sine suffragio*, Cumae had a long and close-knit relationship with Rome, and Hannibal made no impact on its loyalty. Rome also retained Cales and Grumentum and recaptured some Hirpinian cities, after which Hannibal abandoned Campania for the time being and embarked on a campaign in Apulia. Despite the communications problems engendered by lack of access to a good harbour, there seem to have been no immediate attacks on any of the Italiote cities of the South. Tarentum was still being used as a major naval base by Rome, and was well guarded.[35]

However, there were attempts to capture Rhegium, Croton and Locri, all of which were garrisoned by Rome at this stage. It is significant that the impetus came not from Hannibal or Hanno but from their Bruttian allies, as an independent operation undertaken as part of their long-standing hostility to the Greeks.[36] The attack on Rhegium was unsuccessful, but Croton and Locri agreed to secede, partly due to pressure from the Bruttians and to a change of government which brought the supporters of Carthage into power. There is a slight chronological problem in Livy's account of the defection of Locri, since he records that Carthaginian reinforcements landed there, and were admitted in defiance of the Roman garrison, earlier in 215. The actual defection of the city is mentioned as having taken place later in the same year. Clearly this is impossible: Locri must either have defected earlier in 215, or received reinforcements later than suggested by Livy.[37]

One effect of the secession of Croton was to give Hannibal access to the wealth of the sanctuary of Hera Lacinia[38] – a shrine which also had great symbolic importance for the whole of southern Italy – as well as control of the city itself. The manner of the secession, involving the removal of the anti-Bruttian party to Locri, may have contributed to Croton's staunch loyalty to Carthage during the later stages of the war. The city was a Carthaginian base during the retreat into Bruttium in 204/3,[39] and there was a major redistribution of the population. However, Livy's statement that the city was entirely evacuated is unlikely to be true.[40] The departure of some of the population to Locri seems to have been the result of the political upheaval which took place, and it is likely that they returned after the war, as did the exiles in other Greek cities.[41]

The years 214 and 213 were occupied largely by further campaigns in Apulia and Campania. As far as the Italiotes go, these years are chiefly

remarkable for the protracted build-up towards the defection of Tarentum, which finally seceded to Hannibal, together with Metapontum and
Heraklea, in 212, although an initial approach by the anti-Roman
faction was made as early as 214.[42] Despite the secession of the city, the
Roman garrison managed to hold the acropolis, thus effectively tying
down Carthaginian and Tarentine troops by a protracted siege.[43] Nevertheless, the Tarentine navy was useful to Hannibal's forces, as
demonstrated by a decisive victory over a fleet composed of Roman and
loyal Italiote ships in 210 BC.[44] By this date, however, the tide was clearly
beginning to turn against Hannibal. Capua was recaptured by Rome in
211, with severe reprisals. Tarentum fell in 209, after a pro-Roman *coup*,
and Locri was retaken by a force of exiles with some assistance from
Rome in 208.[45] The years between 208 and Hannibal's final departure in
203 were marked by an increasing loss of support from Italian communities. Roman gains in Campania, Lucania and Apulia effectively forced
him to retreat into Bruttium, where his staunchest allies were to be
found. Croton and Thurii were his main base of operations for a while,
but were abandoned shortly before his final departure from Italy. A
proportion of the population of Metapontum, Thurii and Croton chose
to accompany him on his final retreat into Bruttium.[46]

This brief narrative raises several interesting possibilities concerning
the reasons for Greek support for Hannibal, and for his failure to hold
on to it. Although the evidence is sporadic and sometimes contradictory, it is possible to suggest some reasons why the cities which seceded
from Rome did so, and equally, why those which remained loyal did not
follow suit. Similar factors also seem to govern the process of reversion
to Rome. Accordingly, reactions to Hannibal, and to Rome, must be
discussed on a region-by-region basis.

The internal workings of the Greek cities of Campania and northern
Lucania are less well documented than those in the South, but there is
no overt sign of *stasis*. In addition to being politically more stable, they
were also on better terms with their Italian neighbours and had a longer
history of contact with Rome, and were thus free from the three main
causes of tension elsewhere. Cumae, in any case, was partially incorporated in the Roman state by this date, having been awarded *civitas sine
suffragio* in 334 BC,[47] and it is notable that none of Rome's colonies, Latin
allies or *cives sine suffragio* revolted. Ties with Rome seem to have been
that much stronger for these groups than was the case with other allies.
The other feature which sets Cumae apart from the other cities of Magna
Graecia is its predominantly Oscan character, attested by both literary
and epigraphic evidence.[48] This degree of cultural integration is strik-

ingly different from the experience of the southern cities. Ultimately the reasons for Cumaean loyalty to Rome, at a time when much of the Greek South seceded along with Oscan Campania, remain somewhat inexplicable, other than by the fact that it was very much on the fringes of the Greek area of Italy but may never have been fully absorbed by the network of Oscan cities in Campania.

Unlike Cumae, Naples was still distinctively Greek in character,[49] and had maintained close connections with other Greek cities until at least 327 BC.[50] However, the treaty concluded with Rome in 327/6 seems to have guaranteed the city's loyalty thereafter.[51] Indeed, the concept of Naples as a notably faithful ally of Rome appears to have become one of the literary commonplaces associated with Magna Graecia.[52] Certainly, there is no evidence that Neapolitan loyalty to Rome was in question at any stage during Hannibal's invasion, despite intense military pressure in 215/14.

Northern Lucania shows a similar pattern to Campania, with Paestum and Velia remaining loyal to Rome throughout the war. Paestum similarly had close connections with Rome, having become a Latin colony in 273 BC,[53] into which the Graeco-Lucanian city was incorporated. It was significant to the Roman war effort in that as a Latin colony[54] it was an important sources of troops for the Roman army, and was also requested on one occasion to supply ships *ex foedere*.[55] Paestum also offered a donation of plate from the state treasury. Although this came shortly after the acceptance of a similar offer by Naples, it was refused by the Senate.[56] As with Naples and Cumae, Paestum had a history of good relations with Rome, and also of integration with the Lucanians. The archaeological evidence for the Oscanising phase of the city's history suggests a gradual but thorough long-term integration, with co-existence of Greek and Lucanian elements.[57] Velia appears on only one occasion in the sources relating to the Punic War. However, it had close religious connections with Rome (the priestesses of Ceres at Rome were always from Velia or Naples),[58] and appears to have remained loyal. It is known to have supplied warships to the Roman fleet on one occasion,[59] but this is the only military contribution known, again suggesting a rather marginal role in relation to Rome.

Rhegium was the only one of the Greek cities of the far South to remain in alliance with Rome, and was a Roman base for operations in Sicily. As such, it was of major importance, particularly since the defection of most of the other Italiotes along the Calabrian coast left Rome very short of access to harbours. There is no mention of political dissent, as there is elsewhere, but this may simply be a Livian omission.

However, it is significant that Rhegium may not have been part of the Tarentine hegemony of the fourth century,[60] and had enjoyed a closer diplomatic relationship with Sicily, owing to its geographical situation, than with most other areas of Magna Graecia. The intervention of Rome in 270 to free the city from the rebel Campanian garrison may also have given an opportunity to establish a more solidly pro-Roman government than was the case in many other cities.[61] Thus the patterns of alliance in the late third century were to some extent mimicking those of the fourth century, with the group of cities under Tarentine influence defecting to Hannibal, and the rest remaining loyal. Evidence for skirmishes with the Bruttians indicates that for the Italiote cities the war was to a large extent a renewal of the older conflict between the Greeks and their Italian neighbours. The Bruttians attacked Rhegium in 214 but met with a determined resistance. Later in the war, however, a group of slaves and criminals who had been rounded up were sent by Laevinus to Rhegium for use as irregular troops against raiding Bruttians. Clearly hostilities were still going on between Greeks and Oscans.[62]

One of the fullest accounts given by Livy of the behaviour of any city concerns Locri.[63] He describes the Locrians as being caught unawares by a surprise march from Rhegium, while they were in the process of preparing for a siege. Hannibal's troops cut off a large number of Locrians who were bringing in supplies from the territory, and Bruttian troops were sent to besiege the city. Initially, the Locrians refused to negotiate with the Bruttians, until it was understood that they were under Carthaginian command. An assembly was called, and the terms proposed by Hannibal were accepted at the insistence of a pro-Carthaginian faction. The Roman garrison was given safe conduct, much to the annoyance of Hannibal, and later events make it clear that pro-Roman Locrians also left the city and took refuge at Rhegium. The terms proposed by Hannibal seem very similar to those of extant Greek and Roman treaties – a recognition of Locrian autonomy, with the proviso that Hannibal had the right of entry into the city, and an agreement that each side was obligated to assist the other in peace and war.

Meanwhile, a Bruttian army mounted an independent attack on Croton, which was suffering from severe political instability. The Bruttians' attempts to gain an assurance that the city would belong to them, not Carthage, if it fell, were met with a rebuff, but Hannibal was clearly hoping to benefit from Greek fear of the Bruttians. Contact with an anti-Roman faction led by Aristomachos allowed the Bruttians to take possession of an uninhabited part of the city, but the citadel held out and the Bruttians turned to Hanno for assistance. In the event, the faction led by Aristomachos agreed to an alliance with Carthage, although not to Hanno's proposal to settle Bruttians in Croton, and his opponents fled to Locri.

This account is of interest for two reasons, namely that it provides evidence for collusion between two cities and because it preserves details of the settlement made when the city reverted to the Roman alliance. The secession here is closely linked to that at Croton, and Livy seems to imply some sort of connection between the two cities.[64] It is also an instance in which political instability was a major cause, with a change of government and the exile of pro-Roman politicians to Rhegium.[65] However, it is debatable whether this episode can be explained in the terms which Livy employs, which are essentially those of the first century BC.[66] Livy asserts that the exiles were an aristocratic faction, a plausible scenario since both Locri and Rhegium, to which the exiles fled, are thought to have had oligarchic constitutions at this time.[67] However, this model does not work for all the cities for which this pattern is suggested.[68] Nor does it imply that the democrats necessarily gained power as Livy would have us believe. The fact that the majority of the population were originally against supporting Hannibal rather suggests that they did not. The other factor which seems to have been influential is the animosity between Locri and the large number of Bruttian troops in Hannibal's army.[69] Fear of a Bruttian attack was the decisive factor. The significance of political changes is further under-lined by the fact that reversion to alliance with Rome was caused by another bout of *stasis*, culminating in the recapture of the city by the Locrian exiles on their own initiative,[70] rather than by Roman troops. This, and the replacement of the pro-Carthaginian party by the exiles as the governing body, strongly suggest that the politics involved the use of foreign policy as a platform by two conflicting factions of the élite rather than the democratic/oligarchic division suggested by Livy.

In many respects, the factors which influenced the Locrian decision to defect were also influential in the case of Croton. The activities of political factions were important, but the decisive element was distrust of Hannibal's Bruttian allies.[71] Apart from the divisions between pro-Roman and anti-Roman factions, there was a division within the anti-Roman faction as to whether to negotiate with the Bruttians or to insist on dealing only with Hannibal, with the overwhelming majority in favour of the latter option.[72] The Bruttians seem to have taken the opportunity to pursue their traditional hostility to the Greeks in the area,[73] and it seems quite likely that their presence had a decisive effect on the decisions made by each city.

Hannibal seems to have played on local rivalries to gain more allies, here and in other regions. In this instance, Hannibal and Hanno were making political capital out of their role as mediators in a conflict between Greeks and Bruttians.[74] A similar phenonenon occurred in Apulia, where neighbouring (and rival) groups of cities, notably Arpi and Sipontum (anti-Roman) and Luceria, Canusium and Venusia (pro-Roman), adopted opposite policies.[75] In particular, there seems to have been great hostility to the possibility that Hannibal would repopulate the city by means of introducing Bruttian colonists.[76] It is notable that the whole episode hinges on the issue of antipathy to the Bruttians rather than on support for Rome or Carthage. This is particularly reflected in the fact that the Crotoniates who chose to leave the city elected to move to Locri, which was by this time a Carthaginian ally, rather than move to a ccity which was still under Roman control.

This is not the only example of interlinked secessions, further supporting the possibility of collusion or a resurgence of Tarentine imperialism. The defection of Thurii is closely connected with that of Tarentum, but the sources disagree on the extent to which one was a direct result of the other, and Livy and Appian appear to follow different traditions. Livy ascribes the decision to join Hannibal to the execution in Rome in 215 BC of Thurian hostages, whose relatives organised an ambush of Roman troops and negotiated a settlement with Carthage.[77] He also implies that the execution of the Tarentine and Thurian hostages was the work of a Tarentine *agent provocateur* named Phileas who used subterfuge to persuade the hostages to escape. Appian, however, ascribes the defection to pressure by the Tarentines, who used the crews of some captured Thurian ships as hostages to ensure that Thurii seceded.[78] In both these cases, the pressure to secede seems to have come from the Tarentines, which argues strongly that Tarentum was actively pro-Carthaginian,[79] and was reasserting hegemony over Magna Graecia. Certainly the Carthaginians do not feature as a significant factor in either tradition. In fact, the two accounts are not totally irreconcilable, although the version preferred by Appian seems to be influenced by a more anti-Tarentine tradition than that of Livy. The escape of the Tarentine and Thurian hostages referred to by Livy is described in terms of Tarentine duplicity, but the existence of this group of hostages and of Tarentine envoys rather suggests that relations with Rome were already strained and that this incident is not an escape engineered to provide a *casus belli* but part of a declaration of hostilities.

The apparent contradiction in the Thurian action of supplying grain to the Roman garrison at Tarentum may reflect some division within the city.[80] Other references to Thurian action during the war suggest continued support for Hannibal,[81] which would be unlikely in the case of a city which had been forced to change alliance against its will.

Heraklea is one of the least well-documented cities of the South at this period, and its attitude to Carthage is known from only one reference.[82] Like Metapontum, Tarentum and Thurii, it seceded from Carthage in 212 BC, apparently from fear rather than from positive hostility to Rome, although it is not specified whether this was fear of the Carthaginians, the Italians or neighbouring Italiote states which favoured Carthage. Metapontum also defected in 212, following the removal of a large part of the Roman garrison to Tarentum.[83] Here, there seems to have been strong anti-Roman feeling. The defection occurred as soon as there was a suitable opportunity, and the remainder of the garrison was massacred, something which did not occur elsewhere. There is a consistent record of Metapontine hostility to Rome throughout the war, and many Metapontines elected to abandon the city and follow Hannibal into Bruttium in 204/3 rather than surrender to Rome.[84]

The sources for the secession of Tarentum, also in 212, are more detailed than those for other Greek cities, but there are conflicting traditions.[85] All agree that Tarentum was the first of the more easterly Greek cities to defect, and that this had the effect of provoking several other secessions. There is no evidence of particular animosity towards the surrounding Italians and the Carthaginian army does not appear to have been near the city when the first moves against Rome were made. Clearly, the defection was a spontaneous act on the part of Tarentum,[86] not undertaken in response to external pressure. It is possible to argue, on the slight evidence available, that Tarentum was entering a more expansionist phase, and may have been attempting to reassert Tarentine authority in south-east Italy. The fact that it was garrisoned very early in the war, and also had to give hostages, suggests that it was an area of suspect loyalty as early as 218 BC.[87]

The approach made to Hannibal is clearly linked with a political *coup*. Nevertheless, Livy's model of pro-Roman aristocracies and anti-Roman demagogues in the South does not work in the case of Tarentum, since the conspirators who made the approach to Hannibal were young aristocrats.[88] It has been suggested that this incident is merely a projection forward, by Livy or his sources, of earlier political trends involving the fourth-century Pythagoreans,[89] partly on the basis that the conspirators, described as *neaniskoi* or *nobiles iuvenes*, recall the young aristocrats who took a large part in the Pythagorean politics of the fourth century.[90] However, the incident cannot be dismissed as a doublet of some earlier political *coup* described by Timaeus or one of the other fourth-century Greek historians.[91] The political pattern described is common in the Greek world, and not implausible. Given the continued strength of Pythagoreanism as a political force at Tarentum,[92] it is not at all impossible that the conspirators were a group of Pythagorean aristocrats who were intent on overthrowing the democracy. The fact that the motive for secession was largely one of internal politics, the group of aristocrats having used opposition to Rome as a political platform, is made clear by Polybios.[93] Livy cites the execution of the Tarentine hostages in Rome as the initial cause, but this is more likely to be simply a *casus belli* and it is open to doubt as to whether the incident was deliberately engineered, as Livy suggests, or was a Roman act of aggression consequent on Tarentum breaking off diplomatic relations.[94]

The evidence for Tarentine behaviour in the later part of the war is fuller than that for most of the Italiotes. In 210, a joint Romano-Greek fleet was defeated very decisively by the Tarentines, and a successful blockade was mounted against the Roman garrison, which was besieged in the citadel, together with a group of Tarentines who had refused to accept the alliance with Carthage.[95] The recapture of the city by Rome in 209 appears to have been influenced less by political considerations than was that of Locri. Livy ascribes it to the blackmail and subversion of the commander of the Bruttian units of the garrison,[96] but it is unlikely that the city was betrayed by him single-handedly. However, it is notable that most of the Tarentines were unwilling to revert to Rome and put up a considerable degree of resistance, culminating in the sack of the city.[97] In the aftermath of the reconquest, it becomes clear that Rome retained contact with the exiles from Tarentum, and seems to have had a policy, in this case and that of Locri, of exploiting internal divisions in order to secure a reversion of these cities to alliance with Rome. In particular, there were negotiations with a group of exiles at Olympia in 207,[98] and there seems to have been a contingent of Tarentine troops in the Roman army.[99]

Thus, the evidence for Magna Graecia in the second Punic War indicates a number of common factors. In general terms, the response of these cities to Hannibal's attempt to undermine Roman alliances was very mixed. In some cases, it is clear that the Carthaginians were

72

attempting to play on local rivalries and grievances, both in internal politics and in relations between Greeks and Italians, in order to bring about a revolt against Rome. He also skilfully used the Hellenistic rhetoric of *eleutheria* to appeal to the Greek and Hellenised allies of the South. Most of these cities seem to have been very isolated from Rome, and even those who remained loyal were not closely connected with the Roman war effort, being left to fight their own campaigns, but not included in the Roman army on a large scale. Most of the sources reveal an almost complete lack of interest in the wider issues at stake on the part of most of the Greek states, a fact which is not surprising given that they had apparently had little contact with Rome since 270, and also that the presence of the Carthaginians as a major factor in foreign affairs was a familiar feature in Magna Graecia and Sicily. The likelihood that the settlements made in the 270s had been fairly lenient and that many of the cities of the South had enjoyed some resurgence of prosperity seems to have created conditions in which at least one city, Tarentum, was able to pursue a more expansionist foreign policy. The sources are not sufficient to allow this to be argued in detail, but it does seem that Tarentum was instrumental in provoking the secession of at least one other city, and probably more, as well as being one of the few voluntarily to open negotiations with Hannibal.

There is less information about the settlements contracted with the secessionist states when they reverted to being Roman allies. At Locri, the settlement which followed the second change of allegiance in 208 involved a period of martial law under the governorship of Pleminius,[100] possibly to support the new regime. The final settlement, made after complaints to the Senate regarding his conduct, involved the affirmation of the liberty and autonomy of the city and recognition of the new government as '*viros bonos sociosque et amicos*',[101] a formula which may echo Greek diplomatic terminology. In addition, compensation was paid for the damage caused by Pleminius, the Roman garrison was withdrawn and the sanctuary of Persephone, which had been desecrated during the occupation, was purified. Despite the initial occupation, there seems to have been recognition of the decisive part played by the change of government. The new regime received generous reparations from Rome after the Senatorial enquiry into Pleminius' abuse of his governorship. Significantly, the decree of *amicitia* in honour of the Locrian envoys is one of the earliest instances of Rome using the Hellenistic formula of a grant of *libertas* or *eleutheria*. Gruen rejects this as a true parallel for Greek *eleutheria* decrees, but it seems, nevertheless, that Rome was acknowledging the Greek culture of southern Italy.[102]

Tarentum seems to have been dealt with in a similar manner. Little is known about the settlement with Rome, but the city was left under military rule for a considerable period of time. The initial feeling in the Senate was in favour of imposing the same harsh settlement on Tarentum as on Capua,[103] that is, total loss of civic autonomy and identity, but in the end the terms appear to have been considerably more lenient.[104] It is possible that the delay may have allowed more moderate opinion to prevail. The evidence for Tarentum in the second century seems to indicate that its alliance with Rome was on very similar terms to those of other cities in Italy and Greece, with occasional, although not heavy, military contributions. There was a considerable amount of land confiscation, however, as the amount of *ager publicus* in the area appears to have been high.[105] In effect, it is likely that the settlement was very similar to that made with Locri, including a period of martial law, during which Rome governed the city directly by means of a *praetor* and military garrison.

Thus the specific cases for which we have evidence indicate that treaties were imposed on much the same basis as those of 270 BC, but with additional penalties. These seem to have included Roman military and administrative supervision during the war and the years immediately after it, the confiscation of tracts of land as *ager publicus*, and the imposition of a pro-Roman government. There is uncertainty as to whether this change of regime involved a formal alteration to the constitution of the cities which seceded. Equally, there is no sign that a war indemnity was imposed as there was on Carthage itself.[106] It is not impossible, but it seems unlikely given the general nature of the settlements as far as they can be reconstructed. Unfortunately we have no evidence for the settlements made with the cities which supported Hannibal until the very end of the war, notably Croton and Thurii. However, it seems likely that they were on similar lines.

Although the reactions of the Italiote cities to the presence of Hannibal were both complex and very disparate in nature, a number of conclusions can be reached as to the possible reasons for their actions and their relationship with Rome. It is clear that the cities which entered the Roman sphere of influence at an earlier date were much more likely to remain loyal than those which only became allies in 270 BC. This strongly suggests that these were much less assimilated into the Roman system of control of Italy. The slight evidence that we have certainly supports the notion that Rome was not in close contact with southern Italy and had little connection with the area in the period before 218. The Italiote cities also seem to be more stable in terms of internal politics and to be more integrated with the Italian population of the area.

In contrast, the cities of the South were more notable for their political instability, with frequent changes of governing faction which were reflected in changes of allegiance between Rome and Hannibal. Motivation for a change of sides seems to come partly from this, which in itself may reflect other factors, and partly in response to the actions of the neighbouring Oscan communities. Relations between the Greeks and the Italian population had a far-reaching effect, and it may be true to say that local considerations of the network of alliances and enmity between the Greeks and various groups of Italians were in some cases more important than the wider issues concerning Rome and Carthage. In addition to this, there is the more specific factor that while Rome was a new power in south Italian terms, Carthaginian influence was well established. Although not the central problem that it was in Sicily, Carthage had contacts in southern Italy, and particularly with Tarentum, probably dating to the fourth century. Indeed, Tarentum appears to have had an alliance with Carthage and was offered help against Rome by a Carthaginian fleet during the Pyrrhic War. There are a number of reasons why the Greeks of southern Italy might find Hannibal's rhetoric of liberation attractive and view Carthage as a more natural ally than Rome.

The extent to which Tarentum consciously tried to resurrect the Italiote League as a Tarentine hegemony must remain in doubt, but it is worth noting that Tarentum was the only city to make an entirely voluntary approach to Hannibal and that the pattern of secessions corresponds closely to the membership of the League. The settlements with the cities which revolted are not well documented, but the evidence we have suggests that they were largely a return to the *status quo*, with additional punitive measures such as land confiscation and installation of pro-Romans as the governing faction. In military terms, the conduct of the war illustrates to some extent the workings of the relationship with Rome in the case of those cities which remained loyal. Direct military contributions were rare but there is some circumstantial evidence for contingents of Greeks with the Roman army, and there are instances of naval levies, as well as financial contributions. In all, there is enough evidence to belie the assertion that the Greeks were without any significant military capacity. Clearly it is only possible to generalise up to a point when dealing with a complex sequence of events, and there is no single adequate explanation for the Greek reaction to Hannibal. It is possible to assert with some degree of plausibility, however, that this period shows a similar range of preoccupations on the part of the Greeks as did the fourth century, and that the impact of Rome on the Greek South before 200 BC was relatively slight.

4

Treaties and Diplomacy: The Formalities of Relations with Rome 270–89 BC

The framework of relations between Rome and southern Italy and the means by which it was negotiated and guaranteed – treaties, *amicitia* and diplomatic contacts – are very poorly understood. Historiographically, this area is a minefield of problems caused by the inadequacy of the evidence for the third century and the necessity of extrapolating from later material and evidence from other regions. For the second century BC there are detailed accounts of treaties in ancient authors and abundant epigraphical evidence for treaties, letters, edicts and *senatusconsulta*,[1] which illuminate the diplomacy of the period and allow close study of the mechanisms of Roman control. However, there is no comparable body of evidence relating to the conquest of Italy. Studies of the framework of Roman relations in Italy, the nature of alliances, how they were established and how they operated, must rely on snippets of evidence drawn from later, and sometimes anachronistic, literary sources, with little or no epigraphic corroboration. This holds good for Magna Graecia as much as for other regions of Italy. Our understanding of how the alliance worked, and the terms of treaties between Magna Graecia and Rome, must be pieced together from many fragments of information. Nevertheless, it is possible to build up some sort of picture of Italiote diplomacy and the formal framework of relations with Rome.

The basic scenario for Roman expansion has been studied and expounded by numerous eminent scholars, and given its most definitive full-length treatment in English by Sherwin-White.[2] The inhabitants of Italy were divided into three categories – Roman citizens, Latins and allies – each with a different status. The terms of relations with Rome in the case of Latin colonists were determined by the colonial charter of each individual foundation. Relations with allies were governed by treaty, and were formed by process of voluntary negotiation or military conquest. The prototype on which these were notionally based was the fifth-century *Foedus Cassianum*, a text of which is quoted by Dionysios of Halicarnassus.[3] The core of it is a declaration of peace and friendship, with no chronological limit, and the requirement that Rome and the other signatories must assist each other if attacked, with the full military strength of the state if necessary.[4] Within this basic framework, there was obviously room for considerable local variation, depending on the state of relations with Rome and the circumstances under which the treaty had been negotiated. Without extant examples of treaties, however, these must be deduced from circumstantial evidence.

Naples had clearly gained exceptional terms for breaking an alliance with the Samnites and forming one with Rome in 327/6 BC. The treaty is habitually referred to as a *'foedus aequissimum'*.[5] Without further evidence of the terms, it is impossible to say for certain why this should be regarded as more equal than other treaties, but the answer may lie in military exemptions.[6] There is also the problem of chronological developments. The second century seems to have been a period in which inter-state relations were governed by increasingly complex and restrictive treaties, with a great deal more formalisation of relationships and a growing trend towards Roman encroachment on allied autonomy.[7] However, without more detailed evidence, this cannot be explored in any great detail.

This is not to imply that treaties were the only form of inter-state contact recognised by Rome. Early contact with Etruria was regulated by *indutiae*, truces of fixed length, which could be valid for anything between one year and one hundred years.[8] These established a cessation of hostilities but did not provide the basis for any permanent relationship. In other circumstances a peace settlement could be guaranteed by *sponsio*, a formal oath, rather than by treaty.[9]

In a comprehensive reassessment of Roman diplomacy and treaty-making in the Hellenistic world, Gruen has suggested that the negotiation of a treaty was in fact the final stage of Roman involvement with a state and was in most cases preceded by a period of much less defined contact.[10] He identifies a large number of states which were dealt with by means of decrees of *amicitia* (or *philia*, to use Greek terminology), which established friendly relations with Rome but did not carry the mutual obligations implied by a treaty. The replacement of this arrangement with the less flexible device of a *foedus* occurred later and was in part due to the breakdown of arrangements based on *amicitia* and partly on a change of Roman policy which entailed more direct intervention in the East.

Gruen does not apply this model to the history of Roman expansion in Italy, partly because of lack of evidence and partly because of the different circumstances in which alliances were concluded.[11] Both of these observations are valid. We have very limited evidence for diplomacy in the fourth and third centuries and the military character of most Italian alliances means that they must have been based on treaties which defined obligations, if only in a very broad sense. Nevertheless, this does not invalidate the general point that even within a framework of alliances based on treaties, the impression given by the evidence is that Roman policy became much more restrictive and interventionist in the second century, in Italy as well as in Greece. Gruen's analysis of Hellenistic diplomatic conventions and their impact on Roman practice also raises interesting questions about the ways in which Rome dealt with the Hellenised areas of Italy, which will require further examination.

Not all the cities of Magna Graecia had allied status. Cumae became a *civis sine suffragio* in 334, and Paestum was colonised in 273, after which it had Latin status.[12] Nevertheless, most of the Italiotes had allied status, gained during the Pyrrhic War. Leaving aside the treaties between Rome and Magna Graecia before 270 BC, which were intended (as far as we can tell) to define spheres of influence rather than establish a permanent relationship, the gist of a *foedus* with Rome was a declaration of freedom and autonomy, presumably with some military strings attached. Livy, the only authority to comment on the peace settlements after the Pyrrhic War, says that the Tarentines (and presumably the other Italiote cities as well) were granted '*pax et libertas*'.[13] Rhegium was granted additional reparations to make good the damage caused by the renegade Campanian garrison.[14] The restoration of *libertas*, not just to the Greeks but also to the Samnites and other allies, was the main demand made by Pyrrhus during his abortive negotiations with Rome.[15] A request for the restitution of '*libertas et leges*' was made by Tarentum in 207, as the basis for peace negotiations, but this was rejected, at least initially, and Tarentum remained under military rule. Locri, on the other hand, had '*libertas et leges suas*' restored to them.[16] Clearly, *libertas* was a concept which featured highly in the diplomacy of the third century BC, at least in southern Italy. Significantly, Gruen's discussion of *eleutheria* and *libertas* shows that it was not frequently invoked in Rome's dealings with Italy,[17] and most of his citations occur in connection with the South. This may have been a direct reflection of the Hellenised nature of the Mezzogiorno. Political slogans and propaganda were an important part of Hellenistic diplomacy and one of the most frequent and potent examples was the rhetoric of *eleutheria* – usually concerning the 'freedom of the Greeks'.[18] Assuming that Gruen is correct in identifying *libertas* with the Greek *eleutheria*, it seems that the notion of *libertas* was a Hellenistic device, stressed particularly in dealing with the Greek communities of the South, to whom it would have had particular significance.

The peace settlements after the Punic Wars are also unilluminating in terms of detail. As already noted, Tarentum requested restoration of autonomy but was refused. A debate in the Senate on the arrival of the Tarentine envoys was inconclusive.[19] A group of senators favoured abolishing Tarentum as an autonomous state and introducing direct rule by a Roman *praefectus*, a punitive measure already imposed on Capua, but this was opposed by Fabius Maximus.[20] There were deep divisions over this, and a decision was deferred, leaving Tarentum under martial law. A period of martial law was not unprecedented – it also happened at Locri and Capua – but in this case we do not know how long it lasted.[21] *Praetors* were still being assigned Tarentum as a command as late as 181, but most of these cases are ambiguous. It is unclear whether they were military governors of the city or commanders of the forces left there to defend the city against a possible invasion from Greece or Illyria.[22] On balance, however, it seems unlikely that Tarentum continued to be ruled directly for twenty-eight years. Capua became a by-word for the severity of its punishment and if Tarentum had suffered a similar fate, we would expect some reference to it, but this is entirely lacking. Nevertheless, the wars in the eastern Mediterranean rendered south-east Italy a strategically important area and a sizeable Roman force remained at Tarentum until at least 181,[23] if not longer. The settlement also involved loss of a large amount of land, later redistributed to Gracchan, Pompeian and Neronian colonists.[24]

Settlements with most other secessionist states are undocumented, although it is safe to say that land confiscations formed part of most of them. Some – including Croton, Thurii, Vibo and Buxentum – were colonised in 194–192 BC, and thus changed status altogether. Others remained as allies of Rome, but few details are known, other than in the case of Locri. The fraught peace negotiations between Rome and Locri are of interest because they involved one of the few documented grants of *amicitia* to an Italian state. As at Tarentum, martial law was declared, and the city was placed under the control of Q. Pleminius, a nominee of Scipio.[25] There was also a government-designate composed of pro-Roman Locrians who had been exiled during the secession from Rome.

Pleminius's tyrannical rule and unscrupulous plundering of the sanctuary of Persephone drove the Locrians to complain to the Senate and caused a major scandal.[26] Much of the vituperation against him seems to have come from Scipio's political opponents, but the Locrian complaints and extensive reparations made to them argue that he was less than satisfactory as a governor. In the end, the Locrians were paid compensation for the damage to the sanctuary and were declared '*viros bonos sociosque et amicos*'.[27] It is this clause of the settlement which is of interest, since it seems to reflect Hellenistic rather than Roman custom.

Amicitia as the basis for inter-state relations is rare at this date, although it becomes much more common in the second century. The workings of it are a matter of considerable controversy.[28] The status of *Amicus Populi Romani* clearly became something with a strict legal definition, but the nature of it is obscure. A *senatusconsultum* of 78 BC granting *amicitia* to a group of Greeks mentions that the recipients were to be added to the *Formula Amicorum*, presumably a list of *amici*.[29] Another example, cited by Livy, is a grant made in 169 BC to Onesimos, a Macedonian supporter of Rome.[30] He was awarded a house and some land at Tarentum, probably allocated from land confiscated in 207, and was declared an *amicus* of Rome. All three cases echo the form and language of the proxeny decree, a type of honorific decree which had been a commonplace of Hellenistic diplomacy since the fourth century.[31] These, typically, declare the honorand to be *proxenos kai euergetes* and sometimes contain material rewards, such as tax exemptions and grants of land, as well as expressions of honour and goodwill.[32]

The grant to Onesimos and the *senatusconsultum* in honour of Asklepiades, Polystratos and Meniscos are both awards to individuals and are clearly in the tradition of the Hellenistic proxeny decree. The grant to Locri is more problematic, as Livy does not indicate whether the '*viros bonos*' who are the recipients are the envoys present in the Senate or the entire population of the city. If the former, this is another instance of *proxenia*, which is in itself very interesting as it implies that the Locrians are being treated in a particularly Greek manner. If, however, the grant is to the Locrians as a political entity, rather than a group of individuals, this places a very different interpretation on it. Gruen argues that grants of *amicitia/philia* to cities are extremely rare in Italy but usual in the Greek world. In this case, the treatment of Locri would be more in line with that of a Hellenistic city that an Italian one.[33] In fact, the *amici* are more likely to be the pro-Roman governing faction than the city as a political body, but nevertheless, there are important implications. Rome was clearly adopting the conventions of Hellenistic diplomacy, still somewhat novel at this date, in order to deal with an Italiote city.

The principal question which needs to be considered is the obligations of the Italiote allies towards Rome. Military support for Rome was clearly central to any alliance, and as far as we know, was the main clause of most *foedera*. However, the nature of the military obligations is clouded by the erroneous but persistent notion that the Greeks formed a separate class of allies, known as *socii navales*,[34] whose military contributions to Rome were exacted in ships and crews but not troops. The supposition is that the Greek cities were too weakened and depopulated to provide troops, or anything more than a token naval force, and there is an inference that they were of lower status than other *socii*.

In fact, this is to misunderstand the evidence. An examination of the evidence for *socii navales* reveals that they were not a type of ally, but were units of allied troops which served as marines on Roman or allied ships.[35] Livy uses the term *socius navalis* indiscriminately, applying it to full-time marines, legionaries drafted into the fleet, marines serving on Carthaginian, Rhodian and Pergamene ships, and to the crews of the Roman fleet of 310 BC, a date at which there were no allies serving in the Roman fleet.[36]

The evidence, such as it is, for Greek military strength suggests that the Italiotes were certainly not prevented by weakness or decline from providing troops for Rome. There is plenty of evidence for the continued existence of Greek armies and fleets. There is also no known reason why their treaty obligations should be different to those of Rome's other allies in Italy, namely to assist Rome by supplying troops when requested to do so.[37] The arguments against these points are purely negative, hinging on the omission of the Greeks and Bruttians from Polybios' description of an emergency census of the whole of Italy, taken in 225 BC, and cannot be regarded as definitive.[38] In opposition to Polybios' figures, there is positive evidence that the Italiotes had a naval and military capability. If it was not used, then this must surely have been a deliberate choice made by Rome.

Most of the Greek military assistance to Rome of which we have details is naval – ships and crews, rather than troops – but there is also circumstantial evidence that Greek troops fought, both for Rome and for Carthage, in the Punic Wars.[39] Paestum supplied contingents of troops to the Roman army, as did other Latin colonies. A request for ships in 210 is not necessarily contradictory to this since Roman procedure for requesting naval help does not appear to have been in any way related to anything other than the needs of the particular campaign,[40] and there is nothing inherently difficult in the idea of one city providing both troops and ships. Evidence is less conclusive for other

Italiote cities, but there is an implication that Tarentines loyal to Rome served in the Roman army in 209.[41]

Military obligations on the Greeks to provide allied contingents for the Roman army were not heavy. Rather than serving as an integral part of the Roman forces, the Greek cities, along with many others in Italy, were expected to use their forces to defend themselves and to mount independent campaigns against Hannibal, with or without Roman assistance. It is clear from Livy's account of Hannibal's campaigns in Campania that Naples and Cumae both had forces which operated independently from those of Rome, at least on a local scale.[42] There are also instances of Greek exiles raising their own armies, particularly with a view to recapturing their home city, as in the case of Locri.[43]

After the Punic War, the situation is more complicated. Some secessionist allies lost their right to maintain independent forces, and this may have limited the possibility for military participation in the alliance. The Bruttians fell into this category, and it is possible that the Tarentines were also penalised in this manner.[44] This would partly explain the lack of evidence for Italiote troops, but cannot apply to all cities in the region. Paestum, as a Latin colony, must have continued to supply troops, and there is no reason to suppose that the loyal allies lost their forces. Naples still had an army and a war fleet as late as 88 BC.[45]

There is evidence for the use of Greek ships by Rome in the second century, but only very sporadically.[46] The fact that they are mentioned specifically by Livy suggests that they are an exceptional occurrence. The exact composition of the force is listed in each case, with rather more precision than would be usual if this was a routine part of the levy. The language used is also distinctly at variance with that employed for routine information on the annual levy. The phrase *ex foedere* is cited on each occasion, as if to imply a special invoking of the terms of a treaty to justify the request.[47]

The nature of these naval levies also implies that they were irregular and not integral to Roman recruitment. In no case do they amount to more that fifteen ships, spread over at least three cities.[48] No city is asked to supply more than five ships on any occasion, and usually the number was fewer than this. The type of ships requested also suggest that they were not an integral part of the Roman naval effort, since they were mostly scout ships, with a small number of triremes, while the bulk of the Roman navy was composed of the heavier quinquiremes. In general, these forces are almost certainly supplementary forces, possibly in addition to the levy of troops for the army, although there is no certainty of this.

There are only two instances of naval levies in the third century. In 264, Locri, Tarentum and Naples provided a fleet of transports to ferry the Roman army to Sicily, and in 210, a composite force of Rhegine, Paestan and Velian ships was added to a Roman fleet.[49] This last fleet had a very short life span, since it was wiped out by the Tarentines later in 210, an incident which provides a graphic illustration of the fact that Tarentine naval power was not in eclipse. There were, however, a number of similar cases in the second century, in which Italiotes were asked for naval support by Rome, in 195, 193, 191 and 171.

In addition to any formal levies of troops and ships, and to the supposition that the Greeks would be responsible for their own defence, some cities also contributed money and supplies, apparently on a voluntary basis. Naples donated a large amount of gold plate from the civic treasury to assist in covering the costs of the war.[50] It is possible that the favourable nature of Naples' treaty with Rome lay in an exemption from military impositions,[51] but the description of this incident given by Livy seems to suggest that this was a gesture on the part of Naples which was accepted at the discretion of the Senate. A similar offer was made by Paestum but refused.[52] Naples also made occasional donations of money and grain to the Roman forces at a later stage in the war. Livy makes a passing reference to payment of tribute by the Italiotes.[53] However, it occurs in a speech made by Minnio, the envoy of Antiochus, which seeks to discredit Roman claims to have liberated the Greeks with their supposed treatment of the Italiotes, and names Rhegium, Naples and Tarentum as allies which were forced to pay tribute and provide ships for Rome. This is clearly designed as propaganda and is not sound evidence for punitive treatment by Rome.

Inevitably, reconstructions of the legal and diplomatic framework in which the Italiote cities operated between the third and first centuries BC can only be made in outline, as most details are lost. Relations with Rome varied according to the status of each individual city, and thus Italiote obligations to Rome also varied. Military impositions were for the most part very light. Regular levies were made on Paestum, but not anywhere else as far as we know. Where occasional naval levies were made, they were directed more at keeping alive a right which might otherwise fall into disuse than providing a viable fighting force. This lack of involvement, however, seems to have been by choice rather than by reason of Greek incapacity. Perhaps more significant is the manner in which Rome approached diplomatic relations with the Greeks. These were couched in Hellenistic terms, implicitly recognising the Italiotes as part of the Hellenistic world throughout the third century BC.

5

Decline and Recovery: Magna Graecia 200 BC–AD 14

The aftermath of the Hannibalic war in southern Italy is very badly documented in terms of literary evidence and unlike the period following the Civil Wars, there is little epigraphic evidence to supplement such literary sources as exist. There have been a number of attempts to synthesise the evidence for this period,[1] particularly in terms of the economy of Magna Graecia and the agrarian development of the region. The existence, or otherwise, of *latifundia* in the South has generated much controversy and will be discussed in further detail in Chapter 7. An increasing quantity of archaeological evidence has done much to clarify the economic history of the second century, but the lack of literary and epigraphic sources means that the possibility of writing a linear history of Magna Graecia diminishes after 200 BC and virtually disappears after AD 14. Thus the years after the Roman conquest must be approached as a history of social, economic and cultural structures, rather than as a narrative of events.

Nevertheless, the period 200 BC–AD 14 is one of crucial significance for the question of Romanisation, as it seems likely that during this period Rome's relations with southern Italy became closer than had been the case before 218 BC. This corresponds to the evidence for increasing interference by Rome in the affairs of many of her other Italian allies in the second century.[2] In all areas of Italy, Roman involvement in local administration and judicial processes increased, sometimes by request on the part of Italian cities and sometimes as unsolicited interference by the Senate or individuals.[3] This increasingly apparent lack of equality of the allies in relation to Rome, together with other economic and political factors, resulted in the development of tension and hostility on the part of many cities which erupted into open warfare in 90 BC. One of the intriguing facts about the Italiotes is that they did not participate in overt acts of hostility, despite the region's history of disaffection. The reasons for this will be discussed in more detail below. This trend towards a greater degree of centralisation is something which persists after 89 BC, and which culminated in Augustus' reorganisation of Italy and the administrative supervision exercised by some of his successors.

THE SECOND CENTURY BC

Despite the secessionist policies of some Italiote cities, there is little evidence for legal changes in status in the post-war period, although our evidence is slight and there may well have been changes which have not been recorded. The most that our sources tell us about post-war settlements in the South is that peace and autonomy were restored and treaties were renewed.[4] There was a proposal that the Tarentines should lose their autonomy and be governed directly from Rome, as were the Capuans. The outcome of this is not recorded by Livy, but the debate was postponed and we can assume that the most punitive suggestions were not implemented.[5] As noted in the previous chapter, military obligations by the Italiote allies may have increased, although it is difficult to make any definite judgement on the basis of a few instances of *ad hoc* demands for naval assistance. Increasing amounts of interference in the South and exercise of Roman control can be seen in many other ways. The confiscation of large amounts of territory from secessionist cities affected the social stability and economic standing of these communities. The sack of Tarentum in 209 BC caused considerable loss of wealth and population. Apart from casualties, 30,000 Tarentines were enslaved and 3,000 talents were seized.[6] Some other cities, including Croton and Locri, which did not fight to the bitter end, may have escaped with rather less economic damage, while others, such as Metapontum and Thurii, suffered extensive demographic and economic disruption.[7] Even cities which remained loyal to Rome suffered from the after-effects of being effectively in a combat zone for the duration of the war. The frequent levies of troops, either for the Roman army or for local campaigns,[8] were a constant strain on the manpower and on the financial resources of all Italian cities, while the ravaging of land by both sides and the continuous series of campaigns between 216 and 200 caused extensive damage to the agrarian economy.[9]

Much of the South seems to have been in a considerable state of unrest in the period following the departure of Hannibal, and there are indications of extensive brigandage. Livy reports 'conspiracies' of slaves and herdsmen in Apulia in 188 and 185/4 which certainly represent unrest and may point to more serious disaffection, since the suppression entailed several thousand executions. Tarentum was still volatile and strategically sensitive and may have been the source of some of this unrest. It remained garrisoned by Roman troops and subject to the jurisdiction of a praetorian commissioner appointed to deal with it.[10] Livy (35.23.5, 36.2.7, 40.18.4) makes reference to the military sensitivity of the region and the need to defend the Apulian coast in 192/1 and 181 BC. In 186 BC, the question of public order in Italy was raised again by the so-called Bacchanalian conspiracy, notionally a plot to subvert members of the Roman élite and hatch plots against the Senate under cover of religious rites. The suppression of the Greek cult of Bacchus has long been a historical puzzle, coming at a time when Rome was increasingly open to other Hellenic influences. The handling of it certainly indicates nervousness, possibly prompted by the secretive and inward-looking nature of the cult as much as by the public disorders it supposedly generated.[11] Although it was not a specifically southern problem and had a large impact on Etruria and at Rome, the South was certainly restless. A praetorian commissioner was sent to Tarentum to supervise the region, and southern Italy may have been implicated in the diffusion of the cult.[12] It was prominent in a number of Italiote cities, notably Naples and Tarentum, although other sources point to trans-mission direct from Greece or via Etruria.[13]

The history of the South after 200 BC is closely bound up with the questions of land confiscation and distribution, and with Roman colon-isation. The devastation and depopulation after the Punic Wars was considerable, although opinions about its significance differ. Brunt has argued persuasively that much of the economic damage was short-term.[14] In secessionist areas of Magna Graecia, there was undoubtedly large-scale land confiscation as part of the post-war settlements. There is little explicit evidence for this, but the effects of such confiscations can be seen in the amount of colonisation in the South in the early second century and the activities of the Gracchan land commissioners, which suggest that the amount of *ager publicus* must have been high.[15] The Greek cities which received colonies included Tarentum (123 BC), Croton (194), Scolacium (123), Vibo (192), Buxentum (194), Tempsa (194) and Thurii (193).[16] Colonies were also founded at Volturnum, Liternum, Salernum, Puteoli and Sipontum. Part of the Ager Campanus was divided up, and in Apulia 40,000 veterans were allotted land immediately after the war, with further allotments around Beneventum to 47,000 Ligurians in 180 BC.[17]

The purpose of these varied greatly according to context. The majority were citizen colonies of 300 settlers, and were founded to protect the coast in the event of a further invasion by Hannibal. Those at Buxentum and Sipontum failed to become established at first, and were re-founded in 186. Archaeological surveys at Buxentum show that this colony, at least, survived.[18] The colonies of Valentia, founded at Vibo, and Copia, founded near Thurii, were somewhat larger, with 4,000 and 3,300 colonists respectively.[19] It seems likely that these were an attempt to allocate land to displaced Romans or discharged troops and to repopulate the area, and were not as directly connected with security considerations. However, the South was still a restless place and land allocations may have been made with the intention of creating a stronger Roman presence to offset this. It had a powerful effect on local settlement patterns, as demonstrated in western Lucania, where the flourishing Lucanian site at Roccagloriosa was abandoned shortly after the foundation of Buxentum and settlement density increased markedly in the area around the colony.[20]

The final phase of colonisation before 90 BC occurred in 123/2, as a result of G. Gracchus' programme of colonisation and distribution of *ager publicus*. Two colonies were founded in Magna Graecia, namely Minervia at Scolacium and Neptunia in the territory of Tarentum, almost certainly occupying land confiscated from the Tarentines after 209 BC.[21] These ensured that Tarentum came into closer contact with Roman culture than had hitherto been the case, but the absorption of these colonies into the neighbouring Greek cities in 90/89 BC suggests that the older Greek communities remained the stronger cultural and administrative unit.[22] Although these are the only known colonies, Gracchan *cippi* have been found in the Valle di Diano in western Lucania, and around Grumentum, indicating high levels of viritane land distribution.[23]

Colonisation in Magna Graecia continued intermittently throughout the first century AD. Cumae is a debatable case, but inscriptions containing the abbreviation *D(ecreto) D(ecurionum) C(olonia) I(ulia)* provide some evidence for an Augustan colony, although the colonial status of the city has also been dated to the second century AD.[24] Flavian colonists from a deduction of AD 71 are attested in inscriptions from Paestum, all of them veterans from Misenum. At Tarentum, both Gracchan colonists and veterans from a deduction of AD 60 are attested, but there are no epigraphic traces of a group of pirates pardoned by Pompey, which is said to have been settled there.[25]

There was clearly a high level of immigration and colonisation in Magna Graecia during the Late Republic and Early Empire, which undoubtedly had a profound impact on the region. Most of the colonies founded in the 190s were small, but their impact on an area could be striking. The survey of the Bussento valley has shown that the foundation of Buxentum had the paradoxical effect of strengthening the Greek city at the expense of the Lucanian site at Roccagloriosa. The inland settlements were abandoned and a more intensive pattern of land use developed around Buxentum itself.[26] Unfortunately, the dearth of second- and first-century BC epigraphy makes it difficult to trace the immediate impact of these colonies on existing communities. Such traces as there are suggest that there was no move towards large-scale Romanisation. Linguistically, Oscan persists until the first century BC, even where Latin was the official language. Cumae applied to become Latin-speaking for official purposes in 188 BC, but Oscan inscriptions are found dating to the first century.[27] Religious cults are also remarkably unchanged. It is difficult to draw conclusions on physical changes from a region where so many urban plans are obscured by modern settlement, but Paestum may serve as a useful example. Here, there was a remodelling of the street plan shortly after the deduction of 273. The Greek city may have had a grid-plan before this date, but the alignment of the temples of Hera is at odds with the later grid, suggesting that there had been some changes, and the precinct of the temple of Hera underwent some modifications to accommodate the Roman plan.[28] The earliest phases of the *forum* date to the third century, including the *comitium* building, in which the Senate met, and an Italic temple which has been variously identified as that of the Capitoline triad or of Mens Bona.[29] However, although there was clearly a degree of Roman building in the third century, much urban development did not take place until the Augustan period or later.[30]

In some areas, the gradual influx of individual Romans and Italians may have been an influential factor, but this is less likely to leave physical traces than a full-scale colony. There was extensive viritane land allotment in the South, and also a large-scale seasonal migration of wealthy Romans and their households to certain areas of Campania. This principally affected the area around the Bay of Naples,[31] and was not nearly such a prominent feature of the area in this period as it became in the first century BC, but there is evidence that the trend was beginning in the second century, and also that the same phenomenon can be observed, although to a lesser extent, in other areas.[32]

The topic of land use and settlement density will be dealt with fully in the context of the economic history of Magna Graecia (see Chapter 7), but it is worth noting that archaeological evidence is radically modifying the picture of desertion and decline given by the sources. The villas which spring up in Magna Graecia in the second and first centuries BC are not huge *latifundia* but smaller estates with a mixed economy. Some undoubtedly were owned by absentee Roman landlords but others must have been owned by local notables.[33]

Another phenomenon of the second century BC which is sometimes cited as evidence for the depopulation and impoverishment of the South after 200 is the appearence of large numbers of Italians in the epigraphy of cities in the Aegean, and in particular on Delos.[34] The majority of these have *nomina* which suggest a southern origin,[35] and a proportion are Greeks from southern Italy and Sicily. However, there is no evidence that these represent large-scale emigration from southern Italy. Undoubtedly a proportion were political exiles who were unable or unwilling to return, and some may have been permanent residents in the Greek East, but the majority were traders or bankers who did not sever connections with their cities of origin.[36] Far from being an indication of poverty, the presence of so many Italiotes in the East suggests an expanding network of trading contacts, which must surely be a sign of economic growth rather than the reverse.

Interference by Rome in other spheres also caused fundamental changes in the economic life of Magna Graecia. Before 200 BC, most cities in the region had a flourishing monetary system, minting their own coinage to a variety of local needs and specifications. However, in the period following the war, most local coinages disappeared, in Magna Graecia as in other regions. Velia, Vibo, Rhegium, Copia, Paestum, Heraklea, Brundisium and Ancona were all minting coins in the early years of the second century, but these sequences disappeared by *c.* 180 BC.[37] Roman coinage became the common currency for the whole of Italy, facilitating economic transactions between cities. At the same time it provided Rome with a powerful medium for image-making and propaganda in the selection of coin types, and deprived Italian cities of similar opportunities for self-definition. However, some Italiote cities retained the right to coin money for a considerable period after the end of independent coin sequences elsewhere. Heraklea continued to mint bronze coinage until the Social War and Velia until the middle of the first century BC.[38] Paestum continued to issue bronze coinage until the reign of Tiberius,[39] something which is unprecendented elsewhere in Italy, but it is debatable whether this had a primarily economic purpose.

If it served as a means of exchange, it must have been restricted to local circulation. Crawford's suggestion that these were commemorative issues, serving a euergetic rather than economic purpose, seems plausible.[40]

Paradoxically, the development of a system of arterial roads during the second century and the consequent improvement in land communications may have been an important factor in encouraging the decline of parts of southern Italy. In the third century BC, the only systematically constructed road was the Via Appia, originally linking Rome and Capua, then extended to Tarentum and finally to Brundisium in 244 BC.[41] By 100 BC, however, the road-building activities of Roman notables had created a network of roads radiating outwards from Rome. The two which affected southern Italy are the Via Appia itself and the Via Annia Popillia, which linked Rome and Rhegium on a route which ran via Capua, coastal Lucania and the Valle di Diano. In the second century AD, the building of the Via Traiana added an alternative route to Brundisium, which ran through northern Apulia and bypassed Tarentum entirely.[42]

The decline of some of the cities along the coast between Tarentum and Rhegium may be explicable in terms of the fact that they were now distant from the major lines of communication between Rome and the South, while Rhegium, Tarentum and the coastal cities of Campania and Lucania retained greater access to the main system of land transport and communications. The fate of Paestum seems to support this. Until the second century, it had occupied an important position, dominating the land routes through Lucania and controlling a harbour. However, the building of the Via Annia Popillia in 131 BC bypassed Paestum, passing some miles to the East. Around the same time, siltation began to become a serious problem for the harbour, thus effectively cutting the city off from the main sources of transport and communications.[43] The development of Apulia also shows the same pattern. Bari, which dominated the junction of the Via Traiana and coastal routes through Apulia, rose to greater prominence after the construction of the road, and Herdonia, which was also on the Via Traiana, underwent a notable revival.[44]

This pattern does not always occur entirely by accident. Manipulation of communications is a well-known means of exerting political and economic control. The foundation of Brundisium in 244 BC posed a threat to Tarentine economic and strategic supremacy. This was increased when the Via Appia was extended to Brundisium, creating an alternative port and route to Greece. Political privilege gave Brundisium a further competitive edge, in that it was exempted from the *portoria* at some stage, although the date is not known.[45] Finally, the building of the Via Traiana cut Tarentum off entirely by creating a shorter and more direct route between Rome and Brundisium which bypassed Tarentum. Clearly the privileges offered to the Roman colony of Brundisium and the exclusion of the rebellious ally, Tarentum, were used as a means to curb Tarentine power, and had the effect of undermining the prosperity of the city. This was, however, a long-term result of the changes of the second and first centuries. In the Late Republic, Tarentum was still an important city, and the events of the Civil Wars indicate continuing strategic importance.

THE SOCIAL WAR

One of the most problematic aspects of an attempt to write a history of the South is the minimal evidence for Italiote-Roman relations between the 180s BC and the Social War, and the lack of Italiote reaction during the Social War itself. Tarentum, Rhegium and Naples were called on by Rome to supply ships for the Roman fleet in 173 and 171,[46] but there is no other sign of Greek participation in the Roman wars in the eastern Mediterranean. The colonial foundations presumably had military obligations, but there are no known allied contingents. The sources are almost totally silent on the subject of any other contact between Rome and Magna Graecia. There are no further references to *praetores* based at Tarentum after 181, although Livy (44.16.7) records a grant of property at Tarentum to a Macedonian noble in 169 BC which was administered by a *praetor*. This may suggest that the South was in a more settled state. The foundation of colonies at Tarentum and Scolacium in 122 is proof that the South was affected by the Gracchan legislation, but there is no record of the Greek reaction to these measures, or of their impact on existing communities. In Campania, the growing interest in Greek culture on the part of the Roman élite during the second century attracted an increasing Roman presence, and the earliest aristocratic villas on the Bay of Naples appear in this period. There was also an increased amount of political interference, as attested by a boundary dispute between Naples and Nola.[47] Rome sent a commissioner, Q. Labeo, to arbitrate, at the request of the cities concerned. He promptly solved the problem by declaring that the land belonged to Rome, not to either of the disputants. The reaction of the Nolans and Neapolitans is not recorded. Cicero does not give a date, but it seems to belong to 133–123, when the Gracchan land commissioners were active and land tenure was a politically sensitive topic. However, there is no indication of the growing frustration and anger experienced by other allies of Rome between c. 150 and 90 BC. Nor is there any positive indication of support for the Italian cause before, or during, the Social War.

This silence is puzzling, since the Mezzogiorno, like Samnium, was a region with a history of insurrection. The traditional explanation – that the area had been so thoroughly crushed in the second Punic War and weakened by subsequent economic decline that it was without resources to rebel – is being steadily undermined as more archaeological evidence comes to light. In view of the lack of literary evidence, it is only possible to hazard guesses at the reasons for Italiote quiescence and apparent lack of interest in grievances which had become very pressing for many of the allies,[48] but there seem to be two major factors which are significant. The first of these is that the greatest hostility to Rome is found amongst the Oscan peoples who were the traditional enemies of the Greeks.[49] As in the second Punic War, it is possible that ongoing local rivalries influenced the behaviour of the Greeks, at least in the South.

The second is implicit in Cicero's assertion that Naples and Heraklea expressed a preference for autonomous alliance rather than citizenship, saying that many of their citizens 'preferred the freedom of their treaties to citizenship' ('*foederis sui libertatem civitati anteferret*'). Once again, the Greek political slogan of *eleutheria* seems to figure largely in the thinking of the Italiotes.[50] It seems significant that the concept of citizenship, which extended on a large scale in this manner and at the cost of local autonomy, was not widespread in Greece and the Hellenistic world,[51] and that it appears to have been a more specifically Roman development. The reluctance of Naples and Heraklea to accept citizenship must be set against this background. The Roman concept of extended citizenship was so far removed from the Greek idea of exclusive citizenship, even when this included *isopoliteia*,[52] that the main issue of the war may have been regarded as largely irrelevant by the Italiotes. As with the major events of the third century, Italiote actions seem to indicate an isolation from, and indifference to, the main issues which preoccupied Rome, as well as a possible difference of concept on the question of citizenship.

Moretti suggests that 90 BC should be seen as a cultural, as well as a political, watershed, marking the end of the Hellenistic period in Magna Graecia.[53] This is a contentious issue, particularly as there is no agreement over the definition of the Hellenistic period in the context of Magna Graecia, and it has been suggested that the term 'Hellenistic' has no real meaning as a political/cultural division for the history of southern Italy.[54] It is certainly true that the Greeks of Italy and Sicily underwent a different process of development from the Greeks of the Aegean and Asia, and did not directly experience the political and social effects of the rise of Macedon and the establishment of the Hellenised kingdoms of the East. However, these are not sufficient grounds to argue the non-existence of the Hellenistic period in the West. The Greeks of Italy and Sicily maintained a network of cultural, economic and political contacts with the rest of the Greek world throughout their history, and in many cases demonstrably retained a sense of their Greek identity. On the level of inter-state connections, Tarentum maintained contact with Epirus and Sparta. There were also networks of religious contacts between sanctuaries in the eastern and western Mediterranean.[55]

On an individual level, large numbers of Italiote Greeks had contact with the eastern Mediterranean and Aegean Greeks are known to have visited the Italiote cities.[56] These religious, political and economic contacts were maintained from the foundation of the colonies, and although the nature of contacts with the rest of the Greek world inevitably changed to reflect wider historical changes, there is no evidence that they ever broke down. The Western Greeks had to co-exist politically with the changes which occurred in the East after the death of Alexander and later, the Roman conquest of the East. They also remained part of the Greek cultural *koine*, the material culture of the West continuing to reflect and adapt the Hellenistic styles of the eastern Mediterranean.[57] Thus it is clear that far from becoming isolated from the Hellenistic world, Magna Graecia remained an integral part of the Greek world from the fourth century onwards by means of direct contact and indirectly through the Roman conquest of the East. The number of contacts with the Eastern Empire which were maintained by some of the cities of Magna Graecia argue that these cities were recognisably Hellenistic,[58] at least until 90 BC, if not later. It is also notable that some cities retained elements of the Greek language and Hellenistic culture even after the Augustan period, which is widely regarded as the date by which Italy can be regarded as fully 'Romanised'.[59] The year 90 BC cannot be a chronological watershed in anything other than a purely political sense.

CIVIL WAR AND AUGUSTAN REFORM

After 89 BC, the Greek cities became incorporated into the Roman State, either as *municipia* or as *coloniae*, as did all other communities in Italy. Clearly this brought about considerable changes to the political structure and civic life of all Italian cities, involving adoption of Roman law and Romanised constitutions, which will be discussed in detail in Chapter 9. Needless to say, however, the cultural diversity of the region engendered many anomalies in the transition from independence to citizenship. Links with the past can also be seen in the Table of Heraklea. This bronze tablet, originally used for a Greek inscription giving details of the land holdings of the sanctuary of Demeter, was reused in the first century BC for a Latin inscription containing Roman municipal regulations. Once thought to be a fragmentary text of the Lex Julia Municipalis, it is now believed to be a collection of excerpts from several Roman municipal laws, including the Lex Julia, and dates to the late first century BC.[60] Significantly, it was set up at the sanctuary of Demeter, the federal sanctuary of the Italiote League. It implies that the sanctuary had retained its importance as an Italiote meeting place, and possibly that the League was still in existence as a cultural unit, although its political functions must have long since disappeared.

The first century also ushered in a period of political upheaval and civil war which disrupted southern Italy as profoundly as any other area. The revolt of Spartacus brought about the devastation of parts of Magna Graecia,[61] in particular the destruction of villas around Metapontum and Thurii, as well as of other parts of southern Italy. Shortly afterwards, the campaigns of Sulla brought further destruction. Few details are known of the extent of the damage, but Naples, which supported Marius, was besieged and sacked, and its fleet, the last surviving Greek war fleet in Italy, was destroyed.[62]

However, the early part of the first century BC was not entirely a time of depression for the South. It is unlikely that these campaigns had such a profound effect on the society and economy of the South as the Punic Wars. There is no record for this period of any severe problems of recovery such as there is for the 190s. In Campania, there was an enormous growth in the late second and early first century in the number of villas built by wealthy Romans. Cumae, Naples, Puteoli and Baiae flourished as centres for those who wished to pursue interests in Greek culture and philosophy. Cicero, Pompey, Caesar, Hortensius and Lucullus were among those who owned property in this area, visited it frequently, and were a valuable source of patronage both to leading families of these cities and to the communities at large.[63] This period also sees an increase in the number of villas in northern Campania, most of them mixed farms or wine producers. A number of the Roman élite also owned estates further south, notably at Velia, Tarentum and Rhegium, although these, being less easily accessible, may have been visited less often.[64]

During the Civil Wars, the strategic position of the ports of Tarentum and Rhegium placed the Greeks in a position vital to the war effort of both sides. Tarentum was used by Octavian as a base for his operations in Greece, and was also the venue for at least one conference between Octavian, Antony and Lepidus.[65] Rhegium suffered during Sextus Pompeius' campaigns in Sicily, and also incurred the wrath of Octavian, possibly an indication of Antonine sympathies. It was designated as one of the cities to be turned over to Octavian's troops as booty, but was eventually removed from the list, along with Vibo.[66] The number of Julian freedmen and women, and inscriptions referring to Augustus' family, known from Rhegium may suggest that Augustus remained a patron of the city.[67] However, this connection with the ruling family may not necessarily indicate imperial patronage. Rhegium was designated as a place of exile for Julia,[68] and thus the connection with the imperial family appears to be with a disgraced member of it. Inscriptions from Tarentum hint at Caesarian sympathies, with a large number of texts in honour of members of the Julian dynasty, including one which commemorates the institution of the Second Triumvirate. Pompey settled a colony of captured and pardoned pirates there, an act which implies superfluous *ager publicus* but may also indicate hostility towards the city.[69]

The reign of Augustus and the reforms engendered by him had a profound effect on Magna Graecia, as on all other areas of Italy. The supremacy of Italy and the triumph of Italic culture over the Oriental connections and Hellenising tendencies attributed to Antony were central both to his political programme and to the iconography and propaganda fostered by him.[70] The introduction of social and religious reforms with a conservative slant and an intent to promote 'traditional' Roman values placed Magna Graecia in an awkward, but ultimately favourable, position. The Hellenism of the Italiotes placed them outside this cultural framework, but their long relationship with Rome and integration into the citizen body also rescued them from the opprobrium heaped on Greek influences from the Eastern Empire. Italiote Hellenism became culturally and politically acceptable to the ruling regime and relations between Magna Graecia and Rome entered a new phase.[71]

The theme of cultural change and integration is one which will be pursued further in later chapters, but it was not the only Augustan innovation to have an impact on Magna Graecia. The administrative reforms enacted by Augustus undoubtedly affected the South, as well as other regions of Italy. The chief of these was the division of Italy into eleven regions, a somewhat mysterious measure which is known only from Pliny's description of Italy. It may have been enacted in AD 6, but little is known about it.[72] These regions respected ethnic boundaries to some extent, but they also cut across them and diminished them in that ethnic groups were no longer the primary administrative units. Most of the Augustan regions included more than one ethnic group, further breaking down inter-regional barriers. Although a concept of Magna Graecia as a distinct cultural and ethnic entity existed, the peculiarly diverse nature of the region is demonstrated by its treatment under these reforms. It was the only region of Italy to be subdivided and broken up entirely. Tarentum, Heraklea and Metapontum were included in Regio II, along with Apulia. The Lucanians, Bruttians and Calabrian Greeks became Regio III and the colonies of the Bay of Naples were assigned to Regio I, along with Campania and Latium.[73] This seems to mark the final demise of any Greek political cohesion, although examination of the workings of the Greek municipalities shows a continuing sense of cultural identification. The end of the Italiote League as a significant political organisation marked the first stage of this, and the extension of the citizenship must have accelerated the process, the final stage of which was marked by the Augustan reforms.

After the Civil Wars, the possibilities for writing a linear account of the history of Magna Graecia are very limited indeed. This does not mean, however, that our knowledge and understanding of this area comes to an end. Literary sources are limited, but this is compensated for by the great increase in the number of surviving inscriptions, which are an invaluable source of information on the social and cultural history of the Italiote cities. However, this necessitates a very different approach to their history. Thus the remainder of this book will focus on the reconstruction of aspects of civic life in the cities which are sufficiently well documented, with a view to tracing the mechanisms of cultural interaction with Rome, and the impact of Romanisation on the region.

6

East/West Relations: Contacts between Magna Graecia and the Eastern Mediterranean

In considering the relations of the Italiote Greeks with Rome, one is essentially considering the Italiotes as part of Italy. It is all too easy to forget that most cities in Magna Graecia retained a strong sense of their Greek identity and continued to play a significant part in the Greek world. An examination of the evidence shows that although the overt signs of Greekness disappeared in some cities as early as the third century BC, and declined in others, many continued to be conscious of their Greek background and to express this in ways adapted to their changed circumstances long after their conquest by Rome. Thus the question of the nature and extent of the contacts between Magna Graecia and the rest of the Mediterranean world has important repercussions for the study of the Italiotes and also for the way in which they interacted with Rome. Nor were the exchanges only one way. If the Italiotes actively maintained contact with the Greek world after the Roman conquest of the South, Aegean and Asiatic Greeks can equally be seen to have been involved with the cities of the West. Magna Graecia was a pivotal region with a central role in the diffusion of Hellenism in Italy.

Unfortunately the study of diplomatic and economic contacts between East and West Greece is obscured, like so much else in Italiote history, by lack of evidence. The impression given by that which does exist is that such relations declined after the Mithridatic War and ensuing massacre of Italians, but this may merely be due to changes in the nature of the evidence. It is partly offset by literary and epigraphic data for the later Republic and the Empire which demonstrates that if direct political and diplomatic activity declined after the second century BC, cultural contacts continued to flourish and even increase. From the first century BC to the second century AD, those cities of southern Italy which remained culturally Greek acted as a magnet for artists, philosophers and athletes from all parts of the Greek world who were anxious to establish a reputation in Italy and at Rome, and in particular to obtain the patronage of the Roman nobility.[1]

The Bay of Naples, and to a lesser extent Velia, also attracted a large number of wealthy Romans. Greek literature and philosophy were an integral part of the sophisticated villa society which developed. Greek poets, philosophers and rhetoricians obtained patronage from emperors and the court, and from other prominent Romans. Greek games had been known in Rome since the third century BC, but prestigious new festivals instituted by Augustus, Nero and Domitian provided a further focus for artistic and athletic activity. There are also signs that cities further south attracted these cultural migrants, although on a lesser scale than did the Bay of Naples. The evidence for contacts between the Greek East and the Greek West indicates that on a cultural level, the cities of Magna Graecia, or those of them that survived the Punic Wars intact, acted as a mediating influence between Rome and the Greek East and played an important role in the Hellenisation of Roman intellectual and cultural life during the period 200 BC–AD 200.

Obviously, the nature of East/West contact changed and evolved to reflect the changing economic and political circumstances of both the eastern and western Mediterranean. As the political independence of both the Italiotes and the Greeks declined, so economic and cultural contacts may have become more prominent. It is salutary to note, however, that this impression may be the result of the chronological bias of the surviving evidence. The changing fortunes of those Italiotes who were conquered by the Oscans and became Oscanised in the fourth century, or those cities which failed to recover from the devastations of the fourth and third centuries, are also reflected in the patterns of contact between West and East. A number of cities – Nicotera, Medma, Buxentum, etc. – disappear from the historical record almost entirely, and little is known of their later history or contacts outside Italy. Others failed to recover from the ravages of Hannibal, including the once-prestigious cities of Metapontum and Thurii. Yet others – Paestum, Cumae, Terina and Vibo – were substantially Italicised after conquest by the Oscans and do not, with the exception of Cumae, feature prominently in the record of East/West contacts. However, there is no simple correlation between known contacts with the Aegean after *c.* 200 BC and a city's level of prosperity, importance, or continuing Hellenisation.

One would expect evidence for extensive contacts with the Aegean at Naples, where Greek language and culture persisted into the second century AD and was underwritten by an increasing amount of patronage from the Roman élite. However, there are surprises elsewhere. There are few signs of contacts with the Aegean at Rhegium, despite the continuation of Greek language and religion, but much evidence for such contacts with Tarentum, where direct epigraphic evidence for the continuity of Hellenism is lacking. There are similar indications for Heraklea and Velia, which are otherwise very poorly documented. Cumae, despite being Italicised to a large extent after the Oscan conquest of Campania, nevertheless features largely in the development of aristocratic villa society on the Bay of Naples.[2] Thus the distribution of Aegean/Italic contacts after the Punic Wars is uneven and somewhat surprising in its implications. It firmly underlines the fact that the inadequacies of both the literary and the epigraphic record may entirely obscure whole facets of the development of some communities.

Prior to the Punic Wars, there are signs that contacts between the Aegean world and the West were very extensive. Given the lack of information about the early history of the Greek colonies, it is easy to overlook the fact that although the Italiotes developed along distinctive lines from the Aegean Greeks, they remained an integral part of the wider Greek world. Their position on the periphery should not be overemphasised. In the Archaic period, the aristocratic culture of the élite of such cities as Tarentum, Croton, Sybaris and Metapontum mirrored that of the Aegean Greeks, although on a more lavish scale. Both the literary sources, despite their exaggeration, and the archaeological record attest to the wealth of this society. The Italiote cities participated in the pan-Hellenic festivals and maintained contacts with the major sanctuaries of Greece in the same way as Athens, Corinth or any other city of Aegean Greece. The victory lists at Olympia contain an impressive list of victors from the Western cities, with a particularly high level of success in the seventh and sixth centuries.[3] Tarentine and Metapontine athletes feature regularly, but the *pankration* is notable for the dominance enjoyed by Crotoniates, of whom the most noted was Milo Diotimou, who won six Olympic titles and later achieved fame as the general who led the Crotoniates to victory against Sybaris in 510 BC.[4]

Contacts with these sanctuaries were not restricted to major festivals. Western cities regularly made state dedications in commemoration of victories. Few of these have survived, but there are a number of notable exceptions. The Tarentines erected two large-scale bronze statue groups to commemorate their victories against the Iapygians and Peucetians

101

early in the fifth century. The bases of these have been found at Delphi, and bronze fragments from Tarentum were probably part of a copy set up there.[5] On a somewhat smaller scale, a dedication by Hieron of Syracuse has been found at Olympia, commemorating the victory of Cumae and Syracuse over the Etruscans in 474.[6] Despite the lack of agonistic evidence, the Western Greeks clearly maintained a significant presence at Delphi.

On the political/diplomatic level, there is no reason to doubt that the Greeks of Italy and Sicily were fully integrated with the rest of the Greek world. The foundation of Thurii in 444/3 BC demonstrates that Aegean Greek cities were still prepared to undertake major ventures in the West, and the Athenian war against Syracuse provides an example of the extent to which Western cities were involved in the network of inter-state relations on the other side of the Mediterranean. In particular, Athenian interest in the West was extensive in the period 479–412 BC. Themistocles, who named his daughters Sybaris and Italia, constantly stressed the importance of Italy.[7] The ill-documented expedition of Diotimos and the Athenian role in the final foundation of Naples is a further indication of expansionism in the West.[8] The most graphic illustration of this dovetailing of Aegean and Italiote political concerns is the Athens expedition against Syracuse, after which the Athenian defeat effectively precluded any resurgence of interest in the West. In particular, the growing pre-eminence of the Spartan colony of Taren-tum, and the Doric origin of many other cities in the West, ensured that the Athenian fleet received a cold reception. Tarentum refused outright to allow the fleet to land, and the only city which gave any assistance was Rhegium.[9]

Magna Graecia also played an important role in Greek cultural and intellectual development in the sixth and fifth centuries. Pythagoras' arrival in the West in the late sixth century marked the beginning of a major intellectual and political movement which had far-reaching con-sequences. The establishment of Pythagorean philosophy was a major contribution to the development of Greek thought, in medicine, music, mathematics and architecture. It was also an important factor in Italiote politics, since many of the known instances of *stasis* in the West revolve around pro- and anti-Pythagorean factions. Apart from the Pythagoreans, there was also the development of the Eleatic school of philosophy at Velia. Although evidence is slight and anecdotal,[10] there is every reason to believe that artistic and intellectual contacts with the rest of Greece flourished.

During the fourth and third centuries, there is no sign of any diminution of these contacts with the Aegean, at least among those cities which managed to retain their independence from the Oscans. Cumae and Paestum, and also probably Vibo, seem to have fallen out of the orbit of the Greek world after the Oscan conquests of the fifth century. Others, however, maintained their contact with the East, although the forms that these contacts took appears to have changed. The run of success enjoyed by Western Greeks in the major pan-Hellenic games seems to have come to an end, since there are few records of Italiote victors after the fifth century. However, this is not to argue that Italiotes did not participate. It would have been rather strange if they did not. Possibly the drain on manpower and resources involved in constant warfare against the Lucanians, Bruttians and others can be seen in the lack of top-class athletes available to compete. Although agonistic documents are lacking, there is still ample evidence for connections with the major sanctuaries. Italiotes are recorded on the list of *Hieropoioi* at Delphi and in the *Soteria* inscriptions.[11] This is also a period of diplomatic exchanges with the sanctuaries of Asklepios at Epidauros and on Cos. The Epidauros inscription contains a list of *Theodokoi* which includes all the major Greek cities of Italy and Sicily. An inscription of 242 BC from Cos records embassies from the Asklepieion to cities in the Greek world to seek recognition of the right of *asylia* and includes Naples and Velia among the respondents.[12] Both of these reflect the continuing place of the Italiote cities in the diplomatic structure of the Hellenistic world.

Despite this, evidence of international diplomatic activity is scarce, although the exchange of correspondence between Cos, Naples and Velia shows that it did take place. International contacts between sanctuaries continue to occur as late as the first century AD.[13] The latest certain example is a Velian inscription which records the presence of an Aeginetan priest as *curator sacrorum* at the sanctuary of Athena at Velia.[14] The date is uncertain, but it is Augustan or later, with some estimates dating it as late as the second century AD. However, the bulk of the evidence for contacts between Eastern and Western Greeks after 270 BC records the acts of private individuals, or their relations with a particular city, rather than contacts between cities.

It is tempting at this point to make the superficial connection between the loss of self-determinism by the Italiotes and the disappearance of evidence for independent diplomatic contacts, and assume that this reflects a loss of independence. However, the reasons may be more complex than this, even leaving aside the likelihood of distortion through lack of evidence. A feature of the Italiote contacts with the Aegean is the extent to which they reflect the behaviour of the rest of the Greek world at the same period. From the third to the first century BC, there is much more evidence for the movement of individuals between states, and for the relations of individuals with foreign states, as recorded by proxeny decrees. Thus it is not surprising that Italiote Greeks should be recorded in proxeny decrees, ephebe lists, dedications at sanctuaries, and in the victory lists of the minor agonistic festivals which developed in this period, along with Aegean Greeks, and also an increasing number of Italians and Romans.

Literary evidence for the presence of Italiotes in the East is very slender. However, there is one exception to this which is worth mentioning, namely the infamous Herakleides of Tarentum. Polybios indicates that he was an architect from Tarentum.[15] The exact details of his career are confused, but he appears to have been exiled at some stage between 212 and 209, during the secession from Rome, although his subsequent career as a double agent may cast doubt on the genuineness of this.[16] He is credited with the invention of the *sambuca* used by Marcellus at the siege of Syracuse,[17] but appears to have been forced to leave Italy entirely after doubts were cast on his loyalty to Rome. Subsequently, he acted as a diplomat and adviser to Philip V and was instrumental in carrying out Philip's anti-Rhodian policy in 204.[18] There is no evidence that he ever returned to Tarentum. He has been tentatively identified with the Delian banker Herakleides Aristionos but there is no evidence to support this apart from an approximate correspondence of date.[19]

There is some further literary evidence for political exiles from Tarentum in the third century.[20] This seems to indicate that the pro-Roman group formed a 'government in exile' to some extent. The approach made to them by Rome at the Olympic Games of 207 suggests that they were perceived as a coherent political group and not simply a collection of displaced individuals. In addition to this, there are references to a musician, Nikokles Aristionos, who was a Tarentine exile living in Athens. A large tomb, which is probably his, has been dated to the middle of the third century BC, which suggests that he was exiled in the 280s or 270s.[21] His son continued his career in Greece and is named as being the favourite kitharist of Antigonus Doson. However, apart from this, the evidence for Italiotes in the eastern Aegean is almost entirely epigraphic. The largest single body of data is from Delos. The island's status as a free port attracted a large number of merchants and financiers, both Greek and Italian, whose contacts with the island can be traced in inscriptions recording dedications, building activities, donations to the sanctuary, participation in festivals and membership of guilds and collegia.[22] However, Italians and Romans appear in many inscriptions from all over the eastern Mediterranean.

While some of the inscriptions mentioning Italiote Greeks are of a fragmentary nature and others make only brief references to individuals, nevertheless it is possible to make some analysis of the nature of the contacts between Western Greeks and the Aegean. Excluding the material from Delos, most of the inscriptions mentioning Italiotes are proxeny decrees or agonistic inscriptions, although a number of examples are funerary or dedicatory in character, and by and large give little information about individuals. In contrast, the material from Delos is primarily composed of dedicatory inscriptions of a more informative character. In general, despite their limitations, inscriptions can provide some valuable insight into the nature of contacts between Eastern and Western Greeks.

One major question which arises out of the abundance of evidence for individuals from Italy in the Greek East, whether Greek, Roman or Italian, is whether or not these people were permanently resident outside Italy, thus representing a degree of emigration. In general, comparatively few of the individuals who appear in the epigraphic record seem permanently to have been resident in the East. Evidence for the existence of *conventus civium Romanorum* (assemblies of Roman citizens) in some Greek cities indicates that there were enough Romans and Italians resident in the East to require some communal organisation.[23] However, so little is known about their function and composition that this cannot be regarded as decisive evidence one way or the other. Nor is it known whether Greeks from the West participated in these assemblies.

On Delos, a number of Greek families from the West can be traced through several generations, together with their slaves and freedmen.[24] However, Delos, with its central position in the Aegean, status as a free port, and high concentration of Italians with their own enclave on the island (the Agora of the Italians), must be regarded as the exception rather than the rule. It is unclear how many even of the community on Delos were permanent residents in the absolute sense of the word. Wealthy men, such as Midas Zenonos of Heraklea and the banker Philostratos Philostratou of Naples,[25] seem to have invested a considerable amount of money in the building of the Agora of the Italians, judging by the number of buildings which they dedicated. Philostratos paid for the construction of a portico and donated money to several other projects, as well as making rich dedications to Zeus, Apollo and

Artemis. A number of these men appear together with their whole family, including wives, children and slaves, which suggests contact with the island for considerable periods of time.[26]

However, in some cases at least, residence on the island was not permanent. The documents simply indicate a hereditary connection with the island rather than actual residence there. The examples which occur of individuals who held the citizenship of more than one city indicate that patterns of residence and citizenship must have been very flexible. Philostratos Philostratou is given as a citizen of Ascalon in the earliest text in which he appears, but in later documents he is referred to as being a citizen of Naples.[27] Similarly, Simalos Timarchou was both a citizen of Tarentum and a citizen of Salamis.[28] These cases seem to imply that the individuals concerned must have lived for a reasonable length of time in the states which granted them citizenship, which in turn implies a considerable absence from Delos.[29] These multiple citizenships, which are much more common in the Hellenistic period than in the fifth century, also obscure the question of origins. Simalos Timarchou occurs on some inscriptions only as a citizen of Salamis and may have acquired Tarentine citizenship c. 100 BC or a little earlier. The population of Delos was clearly cosmopolitan. It may have been used by many of the Italians there as a base for commercial operations with which they maintained continuous contact and where they lived for considerable periods but not necessarily as permanent emigrants from their home cities. Benefactions to the Italian community on Delos, or dedications in the sanctuary, seem to have been a well-developed form of euergetism among families with connections and interests there, and these were clearly hereditary in nature. Three generations of the families of Agathokles Hermonos and Herakleides Aristionos have been traced by Hatzfeld.

Elsewhere, Italians and Western Greeks are a more overtly transient population and not permanent residents. As such, Italiotes are an indicator of contacts between Magna Graecia and the rest of the Greek world rather than a result of emigration from southern Italy. Some of those categorised by Hatzfeld as *negotiatores* engaged in trade may not actually have been so. Inscriptions which record proxeny decrees or games and festivals do not necessarily imply that those present were resident overseas or were engaged in trade. The Cumaeans Abris Kaikou and Attinos Herakleidou, who are included in Hatzfeld's list of *negotiatores*, are known only from an agonistic inscription from Oropus. There is no evidence that they were involved in trade. Similarly, Agathokles Theodosiou of Naples is named as *auletes* in a victor list from Oropus, c. 80 BC,[30] and Philon Philonos of Tarentum appears as *kitharistes* in a victory list for the Sarapeia at Tanagra, also in the first century BC.[31] Two actors are known from agonistic inscriptions, both Tarentine. Drakon the tragedian appears on a choregic list from Delos,[32] and Dorotheos Dorotheou is named by first-century victory lists from Orchomenos and Argos.[33] Dorotheos is included by Hatzfeld in his list of *negotiatores* but it seems more likely that he was a professional actor who toured the dramatic festivals, since he is known to have appeared at more than one festival. Thus it seems that many of the Italiotes known from agonistic inscriptions may not have been involved in trade necessarily but are likely to have been more or less professional athletes or performers touring a circuit of the major games and festivals.[34]

The fact that a considerable proportion of the evidence other than that from Delos comes from Boeotian agonistic inscriptions may be significant. It would suggest that the Greeks from Italy took part in the festivals which became a major feature of some Boeotian cities in the first century BC and were thus still part of the Greek cultural tradition represented by these festivals, and in practical terms were still in touch with the rest of the Greek world. However, it is likely, as noted above, that the participants in these games were athletes and artists and were present in Boeotia for reasons connected with the games, rather than being part of a tendency to emigrate from southern Italy. A single exception to this occurs in an agonistic inscription of 267 from Egypt which includes a Tarentine, Hephaistion Demeou, who appears to have been a *cleruch* resident in the area.[35] Given the date of this inscription, it seems possible that he may have been one of the anti-Roman faction at Tarentum expelled from the city after the Roman conquest in 272. In any case, he is an isolated example, differing both in date and in character from the main body of agonistic material.

A small number of Italiotes were registered as ephebes, later a common form of 'higher education' for the sons of the well-to-do of both the Eastern and Western Empire.[36] Those registered in Athens, on the list of ephebes of non-Athenian origin, are Simalos Simalou of Tarentum (101/0 BC) and Isidoros Isidorou of Naples (100 BC). Simalos also appears on a Delian ephebe list for 102/1 BC along with Ariston of Herakleia and Agathokles of Velia (119/18 BC).[37] The appearance of Simalos of Tarentum on ephebe lists of two states in consecutive years strongly suggests that this is not simply a case of a Tarentine family resident in Athens but a more complex issue. The *ephebeia* was not yet widely patronised by the sons of the Roman élite, but in the Hellenistic world it was a recognised form of élite education and participation was an indication of social status.

107

The number of funerary inscriptions found outside Delos and Egypt is surprisingly small, only eight being attributable with any certainty. Many of these are Athenian, including two of uncertain date, marking the graves of two Italian women, Demetria Aristonos,[38] who is described only as Italiote, and Demo Euphronos from Terina,[39] as well as two Cumaeans, a Velian, and five Tarentines, and most can be dated to the second and first centuries BC.[40] Two further funerary inscriptions, on Lindos and Rhodes, commemorate Neapolitans but do not have any certain indication of Italian origins. A rather larger proportion of the inscriptions from Delos are funerary in character, and there is a group of epitaphs from Egypt, most of them from Arsinoite or the Thebaid, which commemorate Italiote mercenaries.[41]

A large proportion of the evidence from areas other than Delos comes from decrees granting *proxenia* to individuals of Italiote origin. These are all in a standard format and do not give much information on the individuals concerned, being confined to formulaic declarations of goodwill and occasionally including grants of public hospitality to the recipients of the decree. The decrees passed by the *Boule* of Tanagra and of Oropos in honour of Pelops Dexiai of Naples date to *c*. 222–205 and honour him as *proxenos kai euergetes*.[42] Many of these are decrees by Boeotian cities, although there are examples from Delphi, Tenos and Euboea. In general, they are earlier in date than the agonistic inscriptions discussed above. Most of them belong to the third and second centuries, while the agonistic circuit flourished from *c*. 80 BC onwards.

The exact significance of proxeny decrees in the Hellenistic and Roman periods is one which has been much discussed. The title of *proxenos* was largely honorific by the Hellenistic period, granted to individuals as recognition of high standing or services to the state concerned. Roman decrees of *amicitia* are similar in many respects, and there are instances where such decrees are used as translations of the Hellenistic forms, but in other circumstances grants of *amicitia* clearly had much more legal force than the proxeny decrees.[43] The degree to which the institution had lost its original function as a means of securing representation of interests in other states by appointing a citizen of that state to safeguard them is not known. It may not necessarily be an indication of diplomatic relations between Eastern and Western Greeks but it is significant that, whatever the practical implications, the Italiote Greeks were still participating in a characteristically Hellenistic phenomenon in the years after the Roman conquest. Of the Italiote cities which appear on proxeny decrees, the most prominent are Tarentum and Naples, but citizens of Heraklea, Croton and Rhegium are also found in this type of document.

Although many of the Italiotes in the East do not appear in circumstance which suggest political exile, it has been suggested that a substantial number of them had in fact left Italy as a result of political changes in their home cities occurring in 272 and 209. Moretti attributes much of the depopulation notionally suffered by Tarentum to exile of citizens for political reasons and to emigration as a result of the political and economic disturbances of the third century,[44] but the evidence suggests that this aspect has been overemphasised. Undoubtedly some of the Italiotes in the East can be accounted for by political exile, but this cannot explain the entire number of those who appear in inscriptions in the eastern Mediterranean, particularly since a large proportion of these individuals do not come from cities with a history of political disturbance or of hostility to Rome.[45] The fact that many of the people named do not appear permanently to have been resident outside Italy would also suggest that the contacts between Magna Graecia and the Aegean cannot be explained in terms of emigration forced by political and economic decline. Equally, it cannot be assumed that those Italiotes who were exiled remained in exile permanently. The Tarentines who were exiled in 212 were invited to return after the reconquest of the city by Rome,[46] and exiled Locrians staged a counter-*coup* in 209/8.[47]

Several groups of Italiotes do appear in circumstances which may suggest permanent emigration and possibly exile. Of these, the Italiote mercenaries who begin to appear in Egypt in the third century are perhaps the most likely to represent permanent exiles.[48] However, this cannot be assumed. In particular, this migration cannot be connected with the upheavals caused by war with Rome, since the group of known Italiote mercenaries includes Velians and Neapolitans, who were not hostile to Rome in the third century, as well as Tarentines, who were. The presence of Italiote mercenaries in the armies of Hellenistic monarchs seems to be more a reflection of the increased demand for troops, increased rewards, and the continued Greek affiliation of Magna Graecia than evidence for mass emigration from Italy as a response to the Roman conquest of the South, particularly since the same phenomenon can be observed throughout the Hellenistic world. The fact that this process of recruitment of Italiotes by the Hellenistic dynasts seems to have been principally a third-century phenomenon may also be a reflection of the presence of Hellenistic armies in southern Italy during the fourth and third centuries. It is also possible that the apparent concentration of mercenaries in Egypt is a reflection of the strength of the contacts between Egypt and Magna Graecia.[49] Thus there are a large number of factors which need to be taken into consideration, and which suggest that the migration of Italiotes should be seen in terms of continuing contact with the Hellenistic world rather than purely in terms of the political events of the third century.

The heyday of Italian travellers in the East was undoubtedly the second and first centuries BC, no matter whether they were merchants, financiers, mercenaries or members of the Roman or Italian élites. After c. 80 BC, there is much less evidence for the activities of Italians or Italiote Greeks – not surprisingly, given the large-scale massacres of Romans and Italians during the Mithridatic War.[50] The declining number of epigraphic references to Italians in part reflects the decimation caused by these massacres, but it points to a change of emphasis rather than a decline in contact between Italy and the East.

The increasing level of contact and the Hellenisation of Roman and Italian society, at least among the élite, during the first century BC is a well-documented phenomenon. Cicero's letters provide many instances of Roman and Italian nobles who visited the Greek East both for business and for pleasure. The tendency for well-to-do young men to be educated by Greek tutors and to be sent to Greece to complete their education grew steadily throughout the first century BC.[51] Greek artists and intellectuals migrated to Italy in greater numbers, and the notorious money-lending interests of M. Junius Brutus are an indication that Roman and Italian business interests continued to flourish.[52] What seems to take place is not a decline in East/West contacts but a change in the nature of the evidence. One function of this, however, is that it becomes more difficult to trace both the careers of individuals and the presence of particular regional groups. Individual Italiotes largely disappear from the record after c. 80 BC, as far as activities in the eastern Mediterranean go,[53] but there is no reason to believe that this indicates a diminution or cessation of contact with the Greek world. This would seem to be inherently implausible given the overwhelming evidence for the Hellenisation of Italy, which was mediated to a substantial extent through the Greek cities of Campania.

The importance of Magna Graecia as mediator of Greek culture grew steadily throughout the first century BC and the first century AD. This can be traced both by individual careers and in the development of what might loosely be termed the 'Bay of Naples phenomenon'. The first Roman to own, and retire to, a villa on the Bay of Naples was Scipio Africanus, who retired to Liternum c. 184 BC.[54] He proved to be only the first of many wealthy Romans to be attracted to the area. Cicero's dialogues, many of them set towards the close of the second century BC, depict a Hellenised villa culture and show that the process was beginning to gather pace rapidly.[55] By the middle of the first century BC, numerous villas had been built in the area between Naples and Misenum, and the Bay of Naples had become a major cultural and intellectual centre which was regularly visited by many Roman notables.[56] Cicero's letters show that most of his friends and political associates owned property here, and cultivated connections with leading local families. Cicero himself was a friend of L. Lucceius, a notable from Puteoli, and the list of fellow villa owners in the vicinity includes Caesar, Pompey and Varro, to name only a few examples.[57] They also demonstrate that the interest in Greek culture among highly placed Romans and the possibilities for patronage generated by this attracted large numbers of Greek artists and scholars to the Greek cities of the West. Paradoxically, Cicero was of the opinion that the cultural importance of Magna Graecia had declined by the 60s BC and that the region was no longer of importance as a magnet for Greek *litterati*. This may well be part of the anti-Italiote rhetoric of decline and desolation, but if true, it must represent a change of focus away from Tarentum and towards the Bay of Naples, which was clearly a cultural centre of great importance, rather than an absolute decline.[58]

The most notable example of this is the career of Licinius Archias, the Greek poet defended by Cicero in 62 BC on a charge of illegally claiming Roman citizenship.[59] He arrived first of all in southern Italy, where he received artistic acclaim and grants of citizenship from Tarentum, Rhegium and Naples,[60] before settling in Rome. His contacts with the Greek communities evidently persisted, as it was at Heraklea and as a Herakleote citizen that he chose to register himself under the Lex Julia in order to gain Roman citizenship in 89 BC.[61] It is significant that Cicero does not suggest that the arrival of Archias in southern Italy was in any way unusual and he may have been representative of a general trend rather than an isolated example. This is supported by further cases: the granting of Neapolitan citizenship to Philostratos Philostratou; a similar grant to Sosis, an associate of Cicero, who eventually gained the rank of decurion; a grant of Tarentine citizenship to Simalos Timarchou of Salamis.[62] The process was assisted by the relatively liberal attitude of Italiote cities in matters of citizenship. Grants of citizenship to foreigners were much more common in the West than they were in most cities of Aegean Greece. As early as the fifth century BC, Oscans are listed as demarchs at Naples and Messapian names appear among the list of officials on the third-century Table of Heraklea.[63]

Contacts between the Italiote cities and the Aegean world, and the process of mediation, persisted during the first and second centuries AD. Epigraphic evidence indicates that a substantial number of Greek artists and athletes were attracted to Italy by the Greek games which were held at Naples, Puteoli and Rome, and possibly also at Rhegium and Tarentum.[64] These started, with the exception of the *Capitolina* at Rome, as agonistic contests marking local religious festivals but began to attract both competitors and spectators from a wider area during the first century BC. A similar process can be seen at work in the Eastern Empire, where local festivals became increasingly prominent. There is ample epigraphic evidence for the growth of agonistic festivals in Boeotia during the second century BC. In Asia Minor, there is perhaps a more exact parallel, with increasing patronage and lavish civic expenditure on festivals encouraging the growth of a professional circuit of games and competitions. By the second century AD the Italian festivals were very much part of this regular circuit.

In Italy, the impetus and source of patronage for the Greek games was largely imperial in origin, although some earlier examples are known. The Megalensian Games in honour of the Magna Mater were celebrated at Rome from 207 BC, and a guild of the Artists of Dionysos was founded on the Aventine. The impetus for this may have come from southern Italy, where there is evidence of several such associations, and also abundant archaeological evidence for the building of theatres.[65] However, the first of these festivals to gain pan-Hellenic importance was the *Sebasta* at Naples, which became an event of international importance under the patronage of Augustus. It originated as an agonistic festival attached to a Neapolitan cult, although there is no record of which one. The only known games were associated with the cult of Parthenope, but the torch race which was the centre-piece of these games continued as a separate event even after the establishment of the *Sebasta*.[66] It attained its later status as an event of pan-Hellenic importance after being renamed in honour of Augustus in 2 BC. The Puteolan *Eusebia* developed rather later, during the second century AD. The third of the Italian festivals, the *Capitolina*, was celebrated at Rome and was founded by Domitian in deliberate imitation of the *Sebasta*.[67] Other agonistic festivals are attested in southern Italy – at Rhegium and Tarentum – but these were not pan-Hellenic games.[68]

Patronage of artists, philosophers and *litterati* by these and other philhellenic emperors, most notably Nero, was a major factor in the success of these games and the consequent prominence of Naples. The Italian games feature on many epitaphs and honorific inscriptions for athletes.[69] The victory lists of the *Sebasta* and epitaphs of athletes contain a large number of references to individuals from the Eastern Empire, including natives of Berytus, Antioch, Alexandria and Ephesos.[70] Decrees of public condolence on the deaths of prominent residents, found at Naples, give more detailed information. T. Flavius Artemidoros,[71] a citizen of Daphne, Antioch and Adanea, competed in the *pankration* and claimed victories at most of the pan-Hellenic, Asian and Italian games. Clearly Naples featured at an international level as a centre of Greek culture and as a source of high-level patronage, attracting visitors from all over the Greek world. Neapolitan citizens also benefited from this, the best-known example being the poet P. Papinius Statius.[72] Although his name suggests an Oscan origin, Statius considered himself to be Greek and was the son of an eminent grammarian from Velia.[73] His career as an epideictic poet, assisted by aristocratic connections and the patronage of Domitian, is a good illustration of the power of Greek culture and the importance of its survival in this area of Italy.

In the second century AD, Greek culture and institutions received a further boost from the emperor Hadrian. The Panhellenion, a body intended to provide a focus for all cities of proven Greek origin, provoked a great upsurge of interest in Greek culture and customs which was particularly strong in cities on the periphery of the Greek world.[74] As part of this initiative, an embassy led by Callicrates was sent by Sparta to Tarentum in 145–50, apparently to revive the traditional connection, and seems to have been received with enthusiasm although the outcome of this venture is unknown.[75] However, membership of the Panhellenion was a mark of prestige and imperial patronage, at a time when cities were very concerned with maintaining their standing, and it seems unlikely that Tarentum, or any other city in the West, would have rejected the chance to be involved.[76]

The dynamics of civic structures and of cultural interactions and survivals in southern Italy are very complex, and will be discussed further in Chapter 9. However, connections clearly continued between many Italiote cities and the Aegean world, of a type which suggests that many of these cities retained a sense of their Greek identity, in diplomacy as well as in contacts made by individuals. Some cities retained this degree of Hellenism for much longer than others, as is attested by the literary sources, but where it survived, Hellenism and its attendant contacts with the East were a major element in civic life. However, the other evidence available suggests that the cities of Magna Graecia were perceived as having a strong Greek identity. The use of these cities by Greeks from the Aegean as a means of entry into Italy and in some cases as a trading base, strongly suggests that they retained contacts with the Hellenistic world and a Greek identity in the eyes of other Greeks, as well as in their own self-perception.

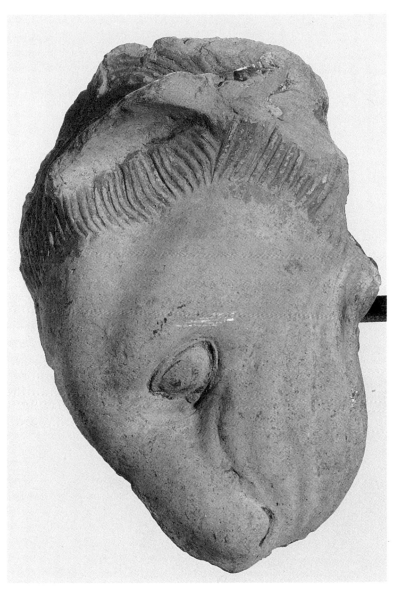

1 Terracotta lion's head antefix. Metapontine, sixth century BC

2 Paestum. Porta Sirena

3 Paestum. Temple of Athena, from south-east, c. 500 BC

4 Ekklesia. Metapontum, sixth century BC

5 Paestum. Amphitheatre, first century AD

6 Red Figure Bell Krater. Paestan, fourth century BC. Signed by Python.

(a) Front

(b) Reverse

7 Terracotta Dionysiac figurine. Tarentine, second century BC

8 Marble stele, with inscription recording sacrifices to Apollo (IG 14.617). Rhegium, first century AD

9 Silver Stater. Locri, *c.* 250 BC (Obv. Head of Zeus. Rev. Roma, crowned by Pistis)

10 Gold Half Stater. Bruttian, *c.* 209 BC (Obv. Head of Poseidon. Rev. Thetis and a hippocamp)

11 Silver Stater. Tarentum, *c.* 300 BC (Obv. Taras, riding dolphin. Rev. Armed horseman and Nike)

12 Silver Stater. Tarentum, *c.* 300 BC (Obv. Taras, riding Dolphin. Rev. Naked horseman)

7

Economic Developments and Agrarian Problems 200 BC–AD 200

Roman authors from Cicero onwards stress the impoverishment and desertion of contemporary Magna Graecia, in contrast to the previous wealth of the region. The entire area is said to be in decline, with many famous cities deserted or so impoverished as to be merely a shadow of their former selves.[1] The reasons why this must be regarded as literary *topos* rather than literal truth have already been discussed (see pp. 13–17), but this still leaves the problem of reconciling the literary and archaeological evidence. Certainly, the cities of Magna Graecia were less wealthy than had been the case in the fourth century, but an economic crisis in the second century BC is much more doubtful, even though there were major changes in the economy of all areas of Italy.[2] The assertion that Magna Graecia entered a period of total and irreversible decline must be rejected: archaeological evidence is casting increasing doubt on the notion of agrarian crises in the second century BC and first century AD.[3] This chapter does not aim to give a comprehensive analysis of the economic history of the region, which would require a book to itself, but will offer a brief summary of the main problems and issues.

Magna Graecia is a diverse area, and it is not possible to make broad statements covering all cities in the region. Some recovered, others continued to decline or were abandoned, while a small number flourished more markedly from the first century BC onwards than they had done previously.[4] Undoubtedly changes occurred in the economic basis of all these cities but these were frequently different in form and result, making it impossible to generalise. Our understanding of the economy of Magna Graecia has been greatly enhanced by the large number of recent excavations and surveys, but of necessity these have concentrated on the territories and cities which were abandoned. Many important centres are also the site of modern cities and have been continuously occupied since Antiquity, a factor which inevitably distorts the historical record. Nevertheless, the results of increasingly systematic programmes of survey and excavation enable a much more thorough analysis of the economy of Magna Graecia.

The economy of most of the region was fundamentally agrarian, but all areas were subject to changes, both in social and political circumstances, and in the natural environment. Given the coastal location, one of the few common factors shared by all the Greek cities of Italy, it is not surprising to find that most had harbours, which allowed for trade and for a fishing industry, and also facilitated communications. What is perhaps more surprising is that so few cities developed this potential. Velia, which had only a small and infertile territory limited by the mountainous terrain inland, was largely dependent on its fishing industry throughout its history.[5] Its harbour was never good enough to attract trade in large quantities and it seems to have been something of an economic backwater until the first century AD. Paradoxically, it is an example of a city which flourished to a greater extent under the conditions of the Early Empire than during its period of independence, thanks to the patronage attracted by the medical school and its vogue as a spa town.[6]

Most of the Greek cities of southern Bruttium and Lucania controlled extensive amounts of territory and their economy rested to a large extent on cereal production. The ear of wheat, which is a common coin type at Metapontum, Sybaris and Croton, underlines the importance of cereal cultivation, as do the cults of Demeter found in many of these cities.[7] At Metapontum, this is corroborated by extensive surveys and excavation of the territory. The Greek system of land division, clearly identified from aerial photographs, is one of the most comprehensive and best preserved in the ancient world.[8] Carter speculates that the fine of 600 talents of silver levied by Cleonymus in 302 BC was not an arbitrary figure, or one invented by later sources, but was based on the annual yield from the territory.[9]

The sources frequently imply that the beginning of decline was connected with the pressures of Oscan expansion, and in some cases the conquest of Greek cities. However, this seems to be negated by the evidence from Paestum, where the fourth and third centuries BC are marked by a period of prosperity rather than decline. The aftermath of the Lucanian conquest saw changes in land use and settlement distribution in Paestan territory, but no sign of economic disruption. Indeed, the pattern is one of increasing settlement density in many parts of the territory, which is hardly consistent with impoverishment.[10] The output of the city's craftsmen also remained high, attesting both to continued activity and Hellenism, since the style of artefacts and the signatures attest the work of Greek artisans. The major economic problems for Paestum were not the result of the Oscan conquest or Roman colonisation, or even the so-called agrarian crisis of the second century, but the drainage and siltation problems which blocked the harbour and the creation of new, Roman, transport networks from which Paestum was excluded. The building of the Via Annia-Popillia in the second century undermined the dominant position of Paestum on the network of roads in northern Lucania.[11]

Elsewhere in the South, Oscan settlements flourished. Greek exports, including pottery, bronzes, terracottas and evidence of Greek architecture, as well as the prevalence of Greek-inspired coinage, suggest an economic relationship, but exactly what was traded, other than consumer goods of Greek manufacture, is uncertain. Wool, destined for the Tarentine textile and dye industry, is a strong possibility, as are slaves.[12] In the other direction, wine may have been exported by the Greeks. Clearly the Greeks had a substantial volume of trade with their Italian neighbours as well as with the Aegean.[13]

At the end of the third century, the Hannibalic invasion caused widespread economic damage, since both Rome and Carthage adopted a 'scorched earth' policy during some campaigns.[14] The traditional view of the Italian economy after 200 BC is one of bleakness, particularly for southern Italy. The second century is said to be characterised by demographic decline, failure of small farms and migration to cities, development of large estates run by cheap slave labour, replacement of subsistence farming by grazing or cash crops, and monopolisation of resources by the élite.[15] The correctness, or otherwise, of this model has long been a matter of heated debate, and it is increasingly questioned as a useful economic analysis.

The core of the controversy is a tension between different forms of evidence, conceptualised by Lepore as a tension between macroeconomic studies (which support the idea of decline) and microeconomic phenomena (individual instances of trading contacts or agrarian prosperity) which undermine them.[16] Essentially the problem lies with the deficiencies of our evidence for the second century. It is difficult to build an entire model of the south Italian economy on snippets of circumstantial evidence, but it is equally unsatisfactory to dismiss all indications which undermine the macroeconomic theory of decline. More recently, however, the whole basis of the macroeconomic model has come under attack. Jongman's work demonstrates that the frequent assertion that Pompeian agriculture was dominated by villas dedicated to the production of wine is incorrect.[17] Estimates of the size of the territory and likely yield of the land indicate that in order to feed a population in the order of 10,000 people, most of the land must have been used for cereal production. In addition, some of the villas have been wrongly identified as such, and most of the rest have been shown to be small estates with an emphasis on mixed farming, not cash crops.[18]

Evidence for large-scale depopulation and migration to larger urban centres is also dubious. Although the ravages of Hannibal's armies would have had a drastic effect on olive cultivation, most other land would have recovered fairly quickly, and the attribution of any long-term decline to the effects of the war is highly debatable.[19] Depopulation can also be overestimated. The sack of Tarentum and enslavement of 30,000 Tarentines, and the large-scale population movements initiated by Hannibal in Bruttium during his retreat,[20] must have had a significant impact at local level, but the level of Roman colonisation between 200 and 180 BC shows that the effects of war casualties and military levies on Italian manpower have been exaggerated. The largest programme of colonial settlement was in northern Italy, but two colonies of 5,000 settlers were established at Thurii and Vibo.[21]

The smaller Roman colonies in the South are usually cited as evidence of decline, since Livy says that a number of them were deserted within a few years of foundation and had to be refounded. This, however, is in contradiction of survey evidence for the vicinity of one of these colonies, Buxentum. Far from failing, the colony re-established the position of the Greek city as an important regional centre.[22] The Lucanian settlement at Roccagloriosa in the Bussento valley, which had flourished during the fourth and third centuries, was abandoned soon after the foundation of Buxentum. There was also a marked shift in the pattern of rural settlement, in which habitations at the upper end of the valley were abandoned and a population developed in the hinterland of the colony. Surveys around Venusia show a similar tendency for a settlement pattern to change in response to colonisation, forming a cluster round a colony.[23] Even Metapontum, the site which was most often cited in support of the decline of Magna Graecia, is not a clear case. Rural settlement began to contract at the end of the fourth century, but the city itself was still inhabited. The Roman 'castrum' occupying the south-east corner of the Greek city was occupied until at least the second century AD. Although much smaller than the Greek city, its area – c. 330 ha – was comparable to that of many other Italian cities which flourished in the Late Republic.[24]

Despite the changes in our understanding of the economic history of the second century, there is still an intractable problem, in the form of our understanding of changes in land ownership and land tenure. Debate is still dominated by the question of the form and function of *latifundia*, and the move to a villa-based agrarian economy. This model is based on the idea that depopulation and the agrarian depression of the immediate post-war years rendered many small farms non-viable and forced farmers of smallholdings to sell their land or give up their tenancies, thus allowing more successful farmers or landowners to acquire more land.[25] These larger holdings could be run cheaply by slave labour, made available by the influx of large numbers of slaves during Rome's wars overseas. This created a vicious circle in which landlords were able to buy out, foreclose on, or simply drive away, their smaller neighbours, thus building up large estates, known to modern historians as *latifundia*, although there is little evidence for the use of the word in ancient times. These could then be farmed for a particular cash crop or used for pastoral farming. The development of these estates was facilitated by increasing amounts of *ager publicus*, which could not be owned by an individual unless distributed as *ager privatus* by the Senate, but it could be leased in units limited to 500 *iugera* per person.[26] The development of large estates by the Roman élite, and probably also by the Italian nobility, indicates an unwillingness or inability on the part of the Senate to enforce the restrictions on the use of *ager publicus*, and the existence of large quantities of undistributed land.[27]

A full discussion of the correctness, or otherwise, of this model, and the broader issues of the Gracchan reforms, lies outside the scope of this work. It is true to say, however, that the view that Magna Graecia was an area depopulated to the point of desertion as the result of the emergence of *latifundia* is a gross oversimplification.[28] Archaeology increasingly shows that the agrarian changes of the second century involved structural changes to the economy, but not a sudden crisis. The pattern which is emerging is one of small and medium-sized estates, most of which had a mixed economy. There are few, if any, examples which support the model of ranch-style farming of livestock or estates devoted to cash crops. Many villas show evidence of wine production – amphora kilns, wine presses, etc. – but not as the only, or even the primary, form of production.[29] What archaeology cannot establish, however, is the nature of land tenure. It is unclear how many estates were owned and how many rented; whether land was leased to smallholders or farmed as a unit; what proportion of the labour was servile; whether the owners were local to the region or incoming Romans. We know from literary references that Roman grandees such as Cicero and Pliny built up huge land-holdings scattered throughout Italy, but there is no means of systematically documenting this process.[30]

The *elogium* from Polla[31] has been used as evidence for the replacement of pasturage by small arable farms, as a result of the Gracchan legislation, but this is somewhat misleading. The text states that the author, either an Annius or a Popillius, was responsible for driving herdsmen out of the area and supervising the distribution of land to arable farmers.[32] In fact, pasturage and herding were important parts of the economy of the South,[33] and the removal of herdsmen to make way for farmers may have represented an innovation. There is literary evidence for herding of sheep in Apulia and Bruttium,[34] and also for the textile industries which probably relied on herding in these areas for a large proportion of their raw wool. Tarentum produced a particularly fine grade of wool, but not in sufficient quantities to supply all the needs of the weaving and dyeing industries.[35]

There were substantial numbers of villas in Magna Graecia, but it would be misleading to assume from this that the literary *topos* of Magna Graecia as a deserted area of large estates and small population reflects the truth. The Metapontum survey shows that there was a fundamental change in the patterns of settlement in the Hellenistic period.[36] From the third century onwards, the number of settlements declined sharply, a fact which may indeed suggest that smallholdings were amalgamated into larger units, that population declined, and that the city became impoverished. In contrast, the preliminary results from a similar survey of the territory of Croton suggest that there was no diminution of the number of settlements and farmsteads.[37] Until the territories of other cities have been systematically explored, there is no way of judging which of these is the more typical pattern, but the data illustrate the dangers of generalising from a single example. There were undoubtedly estates and villas in Magna Graecia, many of which belonged to the Roman élite, but this does not necessarily presuppose depopulation or agrarian decline.[38]

Overall, settlement densities and patterns of land use in Bruttium and Lucania show a high degree of stability from the second century BC to the second century AD. In Bruttium, Guzzo identifies the dominant pattern as one of small farms, with pasturage in upland areas.[39] In Lucania and Apulia, there is more plentiful evidence for the establishment of a villa economy, but with an emphasis on mixed farming, not cash crops.[40] The pattern begins to emerge as early as the third century in some parts of the region, and gathers momentum in the second century. Epigraphic evidence for the territory of Tarentum and the Crotoniate survey both confirm that the territories of cities contained an increased proportion of villas.[41] Kahrstedt's analysis of the Bruttian cities seems to reflect a similar pattern, although his conclusion that many of the Greek colonies had ceased to exist as cities is not justified. Evidence is sparse, but there is enough to refute the idea that civic life disappeared.[42]

Evidence for the economy of Campania is rather more plentiful. Like the rest of southern Italy, it was devastated by Hannibal and the cities which defected to him were severely punished by Rome.[43] However, it seems to have recovered readily. A large number of villas have been identified, including both rural *villae rusticae* and coastal holiday villas. Again, these are mixed farms, not cash-crop *latifundia*, a view which is supported by both literary and archaeological evidence.

Surveys in northern Campania have mapped a series of villas with a capacity for production and transport of wine, oil and grain. Literary sources also note that Campania was a producer of wines, olive oil, grain and fruit.[44] Recent work on Pompeii, however, shows that it is important not to take ancient references to wine-making and olive oil as evidence of economic specialisation.[45] Literary sources give some indication of what crops were grown, but must be used carefully. For instance, they concentrate on specialist crops such as vines, olives and fruit of various sorts, but omit discussion of cereals, which must have been the staple crop on most estates. The reason for this may be partly that production of these 'luxury' items was an élite activity, and partly that ancient agrarian writers did not aim to give a comprehensive description of production. Pliny, for instance, notes regional specialities – olives, chestnuts and shellfish at Tarentum and fruit in Campania. Athenaeus produces lists of fine wines, among other things. Neither of them refers to basic production of foodstuffs.[46]

In addition to agricultural prosperity, the harbours of Puteoli and Naples were entrepôts for trade with Africa, Greece and the East. Puteoli handled much of the grain trade to supply Rome until the end of the first century AD, greatly adding to the wealth and economic importance of the Bay of Naples. Naples itself was not so prominent but the number of Neapolitan traders in the East prior to 80 BC suggests a flourishing trade centre.[47]

The pattern which emerges during the second century is one of structural change in the agrarian economy of Italy, but not necessarily of a crisis. There is a perceptible shift towards a villa economy, based on small estates, and a greater role for slave labour, but this does not presuppose the outright disappearance of tenant farmers or rural depopulation. Archaeology also suggests a greater degree of continuity than is suggested by literature. A high proportion of villas which emerge in the second century BC show continuity of occupation until the first or second century AD, something which rather undermines the idea of an agrarian crisis in the first century AD.[48] This also seems to be true in most parts of southern Italy. Excavation and survey in areas as diverse as the Garigliano valley and the Ager Falernus, the territory of Croton, southern Daunia, and south-east Basilicata, all show a similar pattern.[49]

What may have changed over the two centuries following the Social War is the pattern of land ownership, although this is notoriously difficult to establish. Jongman's recent discussion of the problem of misattribution of Pompeian villas on the basis of amphora stamps highlights the dangers of this approach.[50] Nor is it possible to produce a full list of villas and their possible owners in a volume of this length. Some impression of ownership can be gained, however, from literary and epigraphic references. What this seems to indicate is that there was a steady rise in estate ownership in southern Italy among the Roman élite from the first century BC onwards, perhaps as a direct result of Gracchus' legislation. Cicero's letters contain frequent reference to estates owned by himself and his friends, not just villas in the fashionable areas of Latium and Campania, but also estates further afield. Imperial villas and estates were also numerous. There is epigraphic evidence at Tarentum for imperial estates, and there may have been others in the territory of Croton and Sybaris.[51]

One issue which is central to our understanding of the economy of Magna Graecia is that of pasturage and transhumance. Perhaps the most contentious aspect of the second-century economy is the problem of *latifundia* in the narrowest sense, as defined by Pliny – large slave-run estates on which arable farming had been abandoned in favour of pastoral farming. Tiberius Gracchus is said to have been motivated to introduce his land reforms by the shock of finding large areas of Etruria depopulated and given over to sheep farming.[52] The problem is that literary evidence for this type of estate is slight and archaeological evidence non-existent. Pasturage and transhumance were undoubtedly important in the economy of Apennine Italy, but there is little to support a sudden change in land use in the second century. Much of Apulia and Bruttium are unsuitable for most forms of arable farming, and far better adapted to sheep-rearing. Any changes occurring in the last two centuries BC are more likely to have been changes of degree rather than any fundamental change in land use. The herdsmen whose expulsion is recorded on the *elogium* from Polla may well have been indigenous inhabitants, whose replacement by Roman farmers marked a break with tradition.[53]

Pasturage was undoubtedly important to the economy of the South. There are references to pasturing of flocks at Metapontum, which would indeed mark a change of land use, and a sheep market at Heraklea.[54] Tarentum also produced a particularly fine grade of wool, although this seems to have been an intensive process, involving sewing sheep into 'jackets' to preserve their fleeces. There is epigraphic evidence for shepherds in the *ager Tarentinus*, and references to Tarentine and Canusine wool in Diocletian's price edict show that they continued to command higher prices.[55] Pliny cites the price of Tarentine dye at the considerable sum of 100 denarii per pound, and notes that it was much in demand. Diocletian's price edict quotes Tarentine wool at 175 denarii per pound for fleeces, woven at a cost of 30 denarii per pound.[56] Much of the poetic evidence for the Tarentine textile industry has been dismissed by Morel as a literary *topos*, but there seems enough evidence, even when this is discounted, to suggest that wool production and dyes were still very important to the Tarentine economy.[57]

The existence of large-scale transhumance in the ancient world, and the extent to which it affected Magna Graecia, is a more problematic question. Evidence that transhumance could take place on a very large scale comes from the medieval *dogana* of Apulia, but it is difficult to extrapolate from this. Gabba suggests, very plausibly, that transhumance existed in archaic Italy, although on a relatively small scale, but expanded rapidly, both in terms of size of flocks, number of personnel and distances covered, in the Early Empire. The difference was not the introduction of a new phenomenon but the expansion of an existing one.[58]

Overall, the sum of the microeconomic indicators seems increasingly to contradict the macroeconomic assertions of decline. The economy of Magna Graecia undoubtedly experienced profound structural changes, as did that of the rest of Italy. Patterns of land tenure changed, modes of production shifted, moving towards a villa economy, and long-distance transhumance became a more important part of the economy of the South. However, the picture does not match that of terminal decline given by the sources. There was a shift of wealth from the south of the region to the north – from Tarentum to the Bay of Naples. The patterns of agriculture established in the second century remained fairly stable. There was little sign of vast *latifundia* or of major crises until the upheavals of the third century AD.

8

Ritual and Society: Cults and Cultural Transition

Cults and religious activities occupied a central position in the life of all ancient cities, and those of Magna Graecia were no exception to this. In addition, there is particular reason to examine the cults, priesthoods, festivals and forms of worship which continued into the Roman period. The cities of southern Italy were societies in a state of cultural transition, caught between their native Greek culture, the Oscan elements which had been absorbed to a greater or lesser degree, and the increasing cultural dominance of Rome. The centrality of religious activities to the life of these cities allows us to observe the process of this cultural transition and the ways in which these cities adapted both to Roman influences and to non-Italian influences in an area vital to their existence.

There are a number of reasons why priesthoods, cults and religious activities are useful indicators of a city's social and cultural life, and of the processes of cultural change. At the most fundamental level, these are areas of life which are very conservative and slow to change, with an emphasis on tradition and continuity. This is true in many primitive societies,[1] but is particularly true of Greece and even more so of Rome, with its predominant emphasis on ritual. Having said this, evolution did take place in ancient religion, although at a rather slower rate than other aspects of urban life, but the long time-scale of the process and the conservative nature of religious institutions means that any change is a reflector of fundamental changes taking place in the fabric of society. Given that cults and ritual were a highly politicised area of ancient life and were frequently manipulated as part of the mechanisms of power and legitimation, religion is also very important for our understanding of Roman control and acculturation.

Religion in the Roman world was not as circumscribed a field of activity as it is in most modern Western societies. It was an all-pervasive area of public life with a very high profile. Unlike the Judaeo-Christian or Islamic traditions, Graeco-Roman religion was more concerned with ritual and the public act than with private ethics or belief systems. Cults and their celebration were closely bound up with the political process and with the social dynamics of the city. Priesthoods, as well as magistracies,[2] were important parts of the municipal cursus. Religious activity involved issues such as expression of loyalty to the State, to Rome, and in the case of the imperial cult, to the emperor. Sanctuaries were centres of diplomatic activity and economic power.

Religious festivals were major public events. They were opportunities to express civic identity by the choice of cult and lavishness of the celebrations. They also gave members of the ruling élite an opportunity for euergetism, in financing games, public dinners, processions and all the other trappings associated with these occasions. This could also be displayed to good effect in the financing of temples, cult statues or other offerings and sanctuary buildings as well as in the conspicuous consumption associated with festivals.[3] Apart from the obvious prominence of the urban élite in these matters, religious celebrations were an opportunity for social recognition of important but politically peripheral groups in society. The members of the *Ordo Augustalis*, wealthy freedmen whose libertine status debarred them from the political process, took a leading role in the celebration of the imperial cult, thus gaining social rank and status without encroaching on the jealously guarded political privileges of the decurial order.[4] A similar process can be seen at work, although to a lesser extent, in relation to the various collegia associated with the worship of the Magna Mater.

The processes described so far apply only to the state religion, the cults of the Graeco-Roman Olympian pantheon, to the imperial cult, and to the very small number of other cults to be adopted officially by the Roman State. Some of the more ancient Italic cults retained a certain sentimental value, a factor which was integral to Augustan ideology,[5] but few were of any prominence in Magna Graecia and the trend was for most of these cults to fade in importance after the first century AD. The final element in the religious life of Roman Italy was the increasing number of cults, often mystery cults with an emphasis on personal salvation, imported from the Eastern Empire. Apart from the cult of the Magna Mater, which was officially accepted by Rome in 207 BC,[6] these did not enjoy any official status. Indeed, Gruen has argued that Rome was more open to Greek religious influences before this date, adopting the Sibylline books and the cult of Demeter from Magna Graecia and the cult of Venus Erycina from Sicily. He argues that the suppression of

Dionysiac cults in 186 marked the beginning of a greater caution and strict state control over the adoption of non-Roman cults.[7]

One of the problems for the study of Magna Graecia is that although Greek and Roman religion shared the same pantheon of Olympic gods, and there was no fundamental incompatibility between them, there were also significant differences in ritual, forms of worship and the role of the priesthood. Tripartite cults of three associated deities were peculiar to Roman religion, as were certain divinatory practices such as augury. Greek priests were mediators between the divine and human spheres, as in most cultures, but this may not have been the case in Rome. Beard has argued that the mediator between Rome and its gods was the Senate, with the priestly colleges as expert advisors. Significantly, the Greeks did not translate *sacerdos* as *hiereus*, as would be expected if the functions were equivalent.[8] There is also the problem, in southern Italy, of the intrusion of Italic cults, which were significantly different from both Greek and Roman religious traditions. On the slim evidence we have, it is impossible to assess the impact of Roman cults on southern Italy and the degree of transformation of Greek cults, but the social and political functions of some priesthoods have interesting implications for the cultural history of the region.

As far as one can tell from the evidence, there was a large amount of religious continuity in Magna Graecia between the periods before and after the Roman conquest. There is little sign of any specifically Roman imports, apart from the ubiquitous imperial cult and the Capitoline cult of Jupiter, Juno and Minerva which was introduced into all Roman colonies. Names of cults are sometimes Romanised in Latin dedications, for instance the dedication to Minerva found in the temple of Athena at Paestum and the bilingual dedication to Artemis/Diana found at Tarentum, but this does not necessarily reflect any change to the underlying structure of the cult.[9] This is not in itself surprising, since there was no innate tension between Greek and Roman religion. What does seem significant is the extent to which the Greek nature of civic cults in some cities of the South was emphasised to an increasing degree in the first century AD, a period when local cults were declining in importance in most other areas of Italy. The discrepancy between the pattern of survival found in Magna Graecia and the pattern of change and abandonment of local cults found in many areas of Apennine Italy may be due to the very different structure of cults in the South. Cult centres which were abandoned elsewhere were very often rural sanctuaries and were in many cases associated with the pre-Roman, and non-urban, political structures which began to decline after the Social War and the consequent impetus given to urbanisation.[10] In contrast, the principal cult centres of the Greeks were urban in focus. Even liminal cult places, situated outside the city, were closely connected with the State. The best documented liminal sanctuary is that of Hera Lacinia, situated on a headland and guarding the boundary of Crotoniate territory. It was closely associated with civic life at Croton and with Crotoniate leadership of the Italiote League and as such was closely integrated with the city. It did not by any means provide an alternative to urbanism.

In the period prior to the Roman conquest, a large number of cults of both local and international importance flourished in southern Italy. The evidence available, principally short dedicatory inscriptions, votives and sanctuary buildings, gives little indication of the way in which cults were organised and their place in the wider context of civic life. Study of this material is also hampered by the fact that this evidence is thinly spread over several centuries, from the earliest archaeological evidence, datable to the seventh century BC, to the longer and more informative inscriptions of the second century AD, making detailed investigation of individual cults impossible. Having said this, there is a substantial body of material from which important conclusions can be drawn.

The cults represented are Greek, or very substantially Hellenised. Many of the cults of local gods or heroes such as Taras at Tarentum, Sebethus and Parthenope at Naples or Pandina at Terina and Pandosia may have been local Italic deities but they were all transformed into Hellenised cults.[11] Oscan cults co-existed with Greek ones at Cumae and Paestum, but the Greek influence was predominant in civic life. As was usual in the Greek world, cult epithets and attributes are an indicator of the economic and political preoccupations of a city, and can be valuable evidence for other areas of civic life. At Naples, to cite an example, the cult of Demeter had the epithets Thesmophoros and Actaea, which reflect the Sicilian and Attic influences respectively.[12] The cult of Demeter Thesmophoros continued to be of importance as late as the second century AD, as demonstrated by commemorative decrees passed by the *synkletos* in honour of the priestesses Cominia Plutogenia and Tettia Casta.[13] It is also an interesting illustration of the role of cults in international politics. The cult of Demeter was adopted by Rome as early as 493 BC and in order to retain its Greek character the priestesses were recruited from the temples of Demeter at Naples and Velia. They were granted Roman citizenship and also held in honour in their native cities, as demonstrated by the decrees cited above.[14] Important cults of Demeter also existed at Cumae, where the sanctuary underwent a phase of expansion in the first century AD, at Croton, and at Heraklea. The sanctuary at Heraklea is politically significant as it is thought to have been the federal sanctuary of the Italiote League during the fourth century. The extensive votive deposits at the sanctuary indicate that it was still in use in the Roman period, although excavation has been limited. The Greek text on the Table of Heraklea, which was found at the sanctuary, details its extensive land-holdings. The Roman inscription on the reverse demonstrates the continuing significance of the sanctuary in the mid-first century BC. The preserved fragments may be part of the Lex Julia Municipalis or a series of extracts from this and other municipal laws.[15]

The larger religious sanctuaries wielded a considerable amount of economic and political power both before and after the Roman conquest. The best documented of these, the sanctuary of Hera Lacinia, was the original headquarters of the Italiote League in the sixth century BC, although this function was later lost to the sanctuary of Demeter at Heraklea. It was a shrine of pan-Italiote significance and was of major political significance in the fourth century, for Italians as well as Greeks.[16] Excavation has revealed evidence for expansion of the sanctuary buildings in that century.[17] Cicero mentions a major project to redecorate the temple at a similar period, for which the city employed Zeuxis of Heraklea, some of whose panels were still extant in Cicero's own day.[18] Hannibal chose it as the site of a large bronze stele detailing his forces and dispositions, later consulted by Polybios. Further testimony to the importance of the temple is provided by Livy, who describes an incident in which Fulvius Flaccus removed half of the roof and transported the tiles to Rome to roof the temple of Fortuna Equestris, which he had dedicated and also vowed to make the finest in the Roman world. This incident suggests that the temple must have been large, since only half the tiles were needed, and also that it must have provided strong competition for Flaccus' temple in terms of grandeur. The discovery of this action by the Senate led to a severe reprimand for Flaccus, the return of the tiles and performance of the necessary reparations and purifications, but the tiles are said not to have been replaced as there were no craftsmen at Croton who understood Greek construction techniques. The sanctuary suffered further depredations from pirate raids during the first century, an indication that the sanctuary was rich enough to warrant a raid.[19]

Other sanctuaries which occupied a position of importance were those of Demeter at Heraklea, headquarters and treasury of the Italiote League for most of the fourth century BC, and of Zeus Olympios at

Locri. Both are particularly well known thanks to the survival of significant amounts of epigraphic evidence. The Table of Heraklea contains a Greek inscription of the third century BC, written on the reverse of a first-century Latin legal document and detailing the land-holdings of the sanctuary, which were clearly extensive, and the arrangements for their administration.[20] The financial and administrative affairs of the Olympieion at Locri are equally well known thanks to the preservation of a series of bronze tablets containing part of the sanctuary archives.[21] The transactions recorded include, amongst other things, regular payments to someone referred to only as the *Basileus*. This was almost certainly Pyrrhus, providing corroboration of the literary sources for his robbery and extortion of sacred funds to finance his campaigns. The references to such raids on sanctuary treasuries are a powerful indication that even after the cities of Magna Graecia had passed their economic peak, such establishments were worth raiding.

While it is true that Magna Graecia absorbed remarkably few external influences in the form of major cults introduced from outside, there was a strong tradition in the early phases of Greek settlement for native Italic cults or their sites to be absorbed and 'colonised' by the Greeks. The cults of Taras and Phalanthus at Tarentum are almost certainly an assimilation of pre-Greek cults to the eponymous Spartan heroes of the city's foundation myth,[22] and those of Artemis at Rhegium and Athena at Velia are also likely candidates for pre-Greek origin. Many of these are extramural sanctuaries, of which there are a considerable number in Magna Graecia.[23] These are distinct from other rural temples and sanctuaries in that they are located a short distance outside the city walls and do not seem to bear any relation to patterns of rural settlement. Pugliese Carratelli's analysis of these connects them with pre-Greek religious activity, although there is debate over whether they automatically indicate an Italic cult centre or whether they coincide with the presence of Mycenaean settlers.

The remarkable number of pre-Greek sites in Calabria which were abandoned or destroyed in the seventh century, only to re-emerge as Greek sanctuaries, suggests a degree of syncretism. Excavations at S. Biagio, in the territory of Metapontum, have revealed traces of pre-Greek settlement beneath a rural sanctuary which has produced Greek votives and architectural terracottas.[24] Even where clear archaeological evidence is lacking, there are a large number of very specific and localised deities who look suspiciously like pre-Greek gods loosely disguised as Sirens, nymphs or river gods. On a bilingual inscription from Ischia the Greek text names the nymphs as the recipients of the dedication,[25] while the Latin names the *Lumphieis*, a group of Italic water goddesses. Also at Naples were cults of Sebethus, a local river god, and of the siren Parthenope. The presence of these cults may reflect an East Greek influence at the time of the colonisation, but it has also been plausibly suggested that they may be a Hellenised manifestation of a local chthonic cult.[26] A cult of the siren Leucothea was established at Velia, and coinage from many of the cities of Bruttium depicts local nymphs or water deities, such as Pandina (Pandosia), Terina (Terina) and Krathis (Sybaris).[27] Clearly the impulse to incorporate local Italic deities and to assimilate them to Greek gods was very strong in all parts of the region.

The Oscanised areas of Magna Graecia, principally Cumae and Paestum, show a rather different pattern of religious activity, with much more evidence of Italic cults. This does not represent an attempt to suppress Greek religion, however, despite statements to the contrary by Aristoxenos. The sources describe the Oscan conquest of both Paestum and Cumae as a violent event in which the Greeks were killed or driven out, the remainder being forbidden to speak Greek or to practise their religion.[28] Aristoxenos describes an annual festival at Paestum, held outside the city, which was the only occasion in the year on which the Greeks were allowed to worship their own gods.[29] Unfortunately, this harrowing account of suppression does not fit either the epigraphic or the archaeological evidence. There is no destruction level at either site, as would be expected if the cities had been sacked.[30] The Greek language was still in use and Greek temples and sanctuaries remained in use, with little overt evidence of disruption.

At Cumae, the cave of the Sibyl and the temple of Apollo Kumaios continued to be important religious centres. A Greek dedication to Apollo Kumaios was made by the Oscan Decimus Heius, son of Paccius and sculpted by Isidoros Num[...], a striking example of cultural syncretism.[31] The cult of Zeus is attested by both epigraphic and archaeological evidence. The cult is mentioned by Livy,[32] and is usually equated with a large Doric temple of the mid-fifth century, situated on the summit of the acropolis. There is some confusion about the identification of this temple and that of Apollo, but all the evidence points to a Greek cult. There is an Oscan inscription, however, which records a dedication to Iuvei Flagiui, *'pru vereiiad'* (*'pro iuventute'*).[33] Similar dedications, known as *iovilae*, are found at Capua and other cities in Campania. There has been much speculation about their significance, but one of the more attractive theories is that they may represent an Oscan adaptation of the Greek *ephebia*. The cult of Jupiter Flagiui, or Flazzus, seems to be a case of an

Oscan import, well attested in other parts of Campania, which may have been conflated with a pre-existing Greek cult of Zeus.[34] In both these instances, Oscan cults took root in a recognisably Italic form, unlike the Hellenisation of earlier cults.

Following the Roman conquest of southern Italy, there is something of a lacuna in the evidence. Little is known about cults, or indeed any other aspect of society between the third century BC and the beginning of the first century AD. All the indications are, however, that there was a large measure of continuity in the religious life of many cities, despite the gradual process of Romanisation and the settlement of increasing numbers of non-Greek colonists in Greek cities. Excavation of sanctuaries has shown that there was a high degree of continuity at most of the important ones, and there is epigraphic evidence of exchange of embassies and diplomatic courtesies with sanctuaries in Greece.[35] As would be expected, Rome did not intrude into the religious affairs of other cities. The cult of Jupiter Optimus Maximus is found at Locri and Tarentum, and a cult of the Mens Bona at Paestum,[36] but there are few other signs of Roman cults, despite the increasing level of colonisation in the South after the Punic Wars and during the first century AD. The only controversial incident known is the suppression of the mystic cult of Bacchus/Dionysos in 186 BC on the grounds that it was a threat to public order.[37] Although this was not a uniquely south Italian issue, affecting Etruria and Latium to at least an equal degree, the cult itself may have originated in Magna Graecia. An inscription referring to a special burial place for the adherents of Bakkhos indicates that this mystic and initiatory form of the cult of Dionysos was flourishing at Cumae as early as the sixth century BC.[38] The worship of Dionysos continued here into the Early Empire, with evidence of dedications to Dionysos Hebon, an otherwise unknown form of the cult which may be a Hellenisation of a pre-Greek cult. Dionysos was also worshipped at Tarentum.[39]

Other cults are represented, particularly from the second and third centuries AD, but not in great numbers. Worship of the Magna Mater can be inferred from the presence of colleges of Dendrophori and Cannophori at Cumae, Rhegium and Tarentum. There are also isolated dedications to Isis, Mithras, Horus and the Syrian deity Jupiter Dolichenus.[40] From the second century onwards, there are signs of the diffusion of Christianity in southern Italy. A particularly high concentration of early Christian burials have been found at Naples, in the catacomb of S. Ianuarius and elsewhere, and at Cumae. In general, however, the impression given by the somewhat sparse evidence is that cults from the Eastern Empire did not make much impact on Magna

Graecia, despite its continuing contacts with the East and the cosmopolitan nature of the Bay of Naples. Recent work by Gruen indicates that during the second century Rome became much more circumspect about admitting foreign cults and was willing to suppress them if necessary.[41]

One of the great problems in trying to assess not just continuity of cults but also the extent to which cults and festivals became Romanised is the fact that Latin inscriptions tend to adopt the Roman names for cults, even where other evidence implies direct continuity with a Greek cult. In terms of a basic degree of continuity, there are enough cases where this can be demonstrated to suggest that religious life continued largely undisturbed until at least the second century AD, despite the gradual intrusion of a non-Greek population. The sanctuary of Hera Lacinia, although not as economically or politically important as before the Punic Wars, continued to be an important cult centre. Evidence of continuing activity there can be seen in votives and inscriptions of the second century AD and in additions and repairs to the buildings during the first century BC and throughout the second century AD.[42]

At Cumae, the cult of Apollo Cumanus (or Kumaios, to give it its Greek epithet) was still flourishing in the first and second centuries AD. The temple suffered extensive damage during the Civil Wars, when the acropolis at Cumae was fortified by the Augustan army. It was later rebuilt as part of the restoration of the acropolis by Agrippa and had a significant role in Augustan propaganda and ideology, as the scene of Aeneas's descent to Hades.[43] This particular episode in the Aeneid is significant for two reasons: first, the consultation with the Sibyl at Cumae, and second the chthonic element of the visit to the underworld. The Sibyl, and in particular the Sibylline books, had long been politically important to Rome. Said to have been acquired by Tarquinius Superbus in the sixth century, they were regularly consulted by Rome in times of crisis and represented an important element in the traditional Roman religion favoured by Augustus.[44] The assistance rendered to Aeneas by the Sibyl, and implicitly by Apollo, places the cult firmly with the Augustan ideology of promoting traditional Italian values (despite the Greek origins of the cult), as opposed to the orientalising tendencies of Antony. The chthonic elements of this episode reflect an entirely different aspect of Cumaean religion. The volcanic activity and sulphur springs of the Phlegraean Fields had long given rise to the belief that the entrance to Hades was at Lake Avernus, close to Cumae. These chthonic associations found expression in an Oracle of the Dead at Lake Avernus which was still active during the Augustan period.[45] The political acceptability of these cults had practical consequences for Cumae. Augustus paid for the restoration of the temples and other buildings on the acropolis, and also for the building of a new port to replace the silted-up Greek harbour, which must have provided a boost for the economy of the city.

Similar evidence of continuity is found elsewhere, although without the spectacular degree of imperial patronage enjoyed by Cumae. The cult of Athena at Velia, located outside the walls of the city, was supervised by Athostenos of Aegina, honoured in a Latin inscription set up by the *astynomi*, presumably priests or magistrates. Athostenos was *curator sacrorum* of the sanctuary for forty years and was responsible for some additions to the buildings.[46] Both the significance and the dating of this text are problematic. It is possible that the office of *curator sacrorum* can be equated with an office of the same name which was instituted by Augustus,[47] thus indicating a probable Augustan date. However, several objections have been raised, based on the fact that this was a long-term appointment, rather than an annual office, and that it was tied to one particular sanctuary, rather than involving supervisory responsibilities for all of the city's sanctuaries. The dating of the text to the first century AD has also been questioned on the grounds that Latin does not appear in the epigraphy of Velia in any significant quantities before the second century, although it could be a Latin copy of an earlier Greek text.[48]

One possible explanation is that it was a Greek office, possibly that of an overseer or administrator of the sanctuary rather than a priest, which has been translated into Latin terminology, a phenomenon for which there are numerous parallels. The fact that Athostenos is Aeginetan still poses something of a puzzle. The temple of Aphaia on Aegina was one of the most influential of the Athena sanctuaries at the time of the founding of Velia, so it is not unlikely that Velia would have had connections with this sanctuary and maintained contacts with Aegina.[49] The presence of an Aeginetan certainly seems to indicate some connection with the cult of Aphaia.

There remains the question of whether Athostenos represents a single occurrence of a *curator sacrorum* from Aegina or whether it was a regular custom, which had either survived unbroken from an earlier period or had been revived under Roman rule. Curatorships were civic offices by this date, suggesting that it was a regular appointment. However, it could represent a later revival of a post which had lapsed. If Ebner is correct in suggesting that the post was originally created for a specific purpose and filled a need at a specific point in the history of the sanctuary,[50] it would seem unlikely that it would have persisted for seven, or even eight centuries, although not impossible. However, the revival of such a post, either under Augustus or during the late second century AD, would be perfectly consistent with the archaising revivals of cult practices and also inter-state connections which were taking place in the Greek East during these periods.[51] This movement was typified by connections with other states, in particular colonies. While Aegina was not connected with Velia during the colonising phase of Velian history, as far as is known, this type of religious office is the type of ceremonial connection which was being cultivated between Greek cities, in particular during the second century.

Two further examples of religious continuity merit discussion, namely the medical cults of Apollo and Asklepios, and the festival of Apollo and Artemis at Rhegium. Both are important as they are attested by problematic epigraphic evidence and have peculiarities which have major implications for the questions of Romanisation and for the wider role of religious cults during the Roman Empire.

Healing cults had a long tradition among the Western Greeks. Croton was noted for its doctors in the sixth century BC, and a third-century curse tablet from Metapontum names a group of doctors.[52] A decree of 242 BC from Kos records an embassy from the sanctuary of Asklepios to Naples and Velia seeking the right of *asylia*. At Naples, a dedication to Asklepios and Hygieia suggests that the cult still existed in the Roman period, but we know nothing more about it.[53] At Velia, however, a distinctly odd group of inscriptions provides evidence that an important healing cult continued to exist at least in the first century AD, when the city was popular among the Roman aristocracy as a cold water spa, and possibly as late as the Hadrianic period.[54]

Although the Kos decree clearly concerns a cult of Asklepios, these are associated not with Asklepios but with Apollo Oulios. The evidence comprises six Greek texts, of which two only survive in a fragmentary state, and two Latin texts, of which one is very fragmentary. The four complete Greek texts are inscribed on a togate statue and three herms,[55] of which one is a portrait of the philosopher Parmenides. These were found as a group, together with a number of other statues (some of them of women), and a selection of strigils and medical instruments. They date to the first century AD, and are probably of the Julio-Claudian period, having been found in a building which appears to have been built in the early/mid first century, destroyed by flood, and later rebuilt in the Hadrianic period. The fact that these objects were found in the infill of Insula I, having been used as material for the Hadrianic rebuilding, means that they may originally have been from another area of the city and may not in fact form a cohesive group.[56] However, the form of the inscriptions on the herms and one statue are so close as to be almost identical, which argues for a fairly close interrelation, whatever the connections of the group with the other finds from Insula I. They raise a number of problems, in particular the possible existence of a medical school at Velia, the nature of the cult and/or philosophical group to which these were attached, and the nature of the office of *pholarchos*, which will be discussed below.

Nutton has denied that there was a medical school at Velia in the sense of an institution which was recognised outside the area as being a place where doctors received training,[57] and this seems to be correct. However, it cannot be denied that there was an important healing cult at Velia. The fact that all the Greek texts connected with this cult make reference to Apollo Oulios, the statues of Asklepios and Hygieia and the embassy from the Asklepion on Kos, all point in that direction. The popularity enjoyed by the city during the Augustan period was in part due to its medical reputation. Augustus was cured of a serious illness by cold water treatment, and as a result cold water cures became popular. Velia became a cold water spa much frequented by the Roman aristocracy. Horace expresses some disgust at this new trend which obliged him to abandon the pleasures of Baiae.[58]

The high status enjoyed by doctors is indicated by a decree of the *synkletos* which appears to honour a group of doctors who are described as *Ouliades* (Οὐλιάδης) in terms echoing those of the Hellenistic proxeny decrees which are widely found in Greece and the Aegean.[59] It seems likely, given that the Parmenides herm carries an inscription referring to him as both *Ouliades* and *physikos*, that Parmenides was believed to have a connection with the cult. However, it is impossible to determine whether he was honoured as its founder or whether the cult had connections with Parmenidean philosophy. Given the date of the text, it is entirely possible that the Parmenides herm is a deliberately archaising gesture rather than a true indication of the cult's philosophical background. However, the closeness of the form to that of the cult epithet, *Oulios*, and also the presence of the form *Ouliades*, which must be a title, strongly suggests that *Oulis* was a name adopted on becoming *iatros* rather than an indication of a true hereditary office.

The cults of Artemis Phacelitis and Apollo Archegetes at Rhegium are a further well-documented example of the survival and exploitation of Greek cults in the Roman Empire. A series of eight Greek inscriptions gives details of the participants in the state sacrifices made in honour of these gods.[60] It is not altogether clear which of these cults the

136

inscriptions refer to, and they may record joint ceremonies. Once again, dating is problematic, but the group certainly post-dates Augustus, and is probably of the first century AD, although it could be as late as the beginning of the second century. Pausanias mentions a festival of Apollo celebrated jointly by Rhegium and Messana, to which Messana sent delegates and a choir to participate in the rite.[61] Although there is no certain evidence to connect this with the first century inscriptions, it is tempting to equate this with the occasion for the sacrifices. The unusual feature of these texts is that although they are Greek in form and language, and many of the participants are holders of Greek civic magistracies, the vast majority of the celebrants were Italian, judging by their names.[62] This not only serves to underline the deeply conservative nature of religion in the region, but also hints at another and very interesting trend. It points to a deliberate degree of archaism which is not so very unusual in terms of religious rites but which acquires much greater significance when compared with similar trends in official documents such as decrees of the town council. This issue will be discussed in greater detail in Chapters 9 and 10, but it is worth noting that the revival of archaic traditions, and particularly those related to Hellenism and Greek identity, was a feature of civic life in many cities of Greece and Asia Minor.[63]

Clearly, there was a large amount of continuity in the religious life of southern Italy, although not to the exclusion of all outside influences. As has already been noted, religion and the activities associated with it occupied an important place in the life of the ancient city, and the cities of Magna Graecia were no exception. Religious cults and their celebration were occasions both for the demonstration of euergetism by members of the community and for patronage from outside the city.[64] In southern Italy, this is best documented on the Bay of Naples, not surprisingly given that this was the most prosperous area of the South and had the closest connections with Rome. At Cumae, the Lucceii, a family known to be prominent from numerous references in Cicero's letters, were responsible for additions and rebuilding to the sanctuary of Demeter in the first century AD, including the restoration of the temple, improvements to the area around the temple and the addition of a new portico. The inscriptions, although fragmentary, reveal that this was undertaken by Gn. Lucceius, his son and his two daughters.[65] Less is known about the work carried out at the sanctuary of Hera Lacinia. Licinius Macer and Annius Thraso, both *duoviri* of Croton, paid for the building of a bath house in the first century BC. Other work carried out is known only from archaeological evidence and there is nothing to indicate who paid for it.[66]

The most important source of patronage from outside the city, in religion as in all other areas of life, was the emperor. The patronage extended by Augustus to the cult of Apollo at Cumae and the way in which the characteristics of this cult were subsumed into Augustan ideology have already been mentioned. Naples also received a large amount of patronage from Augustus and other philhellenic emperors, principally in connection with the *Sebasta*.[67] Other agonistic festivals are known to have existed elsewhere in southern Italy, but the evidence is so tenuous that it is impossible to say whether they had the same effect of generating external patronage or euergetism within the city. The festival of Athena at Rhegium had games associated with it but no details have survived.[68] Tarentum also had an agonistic festival, victories at which were noted in a small number of agonistic epitaphs. The epitaph of an Alexandrian athlete who retired to Tarentum and was officially honoured by the city contains further confirmation of the existence of games.[69] It seems safe to conclude, on the basis of the festivals at Naples and Puteoli, that such events did generate a level of euergetism and patronage on a local level but did not attract the same degree of notice as those patronised by the emperor.

So far, nothing has been said about the imperial cult, although it is perhaps the most obvious point at which religion and politics overlap. Curiously, there is little direct evidence for this cult in southern Italy. At Naples the epitaph of a priest of the imperial cult has been found, and also a very fragmentary inscription, from the temple of Augustus.[70] From Velia, there is a dedication to Mercury and Augustus,[71] reflecting a connection found in Augustan art and literature. Representations of Hermes/Mercury which are arguably intended to carry portrait heads of Augustus have been identified on a stucco ceiling of Augustan date, from a building in the grounds of the Villa Farnesina, from a gem and from the Bologna altar, as well as on a number of coins.[72] Literary evidence for the adoption of Hermes as a title or a *persona* suggests that there is a relation between the equation of Augustus with Hermes and aspects of the ruler cult found in the East. For instance, Alexander, Ptolemy III and Ptolemy V are all known to have been equated with Hermes, and Julio-Claudians from Caesar onwards are known to have adopted the names of various Olympian deities. This iconographic connection between Augustus and Mercury which formed part of the imperial cult directly reflects the more oriental aspects of it and is drawn directly from the Hellenistic ruler cults.[73]

Apart from this the cult can only be inferred from the existence of Augustales in most cities of Magna Graecia, with their dual purpose of organising the imperial cult and providing enhanced status and a social role for wealthy freedmen.[74] None of the cult activities of the Augustales has been recorded, most of our evidence being from epitaphs in which individuals record their membership of the *Ordo Augustalis*.[75] However, the Augustales emerged at a particularly early date and occupied a particularly prominent position in coastal Campania, and there seems to be no reason why this should not be true of Greek cities such as Naples just as much as of their Campanian neighbours.[76]

Other religious collegia played an active part in the civic life of Magna Graecia. Like the Augustales, these religious collegia had a considerable social and economic significance, but they also had a religious role. The Magna Mater, one of the very few eastern cults to be accepted officially by Rome, incorporated a number of collegia, each of which had a distinct role in the festivals and celebrations of the cult. Collegia of Dendrophori (Tree Bearers) existed at Cumae and Rhegium, and a collegium of Cannophori (Basket Bearers) at Tarentum. There is also the rather odd cult of the Matres Deae Baianae, found at Cumae but nowhere else, which may be a cult of the Magna Mater.[77]

A further point at which religious and political life overlapped was in the role of priests, particularly those of the Olympian deities. In the Greek world, as in the Roman, the role of most priests was political, at least to some extent. The maintenance of good relations between the city and its gods was vital for civic well-being, thus giving priests an important role in the body politic. In addition, the wealth of some sanctuaries gave their priests considerable economic power. In the Roman world, the close connection between political and priestly office was, if possible, even more marked. Many important priesthoods were offices of state and could be held as part of an official cursus, together with the requisite political offices.[78] This was true in the municipalities of Italy as well as in Rome itself. In Magna Graecia, this trend seems to have become more marked during the first and second centuries AD. Celebration of an important sacrifice by high officials of state occurred in Rhegium – not in itself a remarkable event but unusually well documented.[79] At Naples and at Velia, Greek priesthoods which seem not to have been part of the civic cursus originally, may have become so. The office of *laukelarchos* at Naples is one of the more mysterious of the city's institutions.[80] Nothing is known about the duties of the *laukelarchos*, or even whether the office was religious in function, although it seems very likely that it was. It was probably of great antiquity and the title suggests a possible Etruscan origin. Whatever its origins, by the first century AD it is found in cursus inscriptions, along with the offices of *demarchos*, *prytanis* and *duumvir*, in a context which indicates its role in the political cursus.

A similar and better-documented example is found at Velia. The *pholarchos* was a prominent office in the cult of Apollo Oulios. Its function is not known but the first century AD herms commemorating 'ιατροι' of the cult name all of them as *pholarchoi*.[81] This seems to imply that the *pholarchos*, as his title suggests, was the leader of the cult, and also that the office involved specialist knowledge, since this was a healing cult. It is not the type of priesthood which could normally be held by someone outside the cult. However, two Latin texts,[82] probably later in date, refer to the *pholarchos* in a clearly non-medical and non-religious context, as part of a political cursus. One of these documents is very fragmentary but the other clearly indicates that the office of *pholarchos* was not connected with a medical school or even overtly with a cult but was an office held as part of an official career.[83] Thus it seems likely, from the evidence available, that the office of *pholarchos*, in its Roman form, was adopted into the civic cursus and was held as part of an official career. Both this case and the evidence from Naples seem to show that although some of the more archaic Greek institutions survived, they did so in altered form, evolving to fit into the new context of Romanised municipal life and a Romanised political career for the municipal élite. Significantly, a similar pattern of revival of local cults and priesthoods can be found in the eastern provinces of the empire.

As in other areas of civic life, religion in Magna Graecia shows a gradual process of Romanisation, but retains most Greek cults and festivals with little apparent sign of disturbance. Certainly, pre-Roman cults in this region show a much greater degree of continuity than those of Apennine Italy. Some politically important cults, such as the Capitoline and imperial cults, make inroads, and there is the influx of eastern cults such as those of Isis and Mithras, which are found in most cities of Italy, but there is little sign of fundamental change. Priesthoods and festivals continue to play an important part in the changing identity of cities. Greek festivals such as the games in honour of Parthenope and the *Sebasta* at Naples play a complex role. There is also evidence that archaic Greek priesthoods were given renewed prominence in the first and second centuries AD, and may have been part of the Greek revival which was characteristic of all parts of the Empire. These phenomena served two purposes. For the Greeks, they were a means of reaffirming their Greek identity and attracting patronage from philhellenic Roman notables. For the Romans, they were a means of legitimating Roman rule by adopting local traditions, and of coming to terms with the ambiguities inherent in Greek culture in the Roman world, by adopting a form of Hellenism which was distinctively Italian.

9

Administrative Structures and the Transformation of Political Life

If the religious institutions are conservative and reflect long-term development, the administrative and political structures of a city are much more responsive to changes in internal or external circumstances. In the period of Greek independence, the cities of Magna Graecia frequently underwent adjustments to their constitutions in response to internal and external conditions. Under Roman rule, there was an obvious need for change to conform to Roman norms. Prior to the Social War, there was indirect pressure to promote the interests of the pro-Roman factions in each city, often oligarchic in nature, which led in some cases to structural changes in the mechanisms of government.[1] After 90 BC, or even before it in the cases of the cities which became Roman colonies, Roman legal and administrative structures were imposed as a condition of the extension of Roman citizenship.[2] Clearly this is a simplified version of events. Cities do not fit into a neat pattern of having local constitutions before the Social War and Roman ones immediately afterwards. In all areas of Italy there was a period of transition during which municipal charters were drawn up and the existing machinery of government was adapted to the new circumstances, frequently leaving some intriguing problems.

There is still considerable room for debate on the subject of municipalisation. The traditional view that colonies were governed by *duoviri* and municipia by *quattuorviri* is now recognised as inadequate, but there is little consensus on how to account for the manifest anomalies in the administration of some cities.[3] Sartori makes a case for the continuation or re-emergence of local structures within the framework of the Romanised constitution. In Campania, for instance, the executive power in many cities rested with the *praetor* rather than the more usual college of *duoviri* or *quattuorviri*. It seems likely that beneath the Latin title of *praetor* lies the traditional Oscan magistrate, the *Meddix*.[4] Other

views stress the modifying influence of Caesarian and Augustan legislation. Laffi ascribes quattuorviral settlements to the early first century
BC, and suggests that duoviral constitutions were the product of Caesar's
municipal legislation.[5] None of these explanations, however, caters for
those cities which seem to have both types of constitution, the most
significant of which, for present purposes, is Tarentum.[6]

Magna Graecia poses some particularly fascinating constitutional
problems, touching on the wider issues of civic and cultural identity as
well as on the nuts-and-bolts mechanisms of municipal government. In
this case, some of the anomalies survive well into the second century AD.
A small but significant number of inscriptions seem to suggest the
survival of all or part of a Greek constitution in some cities, which
certainly continued into the first century AD, and possibly even later.
Needless to say, the interpretation of these texts is problematic, given
that there is also evidence for a Roman constitution in the same cities
and at a similar date. The principal problem in studying the political and
administrative history of Magna Graecia is the need to reconcile these
elements. The essential questions raised are whether the Greek texts
represent a working constitution, their relation to the Roman texts, and
if not a functioning constitution, the nature of their role in civic life.[6]
Given that other pre-Roman survivals in other regions had died out by
this date, the balance of probabilities points to something more complex
than a straightforward constitutional survival. Exactly what was occurring in these cases can only be decided on the basis of detailed analysis of
the evidence for each city.

Prior to 90 BC, the constitutional and administrative history of the
region is very shadowy. However, there is enough material to establish a
broad outline for at least some cities. What we do know suggests that
they were constitutionally very diverse and had undergone a number of
changes since their foundation, showing the same pattern of shifts
between various shades of oligarchy and democracy as is familiar from
Aegean Greece. Despite the differences in detail, there were some broad
similarities in structure. All cities had elected magistrates, normally
more than one, who were the principal executive power. Deliberative
bodies included a council with restricted membership, chosen according to a variety of different criteria, and an assembly with wider
membership. The apportioning of power between these elements and
the restrictions on who had the vote, could stand for office, or could
serve on a city council, varied widely according to the nature of the
constitution.[7] The Oscanised cities of Paestum and Cumae may well
have adopted Oscan forms of government. There is no certain evidence

for this, but the apparent dilution of their Greek population and the adoption of Oscan constitutions by other cities conquered in the fifth century expansion makes this very likely.[8] These were rather closer to the Roman constitution in form, with an annually elected *Meddix* as the main executive power, and an assembly, or Senate, with restricted membership.

Of all the Greek cities in Italy, Naples is the one about which we know most in terms of constitutional development. The main magistrate was the *demarchos*,[9] whose title suggests a democratic institution. The most likely date for this is the period of Athenian domination in the fifth century. It was certainly in existence by the end of the fifth century as Strabo claims to have inspected lists of demarchs roughly contemporaneously with the Oscan conquest of Campania.[10] Apart from establishing a date, this is of interest for the nature of the demarchy and for the ethnic composition of Naples. Strabo claims that these lists contained Oscan names as well as Greek, in support of his contention that Naples avoided the fate of Cumae and Capua by selectively admitting Oscans to both the citizenship and the political process. This is further corroborated by Livy, who names the leaders of the pro-Roman faction in 327/6 as a Greek, Charilaus, and Nympsios, an Oscan.[11] After 90 BC, the demarchy continued to survive with a rather different function which will be discussed below. Inscriptions from the first century AD also make reference to the office of *archon*, but there is no evidence for it before 90 BC. Sartori speculates that it was introduced as the main executive office of State,[12] supplanting the more democratically oriented demarchy, as the result of an oligarchic *coup*. It is an attractive suggestion, as is the connection of this with the pro-Roman *coup* implied by Livy in 326,[13] but since there is no direct evidence, it must remain speculation. It could equally well be an older office which preceded the creation of the demarchy. The deliberative bodies of the city are named in later inscriptions as the *Boule* and the *Synkletos*, but nothing can be inferred about them, since all the evidence post-dates 90 BC.[14]

Further south, there is a very large gap in the evidence between accounts of the sixth century, which is characterised by *stasis* between the Pythagorean factions and their enemies, with intermittent periods of tyranny,[15] and the introduction of the municipal constitutions by Rome. Locri had a bizarre and very restricted oligarchy which confined power to one hundred families, but this was modified into something with a wider base early in the fourth century.[16] Most of our information on the third century comes from Livy's account of the Punic War, which is unreliable in its political and constitutional detail. His narrative seems broadly correct but he interprets the constitutional detail and political processes in the light of those of Late Republican Rome.[17] Deliberative bodies are referred to indiscriminately as *Senatus*, while supporters of Rome become *Optimates* or *Boni* and opponents earn a range of uncomplimentary names.[18] There can be no automatic identification between the 'optimate' pro-Romans and an oligarchic faction, although this does seems to be the case at Locri and at Croton.[19]

Tarentum is slightly better documented in terms of its pre-Roman constitution, but many of the details must still be left to speculation. By the late fourth century, the city had a democratic constitution, which implies a powerful role for the popular assembly. Two magistracies are known, the ephorate and the *strategia*.[20] The ephors are clearly adopted from Sparta, as the founding city of Tarentum, and may be relics of an earlier and less democratic constitution. It must have been an important part of the constitution at the time of the founding of Heraklea in 433 BC, however, since Heraklea also had an ephorate,[21] but by the middle of the fourth century it had been superseded by the *strategia*. As its name suggests, this was military rather than political in origin, but by the fourth century it had become politicised to the extent that Archytas was able to use it as the basis of his power.[22] This pattern of politicisation of the *strategia* and a devolution of power to a popular assembly is particularly characteristic of the development of the Athenian democratic constitution in the fifth century, a fact which is curious since Tarentum supported Sparta during the Peloponnesian War and seems to have had little friendly contact with Athens.[23]

Even before 90 BC, a number of cities in Magna Graecia had adopted a Roman constitution as part of a piecemeal process of colonisation. Essentially, these were closely related to the constitution of Rome and those of the Latin cities. The main executive power rested with a college of two or four annually elected magistrates, the *duoviri* or *quattuorviri*.[24] Beneath these were the more junior offices of *aedile* and *quaestor*, forming a political cursus on the Roman model. As at Rome, there was a 'senatorial order', the *Ordo Decurionum*, which had a property qualification.[25] Potential office holders and members of the municipal council, usually known as the Senate, were drawn exclusively from this order, thus imposing a limit on the number of families involved in politics and creating an oligarchic élite, albeit a fairly open one. All adult male citizens could vote, but the extent to which there was much popular participation in politics is open to debate.

The foundation of a colony usually, although not invariably, resulted in the replacement of local forms of government by this type of constitution. The Latin colonies at Paestum, Thurii and Vibo, and the Roman colonies at Croton and Buxentum, all resulted in municipalisation.[26] The colony at Tarentum, founded as part of the Gracchan reforms, was an exception. The city and the colony were physically separate and retained administrative separation until 90 BC, when the colony was absorbed into the Greek city.[27] Cumae was in a very anomalous position, as the only city of Magna Graecia to be designated *civis sine suffragio*, and therefore part of the Roman State, at least to a limited extent.[28] Prior to 200 BC, it was probably self-governing, but after this date it came under direct rule, along with most of Campania, and was administered by the *Praefectus Capuam Cumas*.[29] This was largely due to an accident of geography, since the arrangement was part of the punitive measures taken against the secessionist cities of Campania after the Punic Wars. Capua lost its independent civic status entirely, but the supervisory duties of the *Praefectus* were gradually extended to other cities which retained their autonomy, including some, like Cumae, against which Rome had no grievance.[30]

Whatever the political and administrative machinery of a city prior to 90 BC, this was replaced in the period after the Social War by a Romanised constitution of the type described above. However, the clean division which has traditionally been made between colonies with *duoviri* and *municipia* with *quattuorviri* does not work. It is certainly true in the majority of cases, but there are a number of anomalies which defy explanation, and which must probably be dismissed as simply reflecting local peculiarities.[31] Tarentum is a case in point. The Lex Tarentina, of which we possess a fragmentary and damaged copy, is the charter of the *municipium* of Tarentum, which included both the Greek city and the Roman colony of Neptunia. The extant section concerns regulations for monitoring public finances and penalising fraud and does not describe the constitution in detail, but it refers several times to the co-existence of boards of *duoviri* and *quattuorviri*.[32] In this case, this is clearly a legacy of the fact that the *municipium* was formed by combining two communities of different status. Later inscriptions refer only to *duoviri*, probably a reflection of the grant of colonial status under Nero.[33]

Problems also exist with regard to the status of Naples and Cumae. At Cumae there is some tenuous epigraphic evidence for the praetorship as the main magistracy in the 80s BC, *decemviri* in 49 BC, and *duoviri* thereafter.[34] The *decemviri* mentioned by Cicero are almost certainly

147

erroneous, but the praetorship is an interesting case of the persistence of Oscan institutions. *Praetores* are found in several other Campanian cities in the second and first centuries BC, and seem to be a Latin equivalent of the *Meddix*, the principal magistracy in many Oscan cities. If this is the case, and the inscription in question is indeed from Cumae,[35] then it provides evidence of the persistence of Oscan offices after the Social War. However, replacement by *duoviri* occurred by the first century AD at the latest, and is connected by Sartori with the grant of colonial status. The date of this is problematic. The Liber Coloniarum dates the foundation to the Augustan period,[36] with a later distribution of land to veterans under Claudius, but there is no secure epigraphic evidence for it before the third century.[37] It has been suggested that the earliest colony is the Claudian veteran settlement.[38] The provenance of the earlier inscriptions which refer to Cumae as a *colonia* is disputed but the extensive building work undertaken in the area under Augustus argues for imperial interest in the area,[39] and until it can be proved that the earlier texts referring to the *colonia* are not from Cumae, there seems to be no good reason to doubt the existence of the Augustan colony.

Naples also received colonial status during the second or third century AD, but the date at which this occurred, and its implications for the city, are a matter of debate.[40] The earliest evidence for the grant of the title of *Colonia Aurelia Antoniana Felix Neapolis* is an inscription of Pertinax, dated to AD 222,[41] corroborated by a number of references to *patrones coloniae*, mostly of the later third and fourth centuries.[42] However, the Liber Coloniarum makes reference to a colony of veterans founded at Naples by Titus,[43] and there are references to the city as a *colonia* under Domitian,[44] although the name of the colony indicates an Antonine rather than a Flavian connection. Sartori's suggestion, on the basis of parallels with Tarentum, that the grant of colonial status had become divorced from the actual process of founding a colony, seems to be very plausible.[45] This would explain the continuation of municipal status into the third century. However, the fact that *duoviri* begin to appear in the second century,[46] following the Flavian deduction, may indicate that this deduction had precipitated some changes in the municipal constitution.

Perhaps the most significant development after 90 BC, however, is the apparent survival of elements of the pre-Social War Greek constitutions as late as the end of the first century AD. As already noted, the survival of pre-Roman elements was not unique in southern Italy, but most of these elements disappeared by the first century AD.[47] The existence of Greek magistracies at such a late date seems extremely anomalous, and raises the suspicion that this is not a straightforward case of the survival of Greek elements as a functional part of the constitution. Essentially, only three cities show evidence of this, namely Naples, Velia and Rhegium. All the others had adopted a Roman municipal constitution by the middle of the first century BC, as far as is known. However, the volume of evidence in these three cases shows that an important phenomenon was occurring, which requires some detailed analysis in order to understand the process fully.

Naples is the most important of the Italiote cities preserving traces of the Greek language and practices in civic life after 90 BC,[48] and poses a greater number of problems, since the evidence available is both more extensive and less homogeneous. Unlike Velia and Rhegium, where the Greek elements in public life occur only in special circumstances and as an artificial and self-conscious survival, the epigraphy of Naples suggests that Greek language and institutions continued to be used much more widely, at least until the second century AD.[49] However, the range of constitutional features, and the lack of internal consistency within the body of epigraphic evidence, indicate that this cannot be regarded as the preservation of the pre-Roman constitution, or as a Roman municipal constitution masked by the retention of Greek terminology,[50] but suggest a complex mixture of elements. The magistracies which appear in the epigraphic record include the Greek offices of *demarchos, laukelarchos, archon, antarchon, gymasiarchos, agoranomos,* and *agonothetes* as well as Roman *quattuorviri* (expressed in Greek as τεσσαρες ανδρες). There are also references to the existence of several deliberative bodies, a *boule,* a *synkletos* and a *proskletos.* A small number of Latin decrees and cursus inscriptions exist, which indicate the existence of a duovirate, in addition to the Greek magistracies and the quattuorvirate.[51]

Numerous attempts have been made to integrate these disparate elements, and to relate them to municipal government elsewhere in Italy.[52] The most obvious explanation, that Greek and Latin names were used interchangeably for the same group of offices, can be disposed of quickly, since Greek and Roman titles sometimes occur in the same inscription. There is also a chronological overlap between Greek titles and Latin ones, although Latin comes to predominate by the end of the second century AD. However, some aspects are less problematic than others. *Agoranomos* is the usual translation of *aedile.*[53] The *agonothetes,* an office well documented in the Greek world, was the organiser of the *Sebasta.* The office of *gymnasiarch* is one which is well known from the Hellenistic period, and was an important post in many cities of the

149

Eastern Empire. It also came to be one of the unpopular liturgies, since it entailed heavy expenditure. Significantly for Hellenism in southern Italy, the principal duty of a *gymnasiarch* was usually the organisation of the *ephebeia*.[54] Although there is no corroborating evidence, the Greek cultural ambience means that the survival of an *ephebeia* is entirely possible.

The *boule* probably corresponds to the *Senatus* found in most other Italian cities, and the *Bouleutoi* to the *Ordo Decurionum*. The existence of records of official honours granted by the *boule* and recorded in Greek but with the Latin formula *L[oco] D[ato] D[ecreto] D[ecurionum]*[55] suggests a correspondence between the two. Decrees passed by the *Ordo Populusque Neapolitanorum*[56] also provide evidence for a Decurial order, and supply corroborative evidence for a popular assembly, represented in Greek as the *synkletos*. The *Ordo Decurionum* is also attested in a Greek inscription in honour of the female athlete Seia Spes, referring to her victory in an event restricted to the daughters of *Bouleutoi*.[57]

The magistracies, however, do not lend themselves so readily to assimilation with the municipal magistracies found in other Italian cities. Attempts have been made to match the Neapolitan magistracies and Roman municipal offices by equating the archons, or the demarchs, with the *quattuorviri iure dicundo*, and the *agoranomoi* with the *quattuorviri aedilicia potestate*, the two sets of offices together forming the board of *quattuorviri*, or τεσσαρες ανδρες.[58] However, the evidence for the existence of the τεσσαρες ανδρες is very slight, and rests on only one text, a Greek inscription of the first century BC.[59] It appears impossible to give a single consistent explanation which would include all these different features, and the number of contradictions presented by the data available would seem to suggest that the constitution of Roman Naples should be approached as a dynamic, evolving system.

Perhaps the easiest of the magistracies to assess, in terms of their municipal significance, are the offices of *demarchos* and *laukelarchos*.[60] The origin of both is obscure, and there are few Greek parallels for either. The demarchy was the main magistracy of the city before 90 BC.[61] The office of *laukelarchos* is much more obscure, and nothing is known of its origin or function. It has been suggested that the title is Etruscan, not Greek, and that the office was religious in function.[62] Both literary and epigraphic evidence confirm that these offices continued to form part of the civic cursus in the Roman period.[63] However, there are problematic elements. They could be, and were, conferred on non-Neapolitans, of whom the most eminent were the emperors Titus and

Hadrian.[64] It is possible that both became largely honorific in function, a situation analogous to that of the archonship at Athens,[65] and ceased to have any real political or administrative significance. Nevertheless, there are parallels for the nomination of emperors as honorary municipal magistrates in Italy. Tiberius' son Drusus was a *duumvir* at Pompeii, as were Caligula and Nero.[66] What is certain is that by the first century AD the demarchy, with its long history and Greek background, was being used as a means of honouring prominent non-citizens and consequently of generating patronage. The granting and receiving of such honours by emperors was a means of expressing a particularly close relationship with the ruling regime and of acknowledging imperial patronage of the city.[67]

The date at which the political power of the demarchy declined cannot be pin-pointed, but the earliest extant cursus inscription, that of Seleucus,[68] does not mention it, and the series of decrees of the *boule*, most of which are Flavian in date,[69] name the archons and antarchons as the magistrates of the city. It is worth noting that the offices of *demarchos* and *archon* appear in very different types of inscription and do not appear together in any cursus. Archons and antarchons are named in decrees in contexts which clearly suggest an important civic function, while the offices of *demarchos* and *laukelarchos* occur only in the cursus inscriptions of those who apparently did not hold the archonship.[70] Thus it seems likely that the demarchy lost its practical significance in 90 BC, at the latest.

The relation of the offices of *archon* and *antarchon* to those of *duumvir* and *quattuorvir* remains a major and ultimately insoluble problem. The archonship is known from Latin as well as Greek sources and continued into the third century AD.[71] This would seem to suggest that it was separate from, and parallel to, the offices of *quattuorvir* and *duumvir*, since these are known from the same period.[72] The existence of the office as part of a Latin cursus inscription also suggests that the archonship is not merely a translation of a Roman title.[73] It is possible that one of the functions of the office was to act as president of the *boule*,[74] although it is not possible to establish whether this was its only, or indeed its principal, function. Arguments in favour of this interpretation are first, that the archonship occurs only in the context of the workings of the *boule*, apart from one instance in which it is mentioned in a cursus inscription, and appears to fulfil an important role in initiating decrees, and second, that the office of *antarchon*, which appears in conjunction with it, is normally that of the vice-president of the *boule*.[75] In this context, it does not seem impossible that a Greek

151

archon and a board of *quattuorviri* (later replaced by *duumviri*) could co-exist. Attempts to force these offices into a Roman structure by identifying the posts of *archon, antarchon, demarchos* and *laukelarchos* as *quattuorviri* seem to strain the evidence, given the little that is known about any of them.[76]

However, a possible solution can be reached by placing more emphasis on the cultural context and significance of these survivals and less on the constitutional details. It seems significant, particularly in the light of evidence from Rhegium and Velia, that the Greek offices mentioned occur only in the context of honorific decrees honouring individuals, either of Neapolitan or non-Neapolitan origin. This may be an indication that, as in other cities in southern Italy, the Greek magistracies were retained, and Greek language used, for the purposes of euergetism and ceremonial or honorific functions, in particular the celebration of Greek festivals and proxeny decrees in honour of individuals.

At Velia, valuable documents have also been preserved, although in smaller numbers, which also give indications of Greek survivals in the area, alongside the Romanised structure which formed the basis of administration in Italy after the Social War. On the basis of the persistence of Greek language and culture at Velia, Sartori proposes that the Greek forms of government may have been retained for some time after the Social War, and only superseded by Romanised municipal government during the first century AD.[77] However, the increased amount of epigraphy from Velia since the publication of Sartori's work indicates that this is not the case. The city clearly retained Hellenistic concepts to some extent, but these existed alongside a Roman structure which had developed by the first century BC.

The earliest evidence for the municipal constitution of the Roman city has been dated to the late first century BC and is the epitaph/cursus inscription of Cornelius Gemellus,[78] who was *duumvir* twice, *quaestor*, *quattuorvir iure dicundo* twice, *gymnasiarch*, and *quattuorvir iure dicundo* for a third time. Clearly the city possessed a constitution which featured colleges of *duoviri* by the end of the Republic. Curiously, this is the only reference to the duovirate, as later inscriptions only refer to *quattuorviri quinquennales* or *quattuorviri iure dicundo*.[79] Velia placed no prohibition on iteration of offices, a point which is borne out by the careers of Cornelius Gemellus and Gabinius Menander, who were *quaestor* twice.[80] In addition to the quaestorship, the city also had the office of *aedile*. However, some offices of the Greek city were retained. The post of *gymnasiarch* existed in many cities of the Eastern Empire, apparently fulfilling a largely liturgical function.[81] Parallels from southern Italy include Naples and Rhegium.[82] The main problem posed by the epitaph of Cornelius Gemellus is that of the co-existence of the duumvirate and the quattuorvirate. It is possible that the office could have been *duumvir aedilicia potestate*, since there is no reference to the office of *aedile*, which appears in all but one of the other extant cursus inscriptions. The office of *pholarchus*, which is clearly a Greek office (see p. 140), is included in one of the cursus inscriptions and seems to have become part of the structure of civic offices.[83]

Despite the Roman nature of the municipal magistracies, the local Senate still retained a noticeably Greek character in the first century AD. An inscription of AD 29 which names L. Nonius Asprenas as patron of Velia makes reference to the '*Decuriones et Municip[. . .]*',[84] but there is evidence that the decurions still conducted their business in Greek for some purposes and that the local Senate was known as the *synkletos*.[85] Two decrees of the *synkletos* survive, one a fragmentary Greek text,[86] the other complete and bilingual.[87] These appear to be very similar in form, in as far as the fragmentary text can be reconstructed, both being honorific in character.

The Greek text, which is not securely dated but must, by its archaeological context, be of Julio-Claudian date or later, is in honour of one or more of the doctors associated with the cult of Apollo Oulios. It is fragmentary, but the terminology seems very similar to that of the proxeny decrees which are found in the Hellenistic world from the third century onwards, apparently declaring the recipients '[α]νδρων [. . . ευεργετιας κα]ι αρετ[ης ενεκα]'.[88] There are close parallels from all parts of the Greek world.

The bilingual text is in honour of a Roman dignitary, G. Julius Naso, probably the friend of Pliny the Younger and possibly the same person as the Julius Naso honoured in an inscription from Tenos.[89] The Greek text reads '[η συ]νκλητος και ὁ δημος | Γαιον Ιουλιον Γαιου υἱον Νασωνα | ἀρετης και ευεργετιας ενεκα' and is translated into Latin as '*Senatus et Populus Veliensis | G. Iulio G.F. Nasoni honoris | et virtutis causa*'. It too is very similar to Hellenistic proxeny decrees, which suggests that Velia was still sufficiently in touch with the Greek world to have retained Greek diplomatic forms. However, one notable feature is that despite the use of Greek, all the magistrates known by name have Latin names. Personal monuments, such as epitaphs and cursus inscriptions set up by the municipal élite, all use Latin. This language choice suggests that although Greek was still used for some purposes, and the Greek cultural heritage of the city was actively promoted, the political classes and probably the constitution were Romanised. Greek culture was being exploited for ceremonial and honorific purposes, as at Rhegium and Naples, and does not necessarily imply a Greek constitution.

The nature of the constitution of Rhegium in the Hellenistic period and as a Roman municipium has been much discussed. The essential problem lies in the dating of the documents available, and in assessing the nature of the surviving Greek elements. The main questions to be considered are the relation of the decree of the *boule* to the offices listed in the dedications to Artemis and Apollo; the nature of these offices; the nature of the evidence for the Roman constitution and the date of transition from the Greek to the Roman system of government. In addition, comparisons with other Italiote cities may be valid.

The starting point for any consideration of these issues must be the decree in honour of Gn. Aufidius.[90] This takes the form of a decree, in Greek, of the *halia*, the *boule*, and the *eskletos* which grant honours, possibly in relation to the festival of Athena, to Gn. Aufidius, a Roman general. The general form of this document is that of a Greek proxeny decree, but the language used is unexpected. It is written in Doric Greek, which could not have been the native dialect of Chalcidian Rhegium. It may reflect the Syracusan domination of Calabria in the fourth century and point to a 'Doricisation' of the Rhegine élite.[91] It indicates that at the period at which it was passed, the eponymous magistrate of the city was the *prytanis*, and that the legislative machinery consisted of the *boule*, together with the *halia* and *eskletos*. The date of the document has been a matter of some debate, conjectures ranging from the second century BC to the first century AD, depending on the equation of the Aufidius in question with a variety of possible Aufidii who held office in Rome.[92] However, the later dates suggested seem unlikely, and it is usually dated to the pre-Social War period. Thus the system of government recorded here is that of the Greek city, before the grant of Roman citizenship.

The next series of constitutional documents which have survived belong to the first century BC, although it is possible that one may be as early as the second century.[93] However, these do not give much information about the main constitutional features of the city at this date. They do not refer to the main civic magistracies, but to the office of *gymnasiarch*.[94] In the Eastern Empire, notably at Alexandria, the gymnasiarchy was an important liturgy, particularly concerned with the *ephebeia*. At Velia and Naples it became an integral part of the Roman municipal cursus providing an Italian parallel for this process.[95] However, there have been conflicting interpretations of the Rhegine gymnasiarchy. Bowersock takes the survival of the gymnasiarchy as evidence of a Greek constitution.[96] However, Sartori suggests a minor office, with specialised responsibilities,[97] indicating only a general survival of Hellenistic culture. Although there is little specific evidence, the important liturgical role of the *gymnasiarch* elsewhere points to the probability of similar developments at Rhegium and Velia. Certainly the inclusion of this office in the civic cursus, even if it offered no real power, indicates both its social importance and the process of adaptation of elements from the city's Greek past to present conditions.

A central problem lies in the interpretation of the group of first-century AD inscriptions relating to the cults of Apollo and/or Artemis.[98] The offices mentioned in these inscriptions which may relate to the municipal government are the offices of *prytanis, synprytanis, archon* and *agoranomos*. However, although the title of *prytanis* seems to indicate continuity from the second century BC, the nature of the office appears to have changed. Whereas in the Aufidius decree the only magistrates mentioned were the *prytanis*, apparently the eponymous magistrate, and the presiding official of the *boule*, the first-century texts include a *prytanis*, an *archon*, often the same person, and a group of *Synprytaneis*, usually three in number, but sometimes only two. Only one text makes reference to an *agoranomos*. The fact that the most frequent configuration is a *prytanis* and three *synprytaneis* has led Mommsen to suggest that these magistrates in fact represent a Greek translation of the normal municipal college of four *quattuorviri*.[99] However, there are several major difficulties in this interpretation. The objection of Sartori and Costabile,[100] that elsewhere in southern Italy the terms *duumvir* and *quattuorvir* are literally translated as τεσσαρης ανδρες and δυο ανδρες, is not conclusive, given the lack of standardisation of Italian constitutions and of the translation of local terminology into Latin. The fact that not all the examples contain three *synprytaneis* is a rather more decisive argument.[101]

Other attempts to solve the problem place SEG 29.987, which is rather different from the other texts in beginning with the formula '[πρυτανις και αρχων και αγ]ορανο[μος...]', in the period before the Social War,[102] together with the Aufidius inscription.[103] The remaining sequence of inscriptions (IG 14.617–21) can then be interpreted as a transitional constitution which retained many of its Greek features as a result of specially favourable treatment by Augustus in recognition of Rhegine loyalty during the Civil Wars. The reversion to the Italian quattuorviral constitution can be dated to the end of the first century AD or the beginning of the second century. However, this does not explain the changes in the titles of *prytanis* and *archon*, which would seem to indicate some change in the nature of the magistracies. In the majority of these first-century inscriptions, the *prytanis* is described as εκ του ιδιου. This office is frequently held together with the archonship, which is not documented in the epigraphy of the Greek city, and which is almost always described as πενταετηρικος – presumably a translation of the *quinquennalis*, the holder of censorial powers. These, then, cannot be a straightforward survival of the Greek constitution. The key to the problem lies in the fact that the *prytanis*, and sometimes the *archon*, hold office εκ του ιδιου. Elsewhere in the Greek world, such offices are liturgies, undertaken by the leading families of the *municipium* as a civic duty. As at Velia, the number of *gentes* represented in the lists of *prytaneis* and archons is small, and all of them have Roman names. Costabile suggests that the selection of candidates for these posts was in some way rigged to favour Roman inhabitants rather than Greeks,[104] but there is no evidence to support this. In fact, the pattern of domination of civic office by a comparatively small number of families, often of Roman extraction, is one which is found throughout southern Italy.[105]

So far, a clear pattern emerges from the evidence, particularly the inscriptions from Velia, Rhegium and Naples. The careers of individuals show that these cities were administered on the Roman pattern, with *duoviri* or *quattuorviri*, aediles, quaestors, etc. like any other Italian city. However, it cannot be denied that there are some very odd features of civic and political life which can best be explained with reference to cities in the Greek East. Here, in the great centres such as Antioch, Ephesos, Pergamum and Alexandria, as well as in many smaller cities, two trends developed which were central to the dynamics of civic politics. One was the emergence of the process often termed euergetism,[106] by which the families which formed the urban élite were expected to perform acts of benefaction of many kinds – including provision of essential services, construction of public buildings and monuments, payments for games, festivals and public entertainments, etc. – towards their city and its inhabitants. These were often competitive in nature, with rich families vying to gain increased power and status through these gifts. The occasion for such displays could be either private – commemoration of a birthday or funeral, for instance – or part of a public festival or official duties. Much of this process was driven by peer pressure and unwritten rules and expectations, but the most structured aspect was the system of liturgies in public life. This involved the holding of civic offices or priesthoods at personal expense and the performance of the associated duties with due magnificence, a function which required considerable amounts of money. Offices such as that of *gymnasiarchos* fell into this category, as did those explicitly described as εκ του ιδιου.[107] Most of the civic priesthoods also involved euergetic functions. Many of the more explicitly Greek survivals in southern Italy – the *laukelarchos* at Naples, the *gymnasiarchos* and *prytanis* at Rhegium and the *gymnasiarchos* and *pholarchos* at Velia – fall into this category.

This is not to suggest, however, that this was a purely Greek phenomenon, or that a strict division can be made between offices which were functional and those which were merely euergetic. The élites of Italian cities were under equal pressure to make benefactions and perform acts of civic patronage. In all cities, both of the Eastern and Western Empires, most public offices contained some element of euergetism. Magistrates were unpaid and were expected to pay for public works and entertainments during their year of office, but it is true, nevertheless, that some offices had a more directly euergetic function than others. It is the second major trend in Greek civic life which points to a strong resemblance between the Italiotes and the Greek East. This was a conscious degree of archaism in civic life and an officially encouraged emphasis on elements of the Greek past of these cities which can be found in Greek cities in both the Eastern and Western Empires.[108] Effectively there were two 'waves' of this, both sponsored and encouraged by philhellenic emperors. From Augustus onwards, the Julio-Claudians had taken an interest in Greek culture and had contributed to the popularity of the Bay of Naples among the philhellenic members of the Roman aristocracy.[109] During the second century, Hadrian introduced direct political benefits for cities whose level of Hellenism warranted it. The Panhellenion was an expression of this, as were the new agonistic festivals modelled on the great pan-Hellenic games, and an increase of interest in Greek histories and genealogies.[110]

In the light of this, the form taken by civic euergetism in southern Italy begins to look suspiciously Greek in character. In particular, the process explains many of the peculiarities of civic politics and administration. The decrees in which the city councils describe themselves as the *boule* and issue their proceedings in Greek are not concerned with routine administration or matters of civic government but are usually honorific in character. The proxeny decrees of Velia and Rhegium and the public condolences issued to leading families on the death of one of their members do not reflect the nature of civic government but provide a powerful indication of the impetus towards Hellenisation and the status which could be conferred by Greek culture.[111]

Similarly, the emphasis given to the role of the *gymnasiarchos* and to some of the more idiosyncratic priesthoods underlines the benefits to be gained from having such a strong Greek heritage. The use of the Greek language in official contexts also seems to be very selective, giving the lie to the view that the cities of southern Italy were still primarily Greek-speaking in the first century AD.[112] As far as can be ascertained, it was confined to those types of honorific or euergetic decrees in which the status of both the individual recipient and the city would be enhanced by the emphasis placed on Hellenic identity. The fact that most Greek inscriptions of an official nature are the result of a conscious choice with regard to civic image is underlined by the names of the individuals and by the language of the texts. Most of the names are Latin, not Greek, while the language of the texts frequently reflects that of decrees from cities in the East. This is also underlined in the case of the use of a somewhat peculiar form of Doric in the Aufidius decree (*IG* 1.612), a dialect which was not native to Rhegium and was in any case an anachronism. The evidence of epitaphs and cursus inscriptions leaves no doubt that the administrative structure of these cities was almost entirely Roman,[113] and that the Greek decrees and magistracies were peripheral to this, although serving an important function in the preservation of a Greek civic identity in the Hellenising intellectual climate of the Early Empire.

In essence, then, the constitutions of the Greek cities in Italy underwent a transition to a Roman administrative structure during the course of the first century BC, as did other cities in Italy. The Greek elements which survived co-existed with this, but did not impinge on the territory of the *duoviri* and other magistrates. It is possible that at Naples some magistrates continued to use their Greek titles in some circumstances, and elsewhere the terms *boule* and *senatus* are interchangeable in referring to the local Senate. In most cities, however, it is clear that the Greek magistracies are not Roman ones masquerading under a Greek name but are separate offices with a distinct role of their own.

The political life of these cities, as distinct from the structures of civic government, remains relatively obscure. As far as can be judged from cursus inscriptions and official decrees, the political élite was restricted, with only a small number of *gentes* represented – the Heii and Lucceii at Cumae, the Titinii at Tarentum, the Bennii and Tullii Cicerones at Paestum, to name a few examples.[114] In this, the Italiote cities are not

Table 2 Senators from Magna Graecia

Name	City	Date
L. Cupiennius	Cumae	147 BC
G. Cupiennius Satrius Marcianus	Cumae	Augustan
Gn. Heius	Cumae	Sullan
M. Heius (?)	Cumae	AD 42–5
Gn. Lucceius	Cumae	1st century AD
Gn. Lucceius	Cumae	2nd century AD
Manilius Cumanus	Cumae	52 BC
M. Spurius Gn.F.	Cumae	2nd century BC
Venuleius(?)	Thurii	82 BC
Venuleius Bracchus	Thurii	
L. Vagellius	Locri	AD 47
L. Digitius Bassus	Paestum	AD 145
G. Numonius Vala	Paestum	41 BC
[.............]	Paestum	Augustan
M. Aemilius Flavius Julianus Latinianus	Rhegium	2nd century AD
Q. Laronius	Vibo	33 BC

untypical of the rest of Italy, or indeed the rest of the empire. The iteration of magistracies recorded in cursus inscriptions may be a sign of a shrinking number of men able or willing to take on the financial burdens of office. A clause of the first-century BC Lex Tarentina which stated that decurions must own property of a specified minimum size at Tarentum was designed to restrict the mobility of the political class and prevent emigration by decurions.[115] The increasing impoverishment of the political classes of the empire and the reluctance of the municipal élites to participate in politics is well documented towards the end of the second century AD.

The marginalisation of southern Italy is also reflected in the relatively small number of *gentes* from Magna Graecia who achieved senatorial status. Examples include the Cupienii, Heii, Lucceii, Manilii and Spurii from Cumae, Venuleii from Thurii, Vagellii from Locri, Digitii and Numonii from Paestum, Aemilii Latiniani from Rhegium and Laronii from Vibo.[116] This has been explained as both an indication of the impoverishment of the area, in that so few families had the wealth to support a career in Rome and qualify for senatorial status, and a reflection of the persistently non-Roman nature of the area.[117] Neither of these factors provides sufficient explanation in themselves. Magna Graecia made a modest economic recovery during the Early Empire, and inscriptions attest to a considerable degree of social and political activity on the part of the élite at local level. A number of Southerners, such as G. Lollius Marcianus from Croton, attained equestrian status,[118] which also required substantial wealth. The evidence does not support the theory, therefore, that Magna Graecia was too impoverished to produce a large number of senators. Nor does the idea that they were too Greek to be integrated fully into Roman politics, since they were patently not, although some made capital out of emphasising their Greek antecedents.

The answer may lie in the gradual process of marginalisation of the whole of southern Italy as the centres of economic and political power shifted northwards. Studies of municipal senators and their origins show an intense regionalisation, with relatively small numbers originating in the southern regions of Italy.[119] Greater concentrations are found further north, in Etruria, Picenum and Latium. Seen in this light, the lack of political participation in Rome is not an anomaly or failure on the part of Magna Graecia, but part of a broader trend within Italy. It is also notable that most of the known senatorial families come from cities which had attained colonial status, and very few from cities where Hellenism was a prominent feature of civic life. Within the cities of the region, the local élites seem to have been as active as anywhere else in Italy, but since their activities touch on broader questions of social structure and socio-political interaction, they will be discussed in the next chapter.

10

Urban Society in Magna Graecia: Acculturation and Civic Identity

The social structure of any ancient city was a complex organism which is still only imperfectly understood. Written sources usually reflect the viewpoint of the élite and by and large do not concern themselves with descriptions of the way in which their society was ordered. Not surprisingly, knowledge of the workings of their society is taken for granted. Inscriptions give us a glimpse of a wider selection of social groups but even so, the data are biased towards the more affluent sections of ancient society, including many who express their aspirations and desire to enhance their status by copying the conventions of the élite in the ways in which they record themselves and their deeds. The analytical techniques utilised by sociologists and urban geographers can be used to fill in some of the gaps in our knowledge, but study of the social structure of Magna Graecia must essentially be study of the urban élite, its activities and its ideologies. The purpose of this chapter is to consider the composition of the élite in the cities of Magna Graecia which retained an urban identity during the first two centuries AD, to examine its behaviour, its relations with the Roman élite and with other social groups, and to examine the ways in which the élite constructed and manipulated its own cultural identity and that of the city.

Some comment has already been made on the ways in which the Greek traditions of these cities were perpetuated in cults and religious practices and in the political and administrative structures. An examination of the behaviour of the élite and the ways in which it sought to construct an identity for itself and for its cities places these elements in a wider context, throwing a revealing light on the process of acculturation. The preservation, or resurrection, of Greek elements of civic life and the perpetuation of the Greek language are all part of what seems to be a deliberate fostering of Hellenism by the élites of those cities for which we have evidence. This is not to say that cities such as Naples, Cumae,

Rhegium, Locri and Tarentum did not, at the same time, become Romanised. Strabo, writing in the first century BC, said that with the exception of Tarentum, Naples and Rhegium, Magna Graecia had become barbarised, having been taken over by the Lucanians, Bruttians and Campanians.[1] He goes on to say that in effect Magna Graecia had become Roman, since these groups had themselves become Roman. Clearly, the depth of the cultural and political changes which had taken place in southern Italy was recognised even in Antiquity.

However, Strabo provides something of a red herring for the study of acculturation in the region by setting up an explicit opposition between being Greek on the one hand, and being Roman on the other. This is not necessarily a helpful model for dealing with Magna Graecia, which was nothing if not a multi-cultural society. In addition to the Greek and Roman strands of its history, any model for dealing with acculturation must also take into account Oscan and Messapian elements.[2] Examination of the evidence shows that Hellenism and Romanisation were not mutually exclusive processes, but continued to co-exist within the same cities. There are also indications that even in regions which appear to be highly Romanised, there are traces of an underlying local culture, which can be traced in features such as distinctive local types of building, funerary monument or inscription. Thus any assessment of the urban structures of Magna Graecia must also seek to explore the means by which Roman influences were assimilated and how they interacted with indigenous features, whether Greek or Italian.

The sources for the life and structure of Magna Graecia after the period of conquest are almost entirely epigraphic, with only a small amount of corroborative evidence from ancient literature. This inevitably imposes serious limitations on the sort of conclusions which can be drawn. The volume of material from southern Italy is substantial but not enormous, compared with data from Pompeii, for instance. It is very unevenly distributed, with virtually no evidence from many cities. Even within any given city, epigraphic and archaeological evidence is dependent on many random factors – accessibility of sites to excavators, survival of data, preservation and recording of finds (particularly a problem in dealing with records of very early excavations). The material is therefore not suitable for any form of quantitative analysis. This chapter will therefore concentrate mainly on those cities with a substantial amount of evidence – Cumae, Naples, Paestum, Velia, Rhegium, Locri and Tarentum. This is not to imply that these were the only cities which continued to exist. Sites which have been excavated in Calabria – Nicotera, Tropaea, Medma, Laos, to name only a few – show signs of occupation in the Roman period, and are included in the lists of cities compiled by ancient geographers, but as yet they have yielded too little epigraphic evidence to be studied in detail.

Chronologically, our sample of data is confined to the first two centuries AD, with very few texts as early as the first century BC or later than the middle of the third century AD.[3] In this, it reflects the prevailing pattern throughout Italy and many of the provinces, a feature for which there has yet to be a satisfactory explanation. Macmullen has tried to connect the sudden increase in Latin texts, particularly epitaphs, with an increasing degree of Romanisation in the provinces of the Roman Empire, and therefore suggests that the number of inscriptions should be taken as an indication of the level of Romanisation.[4] Mayer advances a similar but more specific model, arguing that Latin epitaphs were an assertion of legal status by those who had recently obtained Roman citizenship, either by enfranchisement or manumission.[5] Neither of these hypotheses adequately explains the peculiarities of epigraphy in southern Italy. The Oscan and Messapian-speaking peoples of southern Italy had an independent epigraphic tradition which pre-dated the Roman conquest. Messapian inscriptions are usually short epitaphs, but the corpus of Oscan epigraphy includes a wide variety of documents. At Cumae, there are a surprising number of funerary or dedicatory inscriptions in Oscan or Latin, of the second and first centuries BC, including a series of Oscan or bilingual curses.[6] Pre-Roman Greek inscriptions are known from most of the Greek cities of the South, but in small numbers. Many of the Hellenistic cities of the Aegean were prodigious inscribers, recording the deeds of the city or of individuals, but this was not the case in the West. There is no comparable quantity of evidence for the Italiotes, but there are enough texts to indicate that there was an indigenous pre-Roman 'epigraphic habit' (to use Macmullen's terminology).[7] The feature which all the Italiote cities have in common, however, is that there is very little evidence for the transition period between free allied city and Roman *municipium*, so there is very little possibility for comparison.

Any study primarily based on epigraphy must also take into account the fact that it gives an uneven reflection of society, offering more information about the political, social and economic élite and those who aspired to join it, and very little about the poorest levels of society. Even the simplest epitaphs, often those of slaves or freedmen and their families, represent an investment which must have been beyond the poorest section of society.[8] Therefore, there is at least part of the social structure of each city which is inaccessible. However, the inscriptions set

163

up by the civic élites are illuminating, and it is possible, despite the limitations of the evidence, to draw some interesting conclusions about social structure and acculturation in the cities of southern Italy.

The bare bones of the social structure of these cities are similar to those of any other city in Italy in the Early Empire, and were, to a large extent, defined by Roman law and municipal charters. The political power and highest social and economic status lay with the decurial class, open to all free-born citizens who met the property qualification, which had a monopoly of local magistracies and membership of the local senate. As well as direct political power, these families won enormous influence through acts of euergetism – defined by Paul Veyne as 'private liberality for public benefit'.[9]

However, the élite was not just composed of the political classes. It also included families which aspired to the decurial class but had not yet attained this rank, as well as members of élites in other cities who were temporarily resident. The most notable of these were Roman officials and members of the Roman élite who had estates in southern Italy. The frequency of visits to an estate, however, and the extent of involvement in the life of the local community, could be very variable. Villas close to Rome and in fashionable areas such as Campania would be visited frequently by the owner,[10] who may be on friendly terms with the local élite – witness the friendship between Cicero and the Puteolan aristocrat Lucceius – but properties in more distant areas would receive far less attention, with fewer contacts between Roman landowners and the local community.

Less exalted in terms of social status but still influential were the members of the *Ordo Augustalis*.[11] The original function of the Augustales, all of whom were freedmen, was to organise the cult of the emperor and its rituals, and this remained their principal official duty, but they came to have a wider, and possibly greater, significance for the social structure of the Italian city. Membership of the order was consequent on a property qualification, as was membership of the decurial order. Augustales were men of high economic standing, despite their status as freed slaves and their consequent exclusion from the political process. Membership of the *Ordo Augustalis* was a means of giving status and recognition to such men without admitting them to a share of direct political power. As such, the *Ordo Augustalis* became a group of middle status, forming a part of the élite but always secondary to the *Ordo Decurionum*. This is made very explicit in *sportula* inscriptions from Croton,[12] which give details of an endowment to provide an

164

annual public dinner, in which the Augustales receive a larger allowance than the citizens at large, but less than the decurions.

Below the level of these groups which constitute the élite, we have less information on the structure of society. Many epitaphs are those of slaves and freedmen, but many more contain no indication of status. In any case, these texts usually contain minimal information, often only the name of the deceased, that of the dedicator of the monument and the relationship between the two.[13] Given the sporadic nature of the evidence and the lack of consensus on the exact significance of epitaphs and other forms of personal commemoration, it is not possible to use these as statistical evidence for the proportion of slaves and/or freedmen within a city. An exception to this is Tarentum and the Sallentine peninsula, where 40–50 per cent of all epitaphs from the region are those of slaves, and many are from rural rather than urban areas.[14] The number of slaves represented is unusually high, and the non-urban distribution is very unusual. This may simply be due to the vagaries of survival and excavation of sites, but it may also be a reflection of the large number of villas and estates in southern Apulia.[15] Other information which can be gleaned includes an indication of immigration into a city from other areas of the Empire. This line of approach must also be used with caution, however, as only certain groups can be identified. Where colonies of discharged veterans have been established, as at Tarentum and Paestum, epitaphs listing details of military careers are found. At Tarentum, traces of the deductions of both 123 BC and AD 60 are found,[16] while at Paestum there are epitaphs, identical in type to those from the military cemetery at Misenum, of sailors and marines from Misenum, who were settled there in AD 71.[17] Among the inscriptions of Naples are Greek epitaphs which explicitly include ethnic origin, an element which routinely occurs in Greek epitaphs but not in Latin ones. This evidence for citizens of Antioch, Berytus, Alexandria, Cyrene and other cities in the Eastern Empire provides corroboration for other literary and epigraphic evidence for the cosmopolitan nature of Naples and its close links with the Greek world.[18]

One type of social unit whose members are rather more visible than the rest of the population is the collegium. Collegia of different types are found in many of the cities of Magna Graecia, as they are in most other Italian cities. Most examples are religious collegia, many of them connected with the cult of the Magna Mater. There are *dendrophori* at Cumae and Rhegium and *cannophori* at Locri.[19] These played a prominent part in the festivals of the Magna Mater and could be organisations of considerable size. Two inscriptions from Cumae list over a hundred members of the *dendrophori*. Other collegia include the Apollinares, connected with the cult of Apollo, at Cumae.[20] At Rhegium, there was an association of the Artists of Dionysos, a guild of actors, such as is found in many other Hellenistic cities. As a characteristically Greek phenomenon, it cannot be strictly regarded as a collegium, but it fulfilled many of the same functions. The presence of an Association of Dionysos implies some sort of dramatic festival, either as part of a religious or agonistic festival. This correlation is demonstrated in Rome itself, where a college of actors was established on the Aventine shortly after the institution of the first Greek games, the Megalensian Games in 204 BC, in honour of the Magna Mater.[21] Also at Rhegium, there is a series of inscriptions relating to the cults of Apollo and Artemis which may relate either to a civic festival or to the activities of a collegium.[22] Collegia which were essentially trade associations, such as those found at Ostia and Pompeii, are rarely found in Magna Graecia, where the majority of the collegia have religious connections and would have played an important part in civic festivals.

The significant point about collegia and their membership is that they represent a powerful focus for social and economic activity.[23] Membership was usually conditional on being able to pay a substantial fee to the collegium and to contribute to communal meals, the upkeep of a meeting house and any public works undertaken by the collegium. Although members may not have been regarded as part of the élite, they were men (and in some cases women) of considerable means.[24] Socially, collegia provided a focus for this group of non-élite but prosperous citizens, giving them status and enabling them to take an active part in the life of the city. Little is known of their activities in Magna Graecia, but evidence from other cities indicates that they usually had their own meeting houses and cults, and that they provided a network of mutual support for their members. They were also a vehicle for central control of civic activities, since they were closely supervised by the State. The Leges Juliae de Collegiis, enacted by Caesar and Augustus, abolished all collegia which had not been given senatorial approval and set up a mechanism for creating new collegia which involved gaining a patron among the Roman élite who would sponsor a *senatusconsultum* to ratify the new collegium.[25] This cumbersome process was still in place in AD 251. A college of *dendrophori* at Cumae published a list of members eligible for *sportulae*, with the preamble that it was set up by senatorial decree under the patronage of Ampius Stephanus.[26]

One uniquely Greek institution which does not fit into any of these categories is the phratry, which is found only at Naples, although well known from Athens and other cities of the Aegean. The Neapolitan examples are a problem in that they are clearly of archaic origin but are undocumented before the Roman period.[27] There were twelve altogether, although one, the Antinoitoi, may be a Hadrianic renaming of one of the other phratries. The archaic names suggest an ancient origin, and they probably originated as kinship groups. In the first century AD, each had its own cults and meeting house, held meetings and elected officers, and to this extent they resemble collegia in structure.[28] Their function was clearly no longer one of a kinship group, as membership included Roman notables, of whom the most illustrious was the emperor Claudius. Judging by the inscriptions recording gifts and dedications to the phratries, exchanges of honours and grants of membership, they must have been an important part of élite interaction. The deceased son of the Roman notable Munatius Hilarianus was commemorated in a heroon (hero-shrine) by the Artemisioi, and the renaming of the Eunostidoi as the Antinoitoi is a clear bid for Hadrianic favour. Significantly, the revival of kinship groups is also found in the Eastern Empire during the second century AD.[29]

It is clear from this brief review of the social groups represented in the epigraphy that only the élite is sufficiently well documented to be analysed in detail. As in other ancient cities, the dominant *ethos* behind its activities was a mixture of co-operation and competition, frequently manifested in the phenomenon of euergetism. This could take a multiplicity of forms and was a central feature of municipal life in the ancient world, supplying many civic amenities which, in the modern world, would be the duty of the State. Some forms of euergetism were obligatory, consequent on holding a particular magistracy or priesthoods.[30] Elected officials were frequently required to pay for the upkeep of buildings and to pay for games and festivals during their period of office. The amounts of money laid out on these were at the discretion and means of the individual, but there was considerable pressure to make a lavish display. The provision of exotic animals and large numbers of gladiators for the games, or a spectacular procession and public dinner at a festival, gave status both to the individual and his family and to the city. The games given by Veratius Severus at Cumae were lovingly recorded in a large inscription which gives details of his imports for a wild beast show.[31] The burdens of office could be heavy, and evidence from the Eastern provinces shows that the avoidance of public office was a priority for the élites of some cities.[32]

Other forms of euergetism were voluntary, but peer group pressure and a competitive *ethos* seem to have prevailed in Magna Graecia, as in other Italian regions. Leading families were expected to pay for the construction, upkeep or renovation of amenities such as baths, theatres, amphitheatres and aqueducts. Specific works recorded include the restoration and extension of the temple of Demeter at Cumae by Gn. Lucceius, his son and two daughters, the construction of a new bath house at Paestum by Digitius, and the numerous benefactions by the Tullii Cicerones of Paestum.[33] Recent research on Samnium has used the incidence of municipal building as an indication of the economic health of a community and of the prosperity and influence of its élite.[34] By this criterion, Magna Graecia does not score spectacularly well. There are signs of munificence and public building in most cities but not on a grand scale. Magna Graecia, however, is a very different region from Apennine Italy, and there are good reasons for believing that the scale of municipal building is not a reliable economic indicator in this case. Samnium did not become fully urbanised until after the Social War, and therefore lacked the type of monumental public building associated with urban development. One of the interesting features here is the way in which the focus of élite munificence changes, moving from building at the sanctuary sites associated with the Oscan *pagi* to the new, Romanised, urban centres.[35] Magna Graecia, in contrast, was a region where urban structures developed very early, and where planned cities and monumental public building were the norm centuries before the Roman conquest. By the first century BC and the first century AD, the Greek colonies already had a full complement of monumental public buildings.[36] The only room for large-scale munificence of this type was in elaborating or repairing existing buildings or in adding new, specifically Roman, structures such as baths and amphitheatres. Both phenomena are well attested in the region.[37]

Another form of euergetism was the *sportula*, a distribution of money or food, or a dinner at the expense of the donor for all or part of the citizen body. These were usually commemorative in intent, endowing a celebration to mark the birthday or the death of a relative. The Crotoniate inscription in memory of the eques L. Lollius Marcianus records an endowment by his wife, Futia Longina, to pay for a commemorative statue and an annual *sportula* in his memory.[38] A similar inscription honouring Julia Prepis specifies the amounts payable, which are carefully graded to reflect status, from 8 sesterces each for decurions to 6 for Augustales, 4 for other citizens and 2 for women. Frustratingly, many civic benefactors leave no direct evidence of the nature of their euergetism. The majority of inscriptions honouring benefactors refer to their *liberalitas* or *abundantia* in relation to the city but do not give details.[39]

Epitaphs and honorific inscriptions frequently list offices held in the course of a political career, and these inscriptions can give some insight into the composition of the élite. Acts of euergetism by prominent citizens and of magistracies and priesthoods held by them show that the municipal élites of Magna Graecia were as active as those anywhere else in Italy, but also that these cities suffered, like many others, from a small decurial class. The trend throughout the Empire was for municipal élites to decline in numbers and to become impoverished by the constant financial pressures of office and of the demands of civic euergetism.[40] The limited evidence available from southern Italy broadly matches this trend. Only a small number of *gentes* in each city occur in euergetic inscriptions or as holders of municipal office – Futius Onirus and Lollius Marcianus at Croton, the Lucceii, Blossii and Heii at Cumae, the Vagellii at Locri, the Digitii, Bennii and Tullii Cicerones at Paestum. The number of instances of iteration in the holding of offices may also be indicative of a small, and even shrinking, decurial class. Iteration of the quaestorship and quattuorvirate are found in Velian inscriptions, and there is also iteration of the quattuorvirate at Rhegium.[41]

However, statistics for numbers of decurions drawn from inscripions are problematic, particularly in Magna Graecia, where there is a huge imbalance between epigraphic densities in different parts of the region. Duncan-Jones has suggested that a ratio of one decurion per eleven individuals was not uncommon and that in some cities the number could be much higher. Petelia had thirty decurions for an estimated population of between 6,000 and 8,000, while Canusium had over a hundred.[42] However, this does not include any weighting to take account of the chronological distribution of the evidence, size of sample, or nature of the epigraphy used. It is difficult to assess the value of a comparison between Canusium, for which we have an official list of decurions, with other cities where the evidence is largely circumstantial, relying on cursus inscriptions and records of acts of euergetism.[43] If numbers of inscriptions and numbers of decurions are calculated for Magna Graecia (Table 3), the principal correlation which emerges is a close connection between the size of sample available and the number of decurions, with both figures weighted in favour of the richer and more populous areas of Campania and northern Lucania.[44] The oddity is Tarentum, where there are large numbers of inscriptions but few decurial *gentes*. This may be a reflection of the state of the Tarentine élite, but it is worth bearing in mind that a large proportion of Tarentine

169

Table 3 Size of decurial classes in Magna Graecia

City	Notables	No. of inscriptions
Cumae	18	130
Naples	74	276
Paestum	40	300
Velia	15	97
Rhegium	33	71
Locri	5	47
Thurii	4	8
Croton	4	22
Heraklea	0	0
Metapontum	0	0
Tarentum	6	219

inscriptions are rural rather than urban, and therefore weighted against representation of élite activities.[45] Overall, there seems no reason to assume that the decurial classes of Magna Graecia were any smaller than those of other cities.

One of the most noticeable things about urban life in southern Italy is that very few members of the municipal élites from Regio II and Regio III gained entry to the Senate at Rome. In contrast to this, senators of Italian origin from Regio I are much more numerous.[46] The reasons for this are difficult to assess. The relative lack of prosperity of some of the cities of Lucania and Calabria relative to other regions of Italy may have limited the chances of decurions from these areas to gain enough wealth to qualify for senatorial rank, recently estimated as 520 times higher than the daily subsistence wage (compared with a qualification of 52 times the daily subsistence wage for a decurion),[47] and sustain the expenses of a political career at Rome. This argument, however, is much less tenable in relation to the cities of Campania. The sheer remoteness of much of southern Italy from Rome may also have diminished the chances of such moves. It is notable that senators from Magna Graecia tend to come from Naples, Cumae and Paestum rather than anywhere further south, and that the lack of south Italian senators is not specific to the Greek areas but is also true of the entire region. The negative impact of such a lack of contact with the centre on civic development is also something to be considered. Patterson's surveys of Samnium and Lycia illustrate the fact that cities were likely to benefit very tangibly from the absorption of members of the decurial class into the Roman Senate, and that those cities which had few senatorial connections of this type would be cut off from such benefits.[48]

Euergetic activities by the local élite were not the only means of improving the amenities of a city and enhancing its status. Patronage from outside the city was a significant force in civic life, and one which appears to have increased as central interference in civic life grew during the second century AD. The most prominent and prestigious source of patronage was the emperor and members of his family. In this respect, the Bay of Naples scores most highly. The imperial palaces at Baiae were favoured residences of many emperors of the first and second centuries, attracted by the Greek ambience of the Bay of Naples, amongst other things.[49] Cumae and Naples undoubtedly benefited from their proximity. Augustus paid for the rebuilding of the Cumaean acropolis and the renovation of the harbour, paying particular attention to the temple of Apollo, which became central to Augustan ideology after the publication in 19 BC of the Aeneid, which contained the story of Aeneas' visit to the temple and encounter with the Sibyl.[50] The Greek games at Naples enjoyed imperial patronage and several emperors were enrolled in the phratries at Naples.[51]

Emperors were also a useful source of cash in times of crisis. Titus paid for repairs after an earthquake at Naples in AD 81, Septimius Severus paid for repairs to flood damage in 202, and at Rhegium the baths were sumptuously restored in 347, after being damaged by an earthquake.[52] Less prestigious was the connection between Augustus' daughter Julia and the city of Rhegium, which was her place of exile after AD 4.[53] Similarly, there are a large number of inscriptions relating to the Julii at Tarentum, which attest a long history of Julian loyalties at Tarentum, dating to the second triumvirate, and possibly to Julius Caesar.[54] Veyne identifies imperial patronage, and its precursor, the patronage extended to cities by Hellenistic kings, as a system of favours and benefactions designed to enhance the status of the ruler and to create a network of ties which bound cities to him. Acceptance of favours or assistance obligated the recipient to the ruler.[55]

Other notables were equally generous patrons, but many of these acts of patronage are known only from collective expressions of gratitude, which leave the exact nature of the benefaction in doubt. The senate of Velia passed a proxeny decree in honour of G. Julius Naso, possibly to be identified with a friend of Pliny the Younger, who is honoured for acts of patronage by several other cities in Italy and the Aegean, but there is no reference to the cause of this decree.[56] At Naples, the phratries provided a framework for the exchange of honours and benefactions. The phratry of the Artemisioi were involved in an elaborate exchange with Munatius Hilarianus, a benefactor of the phratry and the city, which involved honours to Hilarianus himself and conferred the status of hero, complete with his own shrine and statue, on Hilarianus' deceased son.[57] With the increasing degree of central control over the Italian *municipia* instituted by Trajan, the possibilities for patronage increased. During the third and fourth centuries AD, an increasing number of inscriptions referring to municipal building or repairs show the involvement of a *curator rei publicae* or a *corrector*.[58] Whatever the source of the revenue, there is no doubt given the evidence of inscriptions and material remains that considerable resources were ploughed into building projects which supplied the cities of Magna Graecia with all the standard amenities of a Romanised city – drainage, water supply, baths, temples, theatres and amphitheatres.[59]

ETHNICITY AND ORIGINS: POPULATION CHANGES IN MAGNA GRAECIA

One of the questions posed by the somewhat heterogeneous nature of the epigraphy from Magna Graecia is that of the origin and ethnicity of the inhabitants by the first century AD. Clearly there had been changes of such magnitude that the original Greek population had been considerably diluted. Aside from the admixture of Oscan and Messapian population, varying in the extent of their influence and the means of their arrival, there was extensive colonisation by Rome.[60] Apart from colonies of the third and second centuries BC, there were deductions of discharged veterans in Magna Graecia under the Julio-Claudian and Flavian emperors, easily recognisable in the epigraphic record by their military-style epitaphs. Southern Italy also attracted a good many immigrants form the Eastern Empire. As well as voluntary immigration, slavery provided a means of redistributing population on a mass scale. The inescapable conclusion is that the cities of Magna Graecia underwent a profound change in the nature and ethnic composition of their populations, but this is a change which it is difficult to chart and to quantify. A small number of epitaphs include the place of origin of the deceased, and the victory inscriptions of the *Sebasta* at Naples list the ethnic origin of the competitors.[61]

In the majority of cases, however, it is difficult to discern the ethnic origins of the population. Analysis of the name structures and language use of these cities can give some indications, but does not provide straightforward answers. Both of these fields are obscured by legal, political and social considerations. In the ancient world, the name one was known by and the languages used in any given context were contingent both on legal status and a bewildering set of socio-political conventions.[62] The Roman *tria nomina* could only be used by Roman citizens, but by the first century AD the inhabitants of southern Italy, excluding slaves and non-Italians, were citizens. *Nomina* can sometimes be used to determine regional origin within Italy, but this is not an accurate means of tracing population movement.[63] In any case, a large number of *nomina* found in the South are identifiable only as being of Latin/Campanian origin. Imperial *nomina* were frequently a sign that a person was an imperial freedman, or was a veteran discharged by the emperor whose name had been adopted. There are a number of Tiberii Claudii among the veterans of the Neronian colony at Tarentum, and a high proportion of Gaii Julii at Rhegium, a city which had close connections with Augustus.[64]

The close connection between citizenship and the *tria nomina* meant that use of the *tria nomina* was a political act. Adoption of a characteristically Roman nomenclature implied acceptance of Roman values. This may in part explain the apparent disappearance of the indigenous Greek population of the South. Except in Naples, Velia and Rhegium, there are remarkably few Greek names preserved in the epigraphic record, other than those which are obviously slave names,[65] or those of Greeks from outside Italy. Even the Greek inscriptions which record the activites of the élite – decrees of the *boule*, religious texts, victory lists of the *Sebasta* and honorific inscriptions – include very few non-Latin names. Most of these élite names are of Roman or Campanian origin, rather than being specifically local to Bruttium or Lucania.[66]

This apparent lack of an indigenous Greek élite has mystified scholars considerably, and has lent credence to the idea that the Punic Wars were a watershed, after which Magna Graecia was too impoverished and too Romanised to maintain a significant Greek identity. More recently, on the basis of inscriptions from Locri, Rhegium and Vibo, Costabile has suggested that far from indicating the wholesale demise of the Greek élite and replacement by Italian or Roman colonists, the onomastic disappearance of the Greeks was a political act, not to be confused with a change in population.[67] Greeks anxious to adapt to the presence of Rome and assimilate simply dropped their Greek names in favour of Roman ones when enfranchised in 90 BC, significantly choosing names with a Roman rather than Bruttian affinity. This model has much to recommend it, but the probability is that the truth lies somewhere between the two extremes. With little evidence from the crucial period, the first century BC, it is only possible to hypothesise, but it seems as unlikely that the Greek élite disappeared entirely as that it survived intact. Literary references show that there had been a degree of admixture between Greek and Oscan populations as early as the fourth century,[68] and inscriptions from second- and first-century BC Campania corroborate this. It is not uncommon to find individuals with Greek names and Oscan patronymics or vice versa. An early imperial chamber tomb at Naples contains burials of a family with an eclectic mixture of Greek and Oscan names – Trebios Epilytou, Epilytos Epilytou, Epilytos Bibiou, etc.[69] The effect on social structure of the Roman colonisations has already been commented on. In addition, families died out by process of natural wastage. Studies of the Roman élite show that senatorial families had a comparatively limited life-span, and tended to die out after several generations unless augmented by adoption.[70] A high birth-rate maximised subdivision of wealth within the family and increased the chances of part or all of the family falling below the threshold for maintaining their rank, while a low birth-rate increased the possibility of a family dying out entirely. The Greek population was undoubtedly diluted by the first century AD, but there are no grounds for supposing that it had died out entirely.

ACCULTURATION: THE EVOLUTION OF A NEW REGIONAL IDENTITY

Changes in language distribution can be helpful but not decisive in tracing population movements and changes in ethnicity. Studies in historical linguistics demonstrate that the choice of language in any given context within a multi-lingual society is very much conditioned by social and political pressures within that society.[71] It is part of a constructed personal or collective identity which may have little to do with the actual linguistic and ethnic background of individuals. This is particularly true when dealing with a set of documents which are all, in varying degrees, public records or statements. Even epitaphs, in some respects the most obviously private category of inscription, are public assertions of personal identity. In dealing with the ancient world, it is not possible to do a full-scale study in language distribution because of the restricted number of language fields for which there is evidence.[72] Even within these restrictions, however, it is possible to draw some interesting conclusions about languages and their use.

In essence, Magna Graecia was a multi-lingual society. By the first century AD, the principal languages represented are Latin and Greek. Prior to this, there are also a number of inscriptions in Oscan. Oscan was the principal language of Cumae, and probably also of Paestum, by the fourth century BC although Greek was still spoken in both.[73] Few inscriptions of this date are found anywhere in the region, although small numbers of Greek texts occur at most sites. These provide a clear indication of a pre-Roman epigraphic tradition in Greek, Oscan and Messapian. There are a number of extant Oscan inscriptions from Cumae, Naples and Paestum, however, which date to the second and first centuries BC. Curiously, none of these cities was offically Oscan-speaking by this date. At Cumae, the language change can be dated precisely to 180 BC on the evidence of Livy, who mentions a Cumaean petition to the Senate to use Latin instead of Oscan for official business.[74] Despite this, the existence of Oscan inscriptions dated as late as the first century BC implies the continued use of Oscan as a language after its demise as the official language. There is also a more overtly political dimension to this. The formal application to adopt Latin may be part of a process extending full citizenship to Cumae, a holder of *civitas sine suffragio* since 338 BC.[75] Use of the Latin language had strong political overtones, signalling acceptance of Roman values, and Oscan could be used in a similar fashion to indicate anti-Roman views. It is significant that the number of Oscan inscriptions from southern Italy as a whole rise during the period immediately before the Social War. A particularly striking example is the Tabula Bantina. The Latin inscription on this bronze tablet is considerably earlier than the Oscan one, which is now thought to date from the time of the Social War or slightly earlier.[76] The choice of language does not represent a linear progression away from the Italic languages and in favour of Latin, but a much more complex process in which language choice could reflect the political sympathies of an individual or a city. At Cumae, which did not revolt during the Social War, the issue is less clear cut. The Oscan inscriptions in this case are not state-issued documents, but are epitaphs, religious dedications and curse tablets.[77] Thus the evidence is ambiguous, pointing to the continued use of Oscan as a spoken language, but also hinting, by the chronological distribution of the inscriptions, at a more ideological dimension.

While Oscan disappears from the epigraphic record during the first century BC, Latin and Greek both persist. The relative distribution of these languages, however, is complex. Again, there is no simple chronological replacement of one by the other. The question is complicated still further by the wide variations in geographical distribution. In many cities, Greek inscriptions disappear, or persist in very small numbers. With the exception of Tarentum and Locri, however, these cities are ones from which we have comparatively small amounts of evidence of any sort. There is a small body of Latin inscriptions from Croton and Vibo, but virtually none from Metapontum, Heraklea, Thurii and many other cities, despite evidence that they continued to have municipal status.[78]

The cities in which both Greek and Latin inscriptions have been found in significant numbers are Rhegium, Velia and Naples. In all of these cases, there is a striking division between the circumstances in which Greek is used and those where Latin is employed. The vast majority of monuments set up by private citizens are Latin epitaphs, usually corresponding to one of the relatively standard types found in all parts of the Roman Empire.[79] At Naples and at Velia there is a substantial minority of Greek epitaphs, some of them set up by Greeks from outside Italy. Also at Naples, and at Cumae, there are Greek epitaphs which appear to be literal translations of the D[is] M[anibus] type of Latin inscription. These are headed by the formula θ[ειοις] Κ[αταχθονιοις] and follow the construction of the Latin equivalent, listing the name and age of the deceased and the name of the dedicator.[80] However, the fact remains that the vast majority of epitaphs, particularly those of the élite, are Latin. In contrast, a large number of inscriptions set up by Velia, Naples and Rhegium as civic bodies are in Greek. All of these are primarily honorific or ceremonial in nature, and are couched in Greek terminology as well as being expressed in the Greek language.[81]

Inscriptions relating to the cults of Apollo Oulios at Velia and the cults of Apollo and Artemis at Rhegium use Greek to honour officials of the cults and to record details of sacrifices. At Velia, the inscriptions on statues of *pholarchoi*, associated with the cult of Apollo, show that the incumbents had Greek names and were presumably of Greek origin. Other inscriptions, however, include the office of *pholarchos* as part of a list of offices held by Valerius Caepillio, a Velian magistrate whose name suggests a non-Greek origin. Clearly it was not simply a Greek priesthood, but an office which formed part of the civic cursus for Greeks and Italians alike.[82]

The series of inscriptions from Rhegium which record sacrifices to Apollo and/or Artemis are also couched in Greek terminology, but all the high-status participants are Italian, or at least Italicised. The only Greek names which appear are those of the minor functionaries – the musicians, cook, butcher, etc. – whe are almost certainly slaves. The higher officials, the *prytanis, archon* and *synprytanis*, all have the Romanised *tria nomina*.[83] It was this dichotomy between language and nomenclature which led Costabile to suggest that the élite may have been composed of Greeks using Romanised names. The evidence, however, seems to point to a different conclusion with an emphasis on cultural rather than ethnic implications. Whether the élite of Rhegium, and of other cities in southern Italy, were primarily composed of ethnic Greeks or not, they were certainly Romanised to the degree where they had abandoned Greek names and used the Latin language for many of their inscriptions. On the other hand, these groups of inscriptions also point to a strong Hellenising tendency in the activities of the élites. The cults which are given prominence are the ancient Greek cults of the cities, the sacrifices are celebrated according to Greek custom, and the priesthoods which are singled out are among the oldest in the city. In the case of the *pholarchos* at Velia and the *laukelarchos* at Naples, these are also priesthoods which are almost certainly archaic.[84] The rites are recorded in Greek, firmly underlining their origins and nature.

Other inscriptions confirm this Hellenising element in the behaviour of the élite. From all three cities with substantial quantities of Greek epigraphy, there are examples of Greek euergetic decrees issued by the local senate in honour of benefactors of the city. The most characteristically Greek of these are also the simplest in form, which describe the honorand as *euergetes kai aretes*,[85] a formula found in proxeny decrees all over the Greek world in the Hellenistic and Roman periods. Other examples, notably those from Naples, are more elaborate. A particularly characteristic Neapolitan form is the decree of public mourning and condolence for prominent citizens or foreign notables. This type of decree is of particular interest as it is one of the less common forms of honorific decree in the Greek world, although there is still ample comparative evidence from the Eastern Empire, and it shows an interesting combination of Greek and Roman features.[86]

Of the entire series, the decree in honour of Tettia Casta, a very Greek-sounding *psephisma* of the *boule* passed in AD 71, is perhaps the most deserving of detailed discussion.[87] The text is slightly damaged and has some *lacunae*, but has no gaps which affect the sense.

Τεττίαι Κάσται ἱερείαι τ[οῦ . . . . .]|τῶν γυναικῶν οἴκου διὰ βίου φη[φίσματα]|.

'Επὶ ὑπάτων Καίσαρος Σεβαστοῦ υἱοῦ Δομιτι[ανοῦ καὶ Γαίου]| Οὐαλερίου φήστου ιδ' Ληναιῶνος· γραφ[ομένων παρῆσαν]| Λούκιος φροῦγι, Κορνήλιος Κεριᾶλις, 'Ιούνιος [. . . . . .].| Περὶ οὗ προσανήνεγκεν τοῖς ἐν προσκλήτωι Τρανκουίλλιος 'Ροῦφος ὁ ἀντάρχων, περὶ τού[του τοῦ πράγματος οὕτως εὐηρέστησεν]·| τὴν γνώμην ἁπάντων ὁμολογοῦντας κοινὴν εἶναι λύπην τὴν πρόμοιρον Τεττίας Κά[στας τελευτήν, γυναικὸς φιλοτιμησαμέ]|νης εἴς τε τὴν

τῶν ἁπάντων εὐσέβειαν καὶ εἰς τὴν τῆς πατρίδος εὔνοιαν, ἀργυρῶν ἀνδριάντων ἀνε[κλείπτους ἀναστάσεις τοῖς θεοῖς ποιη]|σαμένης πρὸς τὸ μεγαλοψύχως εὐεργετῆσαι τὴν πόλιν, τιμᾶν ἀνδριάντι καὶ ἀσπίδι ἐγγ[εγραμμένηι Τεττίαν Κάσταν καὶ θάπτειν αὐτὴν]| δαπάνῃ μὲν δημοσίαι, ἐπιμελείᾳ δὲ τῶν προσηκόντων, οὓς δυσχερές ἐστιν παραμυθήσασθαι δι[ὰ .... καὶ τό]|πον εἰς κηγείαν δίδοσθαι καὶ εἰς ταῦτα ἐξοδιάζειν.
Ἐπὶ ὑπάτων Καίσαρος Σεβαστοῦ [υἱοῦ Δομιτιανοῦ καὶ Γαΐου Οὐαλερίου φήστου .... πρὸ καλ.]| Ἰουλίων· γραφ[ομένων παρῆσαν Γράνιος Ῥοῦφος, Λούκιος Πούδης, Ποππαῖ[ος Σεουῆρος]. Περὶ οὗ προσανήνεγκεν τοῖς ἐν προσκλήτωι φούλβιος Πρόβος ὁ ἄρχων, περὶ τούτου τοῦ πρ[άγματος οὕτως εὐηρέστησεν· τὴν μὲν εἰς τὸν ἀνδριάντα]| δημοσίαν δαπάνην, ἥν ἡ βουλὴ συμπαθοῦσα ἐψηφίσατο Τεττίᾳ Κάστᾳ, εὖ [ἔχειν· ἄξιον δὲ καὶ ἐπαινέσαι αὐτὴν καὶ στεφανῶσαι] χρυσῶι στεφάνῳ μαρτυροῦντας αὐτῆς τῶι βίωι δημοσίωι ἐπαίνωι [...........].|
Ἐπὶ ὑπάτων Λουκίου φλαουίου φιμβρία καὶ Ἀτειλίου Βαρβάρου [......., γραφομένων παρῆσαν]| Ἀριστων Βύκκου, Ἀουίλλιος Ἀρριανός, Οὐέρριος Λειβ[εράλις.....| Περ]ὶ οὗ προσανήνεγκεν τοῖς ἐν προσκλήτωι Ἰούλιο Λειουεια[ν]ὸ[ς ὁ ἄρχων (?), περὶ τούτου τοῦ πράγματος οὕτως εὐηρέστησεν·| Τεττ]ία τόπον εἰς κηδείαν ἀπὸ τοῦ τείχους ἐν μετώπωι μέχρι [...... | ...]κουντα ἐξοικοδοεῖν ἐπιτρέπειν καὶ ἀπὸ τῆς στ[ήλης εἰς ...... παντᾶχόσε ἄλλῳ μηδενὶ κηδείαν | ἐπὶ] τῶι αὐτῶι τόπῳ δίδοσθαι. | [...] Δομίτιοι Λέπιδ[ος καὶ .....]| τῆι μητρὶ καὶ Λ. Δομ[ίτιος .... τῆι γυναικὶ ἐποίησαν ......].| L[oco] D[ato] D[ecreto] D[ecurionum]

Decree in honour of Tettia Casta, priestess for life of [......] *oikos* of the women|.

In the consulship of Domitian Caesar, son of Augustus, and G. Valerius Festus, on the 14th of Lenaia. The motion was proposed by Lucius Frugi, Cornelius Cerialis, and Junius [....]|. Concerning the proposal which the *archon*, Tranquillius Rufus placed before the *proskletos*, the following decision was taken: It was agreed by a unanimous decision that there should be public mourning at the untimely death of Tettia Casta, a woman who loved honour and who showed universal piety and goodwill towards the city, and that a silver statue should be set up to the gods for the generous

178

benefactions to the city, and that Tettia Casta should be honoured by a statue and inscribed shields and that the cost of her funeral should be at public expense, but be the responsibility of her family, it being difficult to give comfort by [. . . . . .] and that a place should be given for a tomb and these things paid for.

In the consulship of Domitian Caesar, son of Augustus, and G. Valerius Festus, on the [...] of July, were present Granius Rufus, Lucius Pudes and Poppaeus Severus. Concerning the proposal which the *archon*, Fulvius Probus, placed before the *proskletos*, the following decision was taken. The statue at public expense which the *boule* had decreed to Tettia Casta out of sympathy, is approved. It is good, and worthy of praise and should be crowned with a gold crown, giving testimony to her life with public praise [. . . . . .]

In the consulship of L. Flavius Fimbria and Attilius Barbarus [. . . .], Ariston, son of Bukkos, Avillius Appianus and Verius Liberalis were present. Concerning the proposal which the *archon* (?), Julius Laevinus, referred to the *proskletos*, the following decision was taken. A place for burial was decreed to Tettia [...fragmentary passage detailing the size and position of the tomb and stele], and no one else shall be granted permission to be buried in this place. [...fragmentary passage referring to Tettia's son, Domitius Lepidus and her husband, L. Domitius.]

Most of the elements of this decree are typical of the other examples, but it is the longest and most elaborate surviving example, and it is also unusual in that it is dedicated to a woman. This is not, in itself, unparalleled in the Greek world, but it is infrequent. Tettia Casta herself is a good example of acculturation. The preamble to the decree states that she was a priestess, of a cult which is uncertain as the text is damaged at this point. However, the only Neapolitan cult which is known to have conferred this amount of status on its priestesses was that of Demeter, which was of great antiquity, and which had a long-standing connection with Rome. It would be stretching the evidence too far to suggest that she was one of the Neapolitans who became a priestess at Rome, but this is within the bounds of possibility, and other inscriptions relating to the cult confirm that these women were of very high status.[88]

The grounds on which the decree was passed, namely that Tettia Casta was an exemplary wife (*gynaikos philotimesamenes*) and an exemplary citizen (*kai eis ten tes patridos eunoian*), are a curious mixture of Greek and Roman. To describe someone as a lover of honour (*philotimos*) was a commonplace in the honorific language of Greek inscriptions, but it was not usual in the Greek world to apply such language to a woman, although many Latin funerary inscriptions extol the wifely and familial virtues of women.[89] Praise for being a lover of one's city, however, is very common in all types of Greek honorific inscription. The reality lying behind these generalities and commonplaces is that Tettia Casta was the wife of an important man, possibly the Domitius Lepidus mentioned in the fragmentary last line of the text, as well as priestess of an important cult and probably a benefactor of the city. The honours voted by the *boule* are also a curious mixture of Greek and Roman. The decree provides for a funeral and a tomb at public expense, decorated with a silver statue crowned with gold and an inscribed shield, most of which are found in decrees from the Greek world. Some of these items, however, are also very common from Latin inscriptions. There are many instances from all parts of Italy of statuary in honour of notables, tombs and funerals paid for out of public funds and of the shields or *clipeos* decorating the tomb.[90] Indeed many of the Greek inscriptions from Naples include the Latin formula L[oco] D[ato] D[ecreto] D[ecurionum] which is widely used to indicate a tomb given at public expense.[91]

All in all, the decree in honour of Tettia Casta, and a group of similar decrees, mainly in honour of successful athletes, provide a striking illustration of acculturation in action. Despite their self-consciously Hellenising form and content, they are the product of a Romanised élite, as is clear from the names of all involved – Tettia Casta, the honorand, Domitius Lepidus, her husband, Julius Laevinus and Tranquillus Rufus, the *archon* and *antarchon*. While the form and language of the main part of the decree is closely modelled on that of Greek honorific decrees and *psephismata*, the preamble gives the name of the honorand and the date expressed in consular and imperial years – a straightforward Roman formula.[92] The Roman and Greek strands become increasingly difficult to disentangle when the content of the decree is considered. Most of the honours voted to Tettia Casta are Greek in origin and have parallels in the honorific decrees of the Eastern Empire. At the same time, many of them had by this date become absorbed into the system of honours, symbols, and status indicators used by the Roman and Italian élites, the 'language of power' defined by Wallace-Hadrill.[93] What makes the Neapolitan decrees different from the Romanised adaptations of Greek honours and symbols used elsewhere is the overt exploitation of the Greek language and culture of the city by its self-consciously Hellenising élite. Tettia Casta is not just the recipient of a series of posthumous honours of a generalised Graeco-Roman type, she is the subject of a Greek *psephisma* couched in the language and terms of a Greek city. Nor was Tettia Casta unique. There is a whole series of similar decrees – *dogmata* or *psephismata* – of the *boule* from Naples. None of them is as long and complex as that of Tettia Casta, and the honours are less lavish, often restricted to provision of a tomb at public expense.[94] However, they all contribute to the conclusion that Naples, Rhegium and Velia were all involved in the revival of Hellenism among the élite during the first and early second centuries AD. The Greek language and the Greek conventions of the inscriptions are not a simple reflection of Greek culture surviving in Roman Italy, but are an indication of a very different Hellenism from that of the Classical era. The dichotomy between Greek language and Italic onomastics underlines the fact that this Hellenism is a cultural construct, not something which is consequent on ethnicity. It is also clear that it was largely an élite construct, since it appears primarily in the inscriptions of the urban élite and very rarely in inscriptions of other social groups or in rural inscriptions. The Greek inscriptions of these groups are simple epitaphs and are much smaller in number than their Latin counterparts.[95]

The reason why there was such an emphasis on Hellenism in civic life in cities which were not predominantly Greek in population and were certainly Romanised in their municipal structures lies in the prevailing philhellenism of the Roman élite. This was a phenomenon which transcended the purely cultural sphere and came to acquire a political status which enabled Greek cities throughout the Empire to exploit their history and traditions for political benefits and enhancement of their civic status. From Augustus onwards, Hellenism received some degree of imperial sanction.[96] The amount of active support varied from emperor to emperor, but by and large the emperors of the first and second centuries were philhellenes, who gave active approval to Hellenism and adopted a Hellenising lifestyle themselves. Some, most notably Nero, were censured by their contemporaries for overdoing it, and becoming unroman in their ways.[97] This is the perpetuation of a long tradition of Roman ambiguity towards alien cultures in general and Greek culture in particular, which can be traced back to the the Hannibalic war, and censure of Scipio's Hellenising behaviour while in Sicily.[98] The ambivalent relationship between Romans and Greek culture is clearly demonstrated in the need to be seen to espouse Hellenism only in carefully controlled circumstances, if fashionable Greek ways were not to become unacceptable.

Naples and its environs are perhaps the clearest examples of the process of Hellenism and its manipulation by Romans and Neapolitans alike. Many factors, including proximity to Rome and a history of political good relations, undoubtedly helped in establishing the Bay of Naples as the centre of what might be termed 'villa culture'.[99] The extensive imperial properties at Baiae served to confirm the strength of the connection between the Roman élite and the Bay of Naples. The elements of Hellenism in this area were vital to this development. Greek culture, particularly literature and philosophy, were an essential ingredient of *otium*, the leisured and cultivated lifestyle which was the ideal pursued by Cicero and his correspondents, and later by emperors and senators of the first and second centuries AD.[100] To some extent, this provided the phenomenon of Hellenism with its own momentum. The possibility of gaining imperial or aristocratic patronage attracted large numbers of Greek teachers, philosophers and *litterati* from all over the eastern Mediterranean, of whom the best-known examples are perhaps Licinius Archias, citizen of Heraklea and Naples, but originally from Antioch,[101] and the poet Statius, the son of a *grammaticus* from Velia who moved to the more fashionable Naples to pursue his career, a factor which was instrumental in allowing Statius himself to gain the patronage of Domitian.[102] The Greek games founded at Naples in AD 2 and at Puteoli in 138 both made their imperial connections explicit in their names (*Sebasta* and *Eusebia*) and provided a further point of focus for Greeks from the Eastern Empire, as well as being an expression of civic Hellenism for the host cities.[103] The rewards which could be generated by a display of Hellenism were clearly high, and usually expressed as gains in status or patronage for cities or individuals, although this could be accompanied by more tangible benefits.[104] The high profile of Hellenism on the Bay of Naples is remarked on by Strabo, who makes specific reference to the Greek ambience of Cumae and the Greek civic institutions of Naples.[105]

In this context, the resurgence of Hellenism in the activities of the élite becomes entirely comprehensible, particularly in the voting of honours to prominent Romans or expressing thanks to civic benefactors. The proxeny decree in honour of Julius Naso at Velia, the honorary demarchate for Hadrian at Naples and the inclusion of at least one emperor – Claudius – and numerous Roman senators and officials in phratries at Naples are all examples of the manipulation of Greek heritage by the local élite to give these honours an extra cachet. The question of whether this represents continuity of Hellenism or a resurgence of elements of civic life which had lapsed and been artificially revived is problematic and ultimately unanswerable, in view of the limited evidence. However, parallels with the history of the Eastern Empire in the second century suggest that a deliberate revival is very probable.

The high status accorded to cities with a demonstrable Greek past and Greek culture was not a phenomenon which was peculiar to Italy. In reviving Hellenism in civic life, the Italiote cities were participating in a process which is well documented in the Eastern Empire during the first and second centuries AD. This was characterised by a revival of interest in local history and culture during the second century AD in many Greek or Hellenised cities. Consequent on this there was a revival of ancient magistracies, priesthoods and local cults, and civic divisions such as the Neapolitan phratries, which may have lapsed entirely or faded into obscurity.[106] Ancient kinship ties between cities were formally renewed, particularly between colonies and their founding cities. Sparta revived the ancient cult of the Dioscuri and also the famous *Agoge*. At Cyrene, the sanctuary of Apollo was rebuilt in a predominantly archaic style.[107] In the West, the revival of archaising priesthoods such as the offices of *pholarchos* and *laukelarchos* and the renewed prominence of the Greek magistracies at Naples and Rhegium seem to be part of a similar process.

One of the principal reasons for this was the foundation of the Panhellenion by Hadrian in AD 131/2, since proof of Greek foundation and continuing Hellenism was the main criterion for membership of this League.[108] As a result of this, great emphasis was placed on traditional Greek festivals and forms of government, and many cities developed elaborate foundation myths as a means of proving their Greek origins.[109] The Panhellenion itself had few formal powers, but the status which accrued to a city which obtained membership was considerable,[110] further underlining the connection between civic Hellenism, high status and imperial patronage. None of the Italian cities is known to have been a member, although there is some slight evidence that Tarentum may have been involved.[111] A Spartan ambassador, Callicrates, was sent to Tarentum in AD 145–50, probably in an attempt to renew the ancient ties between the two cities, and received an effusive welcome. Envoys were also sent by Sparta to Naples and Puteoli, probably in connection with the Greek games there. As at Naples and Rhegium, Greek terminology was revived. Writers adopted Greek titles such as *Harmost* and *Satrap* for Roman officials and used archaic Greek place-names such as Dicaearchia (replacing Puteoli) and Hipponion (instead of Vibo) in preference to their Romanised forms.[112] The principle was even extended to personal names with the appearance of characters such as Jason of Argos and Theseus of Corinth in the sources for the second century.[113] Along similar lines, although with historical rather than mythical reference, there is the interesting case of Gn. Nearchus Fabianus at Tarentum. The elements of this name refer to the belief, cited by Cicero, that Fabius Maximus and his *quaestor* were influenced by Pythagorean philosophy acquired from the pro-Roman Tarentine Nearchos, their host after the recapture of Tarentum by Rome in 209 BC. The *quaestor* concerned was, in fact, none other than the arch anti-Hellene Cato.[114]

Clearly the revival and manipulation of Hellenism was important to the élites of southern Italy, and the construction of a Greek civic identity could bring important benefits and was actively encouraged. A factor which differentiates the experience of the Italiotes from that of the Eastern provinces is that the process seems to have begun earlier. In the East, the great Hellenic revival was a second-century phenomenon, given added impetus by Hadrian. In the West, the equivalent process begins a century earlier, with patronage from Augustus and other Julio-Claudian emperors.[115] This, however, makes for a great deal of ambiguity. A conservative, classicising form of Hellenism was an important strand in the iconography and ideology of Augustan Rome, but it was potentially a double-edged weapon. Augustus's propaganda war against Antony had played on Roman and Italian fears of alien rule, presenting Cleopatra as an orientalised despot who had corrupted Antony and was urging him to create a new imperial capital at Alexandria and rule as a Hellenistic king.[116] There was also the question of the mythical Trojan origins of Rome, enshrined in the *Aeneid*. Gruen has demonstrated how elements of genealogy and mythology were employed as political and diplomatic propaganda, and on this level, Augustus's identification of both himself and Rome with a Trojan foundation myth explicitly placed him in opposition to Hellenistic culture.[117] In this context Hellenism was something which had to be handled very carefully, and Magna Graecia was a perfect compromise. It was an integral part of the Roman state, and the cities which had the highest profile in imperial Italy were those which had a history of loyalty to Rome. As such, it was a region where Greek heritage and culture could be encouraged safely without running the risk of leaving the regime and its supporters open to charges of unroman behaviour.

What is not clear is whether or not the Hellenism of southern Italy was a complete revival of features of civic life which had fallen into disuse, or whether it was merely a case of giving greater prominence to institutions which still existed. Unfortunately, there is simply not enough evidence from the Late Republic to allow an informed judgement on this. What is certain, however, is that in a world where the rewards of Hellenism were so great, the élites of Greek cities of Italy would have had a massive incentive to emphasise their Greek culture and history, particularly in their dealings with the Roman élite and the predominantly philhellenic emperors of the first and second centuries AD.

LOCAL TRADITIONS: RESISTANCE AND ACCULTURATION OUTSIDE THE ELITE

So far, this chapter has concentrated on élite culture and the construction of identities, civic and personal, by the élite. The extent to which the poorer sections of urban society were Romanised is much more difficult to judge, and almost impossible in the case of the rural population. This lack of means to study the lower socio-economic groupings in society is particularly unfortunate as they may be able to tell us more about the survival of local culture. Gellner's model of cultural differentiation points to a high degree of cultural homogeneity among the élite of a particular group, but a much more fragmented culture, with greater local variations, among lower-status groups.[118] The epigraphy of Magna Graecia seems to support this model.

There is only one part of the region, however, in which it is possible to get to grips with the question of acculturation and the concept of non-Roman local identities. In the territory of Tarentum and the Sallentine peninsula, there is an unusually high number of rural inscriptions of a somewhat anomalous type.[119] The funerary monuments of the region are also very unusual. Most of them are free-standing *cippi*, often rough-hewn and of local tufa, in contrast to the urban grave markers which tend to include more *stelai*, grave altars and columbaria or chamber tombs containing multiple burials marked by inscribed wall plaques. Some of these *cippi* are undecorated, apart from the inscription, but others are surmounted by a sculpted human head or a flat circle which is clearly intended to represent a head or face.[120] These rudimentary 'portraits' or representations of a human figure are unique to the region, and they may be an attempt to adapt the Roman tradition of funerary portraiture to local needs and customs.[121] The inscriptions, where they exist, are significantly different from those found in other parts of southern Italy. There are very few of the D[is] M[anibus] type of inscriptions which are the most common type of epitaph elsewhere.[122] The type most prevalent in the *ager Tarentinus* and the Sallentine peninsula consists only of the name of the deceased, the age, and the formula H[ic] S[itus] E[st]. The vast majority of the examples date between the first and third centuries AD, and are thus contemporary with the D[is] M[anibus] epitaphs in other areas.[123] The rough execution of both monuments and inscriptions and the somewhat eccentric palaeography of some examples suggests that these are graves of comparatively poor people, many of them probably slaves or freedmen.[124]

It is also significant that this is clearly not just the result of a dichotomy between urban and rural society. Many of the poorer burials with Greek epitaphs which are found at Naples, Velia and Rhegium as well as Tarentum may represent a less Romanised substratum of society. These epitaphs are very different from the Greek inscriptions of the élite, which are almost all connected with the official life of the city. Most of them are very simple in form, usually only the name or name and patronymic of the deceased, and are associated with poor burials.[125] These are frequently multiple burials, in catacombs or columbaria, although there is a series of free-standing *cippi* from Velia which have Greek inscriptions of a very simple type.[126]

A degree of regionalisation of monument types and sometimes of inscriptions can also be found in other areas. In Campania, there is a group of very unusual grave monuments found only in the territory of Capua.[127] These are clearly derived from Greek *stelai* and are characterised by *aedicula* framing the other decoration, but they are very distinctive and localised adaptations of the Greek conventions. The same principle, that of local culture transforming the conventions of an external one into something distinctively and uniquely regional, seems to be at work in the cases of both Tarentum and Capua.[128]

It seems possible that what the Tarentine and Sallentine monuments and inscriptions and the Capuan grave-markers represent is a survival of local culture and identity long after the Roman conquest of Italy was complete. As in all cases of acculturation, this is not a one-way process. External influences, both Greek and Roman, are absorbed, but local products are not simply a copy of the original, executed with more or less skill and fidelity. Outside influences are assimilated and adapted to local conventions, and are used to create a distinctive local culture. They do not overwhelm that local culture although they must, to some extent have altered it. Just as the urban élites forged a distinctive identity by manipulating elements of their Hellenic past while simultaneously embracing aspects of Roman life and culture, so the lower social groups, particularly the rural poor, retained their own distinctive local identity by assimilating external influences and adapting them to their own needs.

In conclusion, the cities of Magna Graecia, or those of them for which there is evidence for the first and second centuries AD, provide an interesting example of the processes of acculturation. The Strabonian scenario of a small number of cities retaining their Greek culture intact while the rest 'become Roman' reflects a superficial measure of truth but grossly oversimplifies the cultural processes at work.[129] Within the framework of the Roman *municipia* or *colonia*, most cities managed to construct a distinctive local identity forged from disparate elements of Greek, Roman and Italic culture. The means by which this was achieved, and the results of the process, inevitably differed from city to city, and also at different levels of society, but all the evidence points to a complex process of cultural interaction, and emphatically not to the development of a monolithic and uniform Romanised Italy.

Epilogue: Magna Graecia in AD 200

By AD 200, the date chosen as the end point for this book, profound changes can be seen to have taken place in Magna Graecia, and even more profound ones were to come during the course of the third century.

The tendency towards administrative centralisation has become more marked, with the introduction of the office of *curator rei publicae* by Trajan. Increasing numbers of these officials are found in the epigraphy of southern Italy during the second century, and the trend increased in the third century, with the creation of the post of *corrector* to supervise Italy on a regional level. This clearly generated a considerable amount of munificence, as these figures are frequently mentioned in the epigraphy of the third and fourth centuries AD, either as donors of gifts to cities or in generalised decrees of thanks for benefactions. Although civic life continued uninterrupted, the impression given by the sources available is one of decreasing civic activity. Cities appear to rely increasingly on acts of euergetism from outsiders, rather than from their own élite. This dichotomy, however, becomes less clear cut. By the end of the second century, a large part of the Senate was composed of men of Italian origin, together with an increasing number of provincials. There is every possibility that what appears to be euergetism from external sources, mainly Roman notables, is in fact a reflection of the regional origins of many of these notables.

Whatever the causes, there is a definite change in the flavour of civic life towards the end of the second century AD, and in the early years of the third. The most immediately noticeable feature in the South is the disappearance of many Greek features of civic life in the course of the third century. The sequence of Greek inscriptions at Naples, Velia and Rhegium dies out around this date, although some of the Greek institutions may have persisted for a time. Latin epitaphs make reference

189

to the archonship and to the phratries at Naples, but elsewhere Greek civic institutions seem to have died out.

There is insufficient evidence to say for certain whether this was also true of priesthoods, festivals and other aspects of religious life, but here, as in other areas of civic activity, the general impression is of the absorption of the distinctive Greek practices into a wider pattern which is common to the whole of Italy. Greek cults continue to co-exist beside Roman ones, with an increasing admixture of cults from the Eastern provinces of the Empire. What does seem to disappear, however, is the high profile given to certain local cults and priesthoods.

Economically, the period 200 BC–AD 200 saw the transition from an economy based on small-scale peasant farming to one based on the villa. The dating of this change, the speed with which it took place, and its impact on the social and economic structure of the region may well have been overestimated, but this is not to deny that the villa was the main economic unit. Towards the end of the second century, however, this pattern begins to break down. Many villas which show continuity of occupation during the first two centuries AD are now abandoned or show signs of disruption, heralding a new period of economic upheaval.

In material culture, there is no doubt that Magna Graecia had undergone tremendous changes following the Roman conquest. Artisanal production of distinctive Greek styles of pottery, statuary and metalwork comes to an end during the second and first centuries BC. By the Early Empire, output of this type is almost completely Italicised in style. Despite this, strong local elements remain in the material culture of the South, something which can be traced with particular clarity in the funerary architecture of the region.

Clearly, the beginning of the third century forms something of a watershed, marking the end of both the economic and political stability enjoyed by Italy as a whole, and the Hellenising impetus among the Roman élite which had been so important to the flourishing Greek culture of southern Italy. After this date, the Greek trappings of civic life die away, but this is not to say that Magna Graecia ceases to be a significant region of Italy. It is very noticeable that there is an upsurge of epigraphy during the fourth century, and literary sources make many references to it during Late Antiquity. Finally, the wheel turns full circle. With the medieval incursions of the Byzantines into the western Mediterranean, Greek culture is once more introduced into southern Italy, where traces of it remain to this day.

Appendix: Italiote Greeks in the East

Name	Date BC	Provenance	Reference
Cumae			
Abris Kaikou	c. 80	Oropos	IG 7.417
Attinos Herakleidou	c.80	Oropos	IG 7.417
Minatos Minatou	180	Delphi	BCH 1880
Zoilos Zoilou	C4	Athens	IG 2/3.9116
Hedeia	Early C3	Athens	IG 2/3.9117
Naples			
Megakles Sosipatrou	275/4	Delphi	Flacelière 1937, 23a
Kyros	C3 (?)	Thebaid	Launey 1950, 2014
Agathokles Theodosiou	c. 80	Oropos	IG 7.416
Dionysios Diphilou	101/0	Athens	
Apollonios Dioscoridou	110/9	Delos	BCH 34, 15
Apollonios Dioscoridou	96/5	Delos	BCH 34, 15
Apollonias	96/5	Delos	BCH 34, 15
Artemo	96/5	Delos	BCH 34, 15
Artemidoros Sarapionos	c. 94	Delos	BCH 34, 17
Chaireas Philostratou	c. 100	Delos	BCH 34, 26
Philostratos Philostratou	c. 100	Delos	BCH 34, 67
Theophilos Philostratou	c. 100	Delos	BCH 34, 84
Sarapion Alexandrou	c. 100	Delos	BCH 34, 73
Sarapion Sarapionos	Late C2	Delos	BCH 34, 76
Sosigenes Theodorou	c. 97/6	Delos	BCH 34, 79
[. . .]les	Mid. C2	Delos	BCH 34, 98
[. . .]ou		Delos	BCH 34, 100
[. . .]ou	c. 94	Delos	BCH 34, 100
[. . .]iaou	C2	Tanagra	IG 7.516
Pelops Dexiai	222–205	Tanagra	IG 7.505
Pelops Dexiai		Oropos	IG 7.342
Isidoros Isidorou	Late C2	Athens	IG 2.470
Gaios Gaiou	Late C2	Delos	IDel 1.2601
Turillas	276/5	Delphi	FD 3.4.414
Velia			
Charopinas Antallou	188/7	Delphi	SGDI 2.2581

ROME AND THE WESTERN GREEKS 350 BC–AD 200

Name	Date BC	Provenance	Reference
Dionysios Degetou	188/7	Delphi	SGDI 2.2581
Eudoxos Aischronos	188/7	Delphi	SGDI 2.2581
Agathokles Hermonos	c. 140	Delos	BCH 34, 11–12
Aphobos	c. 158/7	Delos	BCH 34, 14
Apollodoros Dionysiou	Late C2	Delos	BCH 34, 13
Deiphilos Artemonos	Roman	Athens	IG 2/3.8483
[. . . . . .]tou	Early C2	Egypt	Launey 6012
Hermon Agathokleos	c. 150–40	Delos	BCH 34, 84
Menekles Pankratou	c. 100	Delos	BCH 34, 51
Nikomenes	c. 157/6	Delos	BCH 34, 54
Sosis	c. 158/7	Delos	BCH 34, 79
Theodote Dioskoridou		Delos	BCH 34, 84
Hermon Thrasydeios		Delos	BCH 34, 84
Thrasydeios Hermonos	Mid. C2	Delos	BCH 34, 84–5
Theon Hermonos	c. 100	Delos	BCH 34, 94
Zenon Hermonos	c. 100	Delos	BCH 34, 84
[. . .]ana Thrasydeiou	Late C2	Delos	BCH 34, 11, 97
[. . .]ous	c. 88	Delos	BCH 34, 100
[. . .]ou	Late C2	Delos	BCH 34, 101

Terina

| Megon Agesidamos | 390–339 | Epidauros | IG 4.1504 |
| [D]emo Euphronos | | Athens | IG 2.3387 |

Rhegium

| [. . . . . . .] | Mid. C3 | Tenos | IG 12.313 |
| Alkidamos Zenonos | 390–339 | Epidauros | IG 4.1504 |

Locri

Butios	390–339	Epidauros	IG 4.1504
Zoilos	Mid. C2	Delos	BCH 34, 94
[. . . .]		Athens	IG 2/3.9217
[. . . .]		Athens	IG 2/3.9218
[. . . .]		Athens	IG 2/3.9219

Thurii

Pasillas Phayllou	390–339	Epidauros	IG 4.1504
Damon	390–339	Epidauros	IG 4.1504
Agemos Lysonos	390–339	Epidauros	IG 4.1504

Croton

Diokles	344	Delphi	FD 3.4.
[. . . . .]	Roman	Thespiae	IG 7.1767
[. . . . .]les	Mid. C3	Tenos	IG 12.313
Sosikos Pythonos	390–339	Epidauros	IG 4.1504

Heraklea

Gorgeas Aischylou		Delphi	BCH 1938
Titos Satyrionos	Late C2	Delos	BCH 34, 84
Theodora Krateou	Late C2	Delos	BCH 34, 83–4
Titos Titou	Late C2	Delos	BCH 34, 85–6

Name	Date BC	Provenance	Reference
Satyros Titou	Late C2	Delos	BCH 34, 85–6
Theodora Titou	Late C2	Delos	BCH 34, 85–6
Posidippos Titou	Late C2	Delos	BCH 34, 85–6
Ariston	119/18	Delos	BCH 34, 85–6
Phrasillos [. . . . . io]u		Delphi	IDel 1.2598
Metron		Delos	
Diogenes Protogenou	c. 74	Delos	BCH 34, 39
Gorgias Damoxeno	c. 75/4	Delos	BCH 34, 39
Midas Zenonos	105–103	Delos	BCH 34, 52
Lysippos Lysippou	c. 100	Delos	BCH 34, 48
Posidippos Titou	c. 100	Delos	BCH 34, 70
Theophilos Aristionos		Delos	BCH 34, 84
Metapontum			
Leophron	Late C4/C3	Epidauros	IG 4.1215
Philemenos	390–339	Epidauros	IG 4.1504
Molon		Delphi	Flacelière 26a
Sokrates Molonos		Delphi	Flacelière 26a
Tarentum			
Diokles Diophaneos	C1	Thespiae	IG 7.1726
Dorotheos Dorotheou	C1	Orchomenos	IG 7.3197
Dorotheos Dorotheou	C2/C1	Argos	Vollgraff 1919, 252
Noumerios Leontos	C1	Melos	IG 12.3.1233
Asklepiodoros Pytheou	C1	Orchomenos	IG 7.3195
Hephaistion Demeou	267	Egypt	SEG 29.1114
Epigonos Damokrateos	c. 200	Kyme	SEG 29.1216
Antikrates	C4 or C3	Eretria	SEG 27.275
Aischrion Herakleidou	c. 160	Delos	BCH 34, 42
Nikokles Aristokleos	Mid. C3	Athens	IG 2/3.3779
Memnon Aristionos	C2/C1	Athens	IG 2/3.10412
Kaprion	C2/C1	Athens	IG 2/3.10412
Aristomanos Philaidou	C2/C1	Athens	IG 2/3.10412
Pieria Pythonos	C2	Athens	IG 2/3.10412
Theantas		Thebaid	Launey 601
Lysanias		Arsinoite	Launey 601
Sosibios		Arsinoite	Launey 601
Aristakos Herakleidou	c. 160	Delos	BCH 34, 42
Aristion Herakleidou	c. 160	Delos	BCH 34, 42
Kleano	c. 160	Delos	BCH 34, 42
Nikaso	c. 160	Delos	BCH 34, 42
Herakleides Herakleidou	c. 160	Delos	BCH 34, 42
Menekrates Herakleidou	c. 160	Delos	BCH 34, 42
Demetrios Dazou		Delos	BCH 34, 33
Eirene Simalou	Late C2	Delos	BCH 34, 35
Eukles Herakleidou	c. 157/6	Delos	BCH 34, 35
Herakleides Aristionos	179–169	Delos	BCH 34, 42
Myrallis Menekratou		Delos	BCH 34, 42
Parmenion Dazymou	158/7	Delos	BCH 34, 65

Name	Date BC	Provenance	Reference
Simalos Simalou	102/1	Delos	BCH 34, 78
Simalos Simalou	101/0	Athens	BCH 34, 78
Simalos Timarchou	c. 100	Delos	BCH 34, 79
Sokrates	c. 151/0	Delos	BCH 34, 79
[. . . .]des [. . .]b[. .]ou	c. 200	Delos	BCH 34, 78
[. . . . .]	Late C2	Delos	BCH 34, 101
Philon Philonos	C1	Tanagra	IG 7.540
Leon Pantaleontos	264 or 232	Oreus	IG 9.1127
Drakon Lykonos		Delos	IG 11,108
[. . . . . .]	C2	Clitor	IG 5.368
[. . . . . .]	Mid. C3	Tenos	IG 12.313
[. . . . . .]	205–203	Delphi	FD 3.4.613
Philippos Philinou		Egypt	Launey 601
[. . . . .]		Thebaid	Launey 601
Andronikos Philippou	205/4	Delphi	Flacelière 89
Euandros	272/1	Delphi	Flacelière 26a
Euthymeides	272/1	Delphi	Flacelière 26a
Zopyros Lamiskou	253/2	Delphi	Flacelière 86
Hippos	205/4	Delphi	Flacelière 89a
Xenaithos	234/3	Delphi	Flacelière 64b
Xeneas Xenaithou	234/3	Delphi	Flacelière 64b
Philippides	205/4	Delphi	Flacelière 89a
[. . . . . .]los		Delphi	Flacelière 26a
Lykos Philea	189/8	Delphi	Syll³.585
Pison Damoxenis	390–339	Epidauros	IG 4.1504

Notes

INTRODUCTION

1 '. . . Magna Graecia, which is now deserted, was then flourishing . . .' Cic. Am. 13.

2 The most striking example of the disappearance of a city is that of Paestum, which drops entirely out of the historical record during the Middle Ages and was not rediscovered until the middle of the eighteenth century. Pedley 1990, 14–17, 164–8.

3 Frederiksen 1984, 264–84; Sartori 1953, 143–56, 165–72.

4 Finley 1975a, 61–5.

5 For area studies of other regions of southern Italy, see Salmon 1965 and Frederiksen 1984.

6 Rawson 1985, 3–114.

7 Plut. Cat. Mai. 3.7; Astin 1978, 14.

8 Rawson 1985, 20–37; Cic. Arch. 4–11.

9 Pallottino 1991.

10 Bowersock 1990, 1–13.

11 Whitehouse and Wilkins 1989, 102–26.

12 Bowersock 1990, 2–18.

13 Orr 1983, 93–109; Gellner 1983, 8–23.

14 These changes varied widely from region to region, but a representative selection of examples are given by Bruun 1975, 15–27, Kaimio 1975, 225–9, Frederiksen 1959, 80–130 and Salmon 1965, 387–404.

15 Maddoli 1982, 9–33; Napoli 1978, 29–43; Calderone 1976, 34–50; Ciaceri 1940, 11, 188; E. Greco 1970, 416–20; Cazzaniga 1971, 26–31.

16 Pind. Pyth. 1.146; Eurip. Med. 439–40; Tro. 1110–17; Iph. Aul. 1378.

17 Maddoli 1982, 9–11; Timaeus FGH 566 F 13 (Schol. T.Plat. Phaedr. 279C); Pol. 2.39.1; Napoli 1978, 30–43.

18 Pol. 2.39.1.

19 Plin. N.H. 3.38 and 95; App. Samn. 7.1; Serv. Aen. 1.569; Sen. Helv. 7.2; Strab. 6.1.2; Sil. It. 11.20; Ps. Scymn. 303. On the changing geographical definitions of Magna Graecia, see Musti 1988, 78–94.

20 Dion. Hal. 1.35; Arist. Pol. B296; Thuc. 6.34, 44, 7.3; Herodot. 3.137; Calderone 1955, 77–124; Pallottino 1991, 41–5.

21 Momigliano 1929, 47–52.

22 Strab. 6.2.1–11; E. Greco 1970, 416–20; Cazzaniga 1971, 26–31. On Antiochus, see Strab. 6.1.4 and Musti 1988, 68–74.
23 Just. 20.1.
24 Plut. Cam. 22.2; Plut. Rom. 2; Fest. 326, 329; Dion. Hal. 1.72–3; Ov. Fast. 4.64; Athen. 12.523e.
25 Plin. N.H. 3.42.
26 Calderone 1976, 34–50; Musti 1988, 87–94.
27 Calderone 1976, 34–5; Maddoli 1982, 10–11; Musti 1988, 87–94; Iamb. Vit. Pyth. 166; Nicom. Geras. ap Porph. Vit. Pyth. 20.
28 Napoli 1978, 30–43.
29 Maddoli 1982, 9–33; Calderone 1976, 34–50; Ciaceri 1940, 11, 188; Cantarella 1968, 11–25; Musti 1988, 78–94.
30 Cic. De Or. 2.154, 3.139; Tusc. 1.38; Val. Max. 8.7.2.
31 Plin. N.H. 3.42.
32 Strab. 5.4.7, IG 14.645.
33 Plin. N.H. 3.104; Verg. Aen. 3.401–2; Herodot. 7.170; Strab. 5.1.4, 5.1.9, 6.3.9; Lycoph. Alex. 590–608; Schol. Lycoph. 590–8; Pallottino 1991, 40-5. A discussion of possible sources and a full list of references to Greek heroic foundations in Italy is given by Pearson 1987, 59–90 and Musti 1988, 173–95. The intriguing possibility that the Diomedes myth was adopted by Iullus Antonius and the remains of the Antonian faction, in opposition to Augustus, is offered by Coppola 1990, 125–37.
34 D'Arms 1970; and Chapter 10 in this volume.
35 Strab. 6.1.2.
36 Finley 1975b, 120–33.
37 For discussion of possible Italiote sources for the history of the West to 270 BC, see Pearson 1987 and Musti 1988, 11–60.
38 Von Fritz 1940, 60–1; De Sensi Sestito 1987, 85–113; Maddoli 1982, 9–30.
39 Plut. Pyrr., 13.2–5; App. Samn., 7.1–3; Dion. Hal., 19.5.1–7.3; Dio 9.39.2–10; Zon. 8.2. On the manipulation of the historical tradition to validate Roman actions and deflect the charge of Roman aggression, see Rowland 1983, 749–62.
40 Ath. 1.26e, 4.138d, 13.605a, 6.273b-c, 12.518c.
41 Plato Laws 1.637.
42 Pol. 8.24.1.
43 Plut. Pyrr., 13.2–5; App. Samn., 7.1–3; Dion. Hal., 19.5.1–7.3; Dio 9.39.2–10; Zon. 8.2; Theopomp. ap. Ath. 4.166e-f; Strab. 6.3.4.
44 Zon 8.2; App. Samn. 8; Plut. Pyrr. 13.2.
45 Hor. Sat. 2.4.34; Epist. 1.7.45.
46 Dio Chrys. 33.35; Juv. Sat. 3.2–3; Cic. Am. 13.
47 Juv. Sat. 3.2–3; CIL 10.3682–713.
48 Cic. Am. 13.
49 Strab. 6.3.4.
50 Livy 24.2.8.
51 Sen. Epist. 68.5.
52 De Sensi Sestito 1987, 84–90.
53 Momigliano 1959, 529–56; Pearson 1987, 1–3, 37–51.
54 Pol. 12.3.1–16.14.
55 Petrochilos 1974.
56 Pallottino 1991, 3–21.

NOTES

1 THE GEOGRAPHY AND EARLY SETTLEMENT OF MAGNA GRAECIA

1 Braudel 1973, I, 25–102.
2 Delano Smith 1979, 14–21.
3 Pedley 1990, 29–36; Paget 1968, 152–69; Frederiksen 1984, 14–23.
4 Delano Smith 1979, 159–66.
5 Plin. N.H. 3.60; Strab. 5.4.3; Pol. 3.91.
6 The earliest drainage scheme was attributed to Aristodemos of Cumae (Plut. Mul. Virt. 262a–b), but most of the ancient drainage and land reclamation schemes were of Roman date. Agrippa undertook harbour construction at Cumae, and drainage schemes were undertaken by both Nero and Domitian. Stat. Silv. 4.3.72–89; Suet. Nero 31; Paget 1968, 152–69.
7 Frederiksen 1984, 6–12.
8 IG 14.727 (=CIL 10.1481).
9 Scherillo 1977, 81–116; Frederiksen 1984, 14–17; Beloch 1890, 145–67.
10 Verg. Aen. 6.8–265; Austin 1976, 49–58; Paratore 1977, 9–39.
11 To avoid confusion, Greek cities will be referred to throughout by the Italicised names used by the majority of sources for Italian history, although in most instances these were not the original Greek names. An exception will be made for Naples, for which I shall use the modern (Anglicised) form in order to avoid the complications created by the multiple foundations of different names on the site of modern Naples. A list of the Greek originals is included in Table 1.
12 Strab. 6.1 9; Brunt 1971, 359–61; Toynbee 1965, 545–6.
13 Livy 34.53.1–2.
14 Cic. Am. 13, De Or. 2.154, 3.139; Tusc. 1.38; Val. Max. 8.7.2; Ath. 1.26e, 4.138d, 13.605a, 6.273b–c, 12.518.
15 Plin. N.H. 8.190, 9.137; Ed. Dioc. 21.2, 25.1; Morel 1978, 94–110; Frayn 1984, 20–4; Varro R.R. 2.2.1.8.
16 Ampolo 1980, 175.
17 Susini 1962, 11–15; E. Greco 1981, 196–9; D'Andria 1979, 15–28 and 1990; Yntema 1982, 63–82. Strab. 6.3.5–6 describes Rudiae as a Greek city and attributes Cretan ancestry to the Iapygians.
18 Peroni 1983, 211–83; Kilian 1990, 455–6.
19 Kilian 1990, 455–6 and figs 4 and 6. The highest concentration of sites with Mycenaean material, however, are in Puglia.
20 Kilian 1990, 455–8. The persistence of contacts and their apparent tendency to spread inland, as indicated by the diffusion of Late Helladic IIIC material, suggests a significant degree of contact.
21 Strab. 14.2.10, possibly using a Rhodian source, as suggested by Bérard 1941, 72–5. Pugliese Carratelli 1962, 241–6 suggests that some of the extra-mural sanctuaries of Magna Graecia were sites of Mycenaean cult places.
22 Graham 1990, 45–52.
23 Boardman 1980, 162.
24 Al Mina, once thought to be a Greek colony, is now known to be a Phoenician city, although with a large Greek element in the population. Pithecusae still looks to be a Greek foundation. Boardman 1980, 165–8.

197

25 Herring 1991b, 35–7.
26 Strab. 6.1.14, 6.3.4; Diod. 11.90.3, 12.10.1–11.3; Herodot. 5.45.
27 Diod. 12.35.1–2, 13.3.4, 5.3, 11.1.
28 See Chapters 3–5 in this volume.
29 Dion. Hal. 1.35; Herodot. 7.170; Plin. N.H. 3.104; Verg. Aen. 3.401–2; Strab. 5.1.4, 5.1.9, 6.3.6–9; Lycoph. Alex. 590–608; Schol. Lycoph. 590–8; Pallottino 1991, 40–5; Pearson 1987, 59–90; Musti 1988, 173–95.
30 Susini 1962, 11–15; Herodot. 7.170; Strab. 6.3.6–9.
31 The language spoken in south-east Apulia, Messapian, appears to be Illyrian in origin. Pulgram 1958, 210–16; Parlangèli 1960, 14. For other cultural links, see Nava 1990, 560–78.
32 Hecat. FGrH 1 F 61; Antiochus FGrH 555 F 7; Hellanicus 4 F 79 a–b. Frederiksen 1984, 135-7.
33 The whereabouts of the Opikoi and their relationship to Osci have been debated by both ancient and modern historians. Thuc. 6.2.4, 6.4.5; Plat. Epist. 8; Arist. Pol. 1329a40, 1329b18; Frederiksen 1984, 136–8.
34 La Genière 1979, 60–1.
35 D'Andria 1990; Boersma and Yntema 1987.
36 D'Andria 1989, 63–70; Moretti 1971, 24–7; E. Greco 1981, 218–19, 239–43. For a discussion of the relationship between Greek foundations and Italic synoecism, see Herring 1991b, 37–42.
37 E. Greco 1981, 56–7.
38 Strab. 6.3.6; Thuc. 7.33.
39 D'Agostino 1968, 78–205 and 1977; De Caro and Greco 1981, 120–5.
40 Pellegrini 1903, 204–94; Albore Livadie 1975, 53–8; D'Agostino 1968, 78–205.
41 La Genière 1979, 71–4.
42 Zancani Montuoro et al. 1972, 9–33; La Genière 1979, 76–7.
43 Herring 1991b, 37–42.
44 La Genière 1979, 64–7; Boersma and Yntema 1987.
45 Moretti 1971, 22–34.
46 La Genière 1979, 86.
47 La Genière 1979, 86–7.
48 La Genière 1979, 87; Morel 1983, 123–62.
49 Frederiksen 1984, 117–29.
50 There is also a tradition in the ancient sources which attributes the foundation of Pompeii, Capua and twelve other Campanian cities to the Etruscans (Strab. 5.4.3 and 8; Livy 4.37.1–2; Vell. Pat. 1.7; Plin. N.H. 3.61 and 70; Pol. 2.17.1; Theophrastus H.P 9.16.6; Philistus FGH 556 F 43). Archaeological evidence supports an Etruscan presence but does not conclusively prove Etruscan foundation. Frederiksen 1984, 117–25.
51 Strab. 5.4.3 and 8; Livy 4.37.1–2; Vell. Pat. 1.7; Plin. N.H. 3.61 and 70.
52 La Genière 1979, 87; Whitehouse and Wilkins 1989, 108–16.
53 The two most striking examples of internecine warfare among the Greeks are the destruction of Sybaris by Croton in 510 BC and the destruction of Siris at an unspecified date in the sixth century. Graeco-Italic coalitions were formed by Alexander of Epirus in 335–3 (alliance with the Peucetians, Diod. 12.2.6–12) and Naples in 327 (a short-lived coalition with Nola against Rome; Livy 8.23.1; Dion. Hal. 15.6.1–5).

54 After the initial aggressive phase, Greek expansion inland seems to be limited, although there is ample evidence for flourishing economic contacts. Herring 1991b, 33–54; Whitehouse and Wilkins 1989, 108–16.
55 Moretti 1953 and 1957; Strab. 6.1.12; Paus. 10.10.6, 13.10.
56 Livy 1.18.2; Pol 2.39.1; Strab. 6.1.1, 1.12, 3.4; Diod. 10.18.2; Plut. adv. Coloten. 32.1126a–d; Von Fritz 1940; Musti 1966, 323–5, 328–9.
57 Livy 2.9.6, 2.14.5–9, 2.21.5–6, 2.34.3–4. Relations soured rapidly after the fall of Cumae to the Samnites. Livy 4.44.12, 4.52.6; Ogilvie 1965, 256–7, 269.
58 Ath. 12.522d (= Clearchos, FGrH ll, fr.9); Paus. 10.10.6, 13.10; Herodot. 7.170; Diod. 11.52, Arist. Pol. 1302b33; Wuilleumier 1939, 53–8. Ciaceri 1940, 129 rejects the story of the sack of Karbina and the impious slaughter of suppliants in the temple of Zeus Kataibates, but archaeological evidence from Carovigno seems to indicate destruction of the site early in the fifth century (E. Greco 1981, 200). Fragments of monumental bronze statuary from Tarentum, now in the British Museum, have been identified as being from a copy of one of the Delphic groups. Williams 1989, 529–53 suggests that it was an equestrian figure from the later group, set up in the *agora* at Tarentum.
59 Diod. 11.51; Pind. Pyth. 1.72.
60 Strab. 6.1.6–8, 6.1.10.
61 Diod. 13.3.4; Strab. 6.1.14, 6.3.4.
62 Strab. 5.4.7; Schol. ad Lycoph. Alex. 732 (=FGrH 566 Timeus F98).
63 Rutter 1979, 5–6, 45, 94–5; Lepore 1967, 179; Frederiksen 1984, 103–5; Càssola 1986, 62–5. An Athenian strategos called Diotimos, who held office in 433 BC, is known from epigraphic evidence. Davies 1971, 161.
64 Livy 8.22.5; Vell. Pat. 1.4.2; Plin. N.H. 3.62; Stat. Silv. 5.3.104–6 and 109–11; Lutat. fr.7 (FRH 1.192); Ps. Scymn. 251.
65 Strab. 14.2.10; Steph. Byz. s.v. Παρθενοπη; Frederiksen 1984, 86–7.
66 Livy 8.22.5. Lepore 1967, 228–39 suggests that sources for a division of the city may have their origins in the ethnic division between Greeks and Samnites mentioned by Strabo 5.4.7.
67 Diod. 12.54.4, 13.3.4–5; Thuc. 6.44–50, 7.1; Gomme 1970, 310–16.
68 Pol. 2.39.1–8; Walbank 1957, 222–7; Ghinatti 1961, 117–33; De Sensi Sestito 1984, 41–50; Wuilleumier 1939, 70–1; Ciaceri 1940, 436; Larsen 1968, 95–7. Polybios names the federal headquarters as the sanctuary of Zeus Homarios, but De Sensi Sestito makes a persuasive case for the use of the sanctuary of Hera Lacinia as a federal meeting place. Larsen identifies the Italiote League as a significant entity in the history of Greek federalism as it is an early example of a defensive League.
69 There are no references to the members of the League after its revival, but there is a certain amount of circumstantial evidence that it included Tarentum, Thurii, Heraklea and Naples. Livy 8.25.7–8, 27.2; Dion. Hal. 15.5.2–3; Strab. 6.3.4.
70 Frederiksen 1984, 136–7; Salmon 1965, 28–49.
71 Strab. 6.1.4; Diod. 20.15; Just. 23.1; Salmon 1965, 39–43; Frederiksen 1984, 136–7.
72 Livy 4.37.1, 44.12; Diod. 12.23.2, 76.4, 14.101–3; Front. Strat. 2.3.12; Polyaenus 2.10.2; Frederiksen 1984, 136–9.

73 Diod 12.31.1, 14.15.1. Frederiksen 1984, 137 and 150 suggests a possible Greek source for this chronology but it can only be regarded as an approximation, not as an accurate date.

74 Strab. 5.4.7.

75 Italic names are found in Greek inscriptions as early as the seventh century. A protocorinthian *lekythos* from Cumae is inscribed with the name of its owner, Tataia (IG 14.865; Jeffrey 1961, 240). IG 14.861 records a second-century BC dedication to Apollo by Dekmos Heios, son of Pakios ('Ἀπολλωνι Κυμαιω Δεκμος 'Ειος Πακιου . . .') and the Table of Heraklea (IG 14.645) includes the Hellenised Messapian name Dasumos, son of Pyrrhos.

76 Aristox. ap. Ath. 14.632a–b; Pugliese Carratelli 1972, 37–54; Fraschetti 1981, 97–115.

77 Cic. Leg. Ag. 2.93; Livy 23.2.1.

78 Vetter 1953, nos. 112–18; Frederiksen 1984, 140–8.

79 Sartori 1953, 60–77, 145–56.

80 The chief of these were the Hellenised cities of Consentia and Petelia, both of which are known from literary sources, and Serra di Vaglio, a large site in the Basento valley, which flourished in the fourth century but which is known only from archaeological evidence. Livy 23.4–10 refers to Petelia as an 'urbs' but to other Bruttians as 'ignobiles populi' or 'ignobiles civitates' (25.2, 29.38.1 30.19.10–20.5). Strabo 6.1.3 names Petelia as the 'μητρόπολις . . . τών κώνων', the chief city of the Chones. E. Greco 1981, 161–74.

81 The Greek temple at Canosa provides a good example of Hellenised Italic architecture in a non-military context (Pensabene 1990, 269–350). At Serra di Vaglio, there are Greek fortifications completed by the magistrate Nummelos and commemorated by a Greek inscription (E. Greco 1981, 167–9). On trade networks, see Herring 1991a.

82 Whitehouse and Wilkins 1989, 102–26.

83 Strab. 6.1.8 and 10; Dion. Hal. 20.7.2–3; Diod. 14.44.4–45.1, 102.1–108.6; Ciaceri 1940, 409–42.

84 Diog. Laert. 8.79–3; Diod. 14.109.1–5; Ath. 12.519b; Plat. Epist. 8; Cic. Rep. 1.59–60; Ael. Var. Hist. 7.14; Suda s.v. 'Αρχύτας; Plut. Dion 18.2, 20.1; Strab. 6.3.4.

85 Brauer 1986, 49–51.

86 Vattuone 1976–7, 285–300.

87 Arist. Pol. 1399b33; Sartori 1953, 84–8; Brauer 1986, 44–6, 49–52.

2 ROMAN CONQUEST: MAGNA GRAECIA 350–270 BC

1 Liv. 24.2.8. *Stasis* existed in the earlier history of Magna Graecia, as witness the ejection of Pythagorean factions and various episodes of tyranny, but this is the first point at which we can analyse its effects on external relations.

2 See Chapter 3 in this volume.

3 Strab. 6.3.4; Polyaen. Strat. 4.2.1.

4 Pol. 2.39.1–8; Walbank 1957, 222–7; Larsen 1968, 95–7; Ghinatti 1961–2, 117–33; De Sensi Sestito 1984, 41–50.

5 Plut. Pyrr. 13.5–6 makes it clear that this was an Italiote, not just a Tarentine, initiative.
6 Frederiksen 1984, 207–24; Strab. 6.3.4; Just. 8.2.1.
7 Hülsen, RE 907; Strab. 6.1.2; Fest. 35; Livy 30.19.10, 35.1.2.
8 Diod. 20.104.1, 21.4, 16.63.2, 19.4.1; Brauer 1986, 62.
9 Strab. 6.3.4; Polyaen. Strat. 4.2.1; Plut. Pyrr. 13.2–5; App. Samn. 7.1–3; Dion. Hal. 19.5.1–7.3; Dio 9.39.2–10; Zon. 8.2.
10 Livy 8.27.1–29.1; Plut. Pyrr. 14.3; App. Samn. 8; Dio 10.48.
11 Diod. 20.104.1–105.3; Livy 10.21.15.
12 For example, Plut. Pyrrh. 13.5.
13 Dion. Hal. 20.4.2; Plin. N.H. 34.32; Val. Max. 1.8.6.
14 Giannelli 1974; Lévèque 1957, 452–65.
15 Plut. Agis 3.2; Diod. 16.62.4 and 63.2; Plin. N.H. 3.98 (=Theopomp. FGrH 1.3. Fr.259 and 261); Wuilleumier 1939, 80–1; Ciaceri 1930. For a discussion of the chronological problems, see Giannelli 1969, 1–6; Brauer 1986, 63.
16 Livy 8.3.6, 17.9, 24.4; Diod. 16.15, 16.90.2; Just. 12.2; Aul. Gell. NA 17.21; Strab. 6.3.4; Wuilleumier 1939, 81–7. Brauer 1986, 68–73 gives a discussion of the numismatic evidence. For chronological problems, see Giannelli 1969, 7–22.
17 Livy 8.17.9; Pedley 1990, 108–9.
18 Livy 8.24.4.
19 Strabo 6.3.4 suggests that the ultimate plan was to construct a fortified, purpose-built meeting place. For alternative interpretations, see Giannelli 1969, 11–13. Since there is no corroborative evidence for disagreements between Tarentum and Alexander, and Livy 8.24.4 mentions the recapture of Heraklea from the Lucanians, this seems plausible.
20 Livy 8.24.5–15; Strab. 6.3.4.
21 Diod. 19.4; Strab. 6.3.4.
22 Diod. 19.70.1–71.2.
23 The chronology of the campaigns of Acrotatos, Cleonymus and Agathocles are very uncertain: cf. Meloni 1950, 103–21 and Giannelli 1974, 353–80. The chronology adopted here is that suggested by Brauer 1986, 63–80, and based partly on numismatic evidence.
24 Diod. 20.104.1–105.3; Livy 10.1–2; Leonid. Anth. Pal. 6.129–131; Paus. 4.36.2; Duris ap. Athen. 13.605d; Ps. Arist. Mir. Ausc. 78. The size of the fine has been dismissed as an exaggeration, but Carter 1990, 423–5 estimates that it must have been almost equivalent to the annual agricultural surplus produced by the territory, a large but not impossible sum.
25 Diod. 19.4, 21.4; Strab. 6.1.5, 3.4; Just. 23.1; Wuilleumier 1939, 91 and 96–7; Giannelli 1974, 370–80.
26 Dio 4 (=Zon. 7.12); Dion. Hal. 12.1.9; Livy 8.26.6; Calderone 1976, 60–70. Gruen 1991, 7–9 and 39–40 stresses the importance of religious and cultural contacts with southern Italy and Sicily before the second century BC.
27 Livy 8.22.7–29.5; Dion. Hal. 15.5.1–9.2.
28 Salmon 1965, 215–19; Frederiksen 1984, 206–9.
29 Livy 8.23.1–2; Dion. Hal. 15.7.3.
30 Livy 8.22.7.
31 Livy 8.23.1–3, 23.7; Dion. Hal. 15.5.2–6.5.

32 For the topography of fourth-century Naples and the division between Palaepolis and Neapolis, see Chapter 1, n. 6 in this volume.
33 Livy 8.25.8. However, this may well be an anti-Oscan tradition.
34 Livy 8.26.6–7; Cic. Balb.8.21.
35 Livy 8.22.7–29.5; Dion. Hal. 15.5.1–9.2.
36 Dion. Hal. 15.5.1–9.2; Frederiksen 1984, 210–11.
37 Livy 8.25.8; Dion. Hal. 15.5.2; Frederiksen 1984, 208–12.
38 The so-called Campano-Tarentine coinage provides evidence of economic connections between Naples and Tarentum, being minted at Tarentum using a Campanian weight standard. The date, however, is uncertain and varies between c. 327 and c. 260–50 BC. See Evans 1889, 131–23; Breglia 1947–8, 227–47; Lepore 1967, 225.
39 Livy 8.25.5–9; Dion. Hal. 15.4.1–5; Frederiksen 1984, 208–12.
40 Livy 24.2.8 generalises from this to imply that all democrats were anti-Roman.
41 Frederiksen 1984, 158–79; Pugliese Carratelli 1969, 49–82.
42 Livy 8.25.9. See Dion. Hal. 15.6.2.
43 Von Fritz 1940, 56–61; Frederiksen 1984, 148.
44 Athen. 16.632a; Strabo 6.1.3.
45 There is evidence for continuity of Greek names, language and culture at Paestum long after the Lucanian conquest. Pugliese Carratelli 1972, 37–54; E. Greco 1981, 18–19; Pedley 1990, 97–112.
46 Livy Per. 12; Vell. Pat. 1.14.7.
47 Livy 10.44.8–45.11.
48 Livy 8.27.1–28.11.
49 Livy 8.27.1–4.
50 Frederiksen 1984, 208.
51 Dion. Hal. 5.1.
52 Cic. Sen. 39; Powell 1988, 181–4; Guzzo 1983, 191–246.
53 Frederiksen 1984, 180–1, 207–24.
54 Frederiksen 1984, 207–24.
55 Livy 8.17.10; Braccesi 1974, 196–202; Manni 1962, 344–52.
56 Herring 1991b, 42–4.
57 Livy 9.14.1–9.
58 Livy 9.26.3; Dion. Hal. 17.5.2; Salmon 1965, 231–2. In particular, the Roman colonisation in Apulia seemed to indicate an increasing interest in the South, and a closer approach to the Tarentine sphere of influence.
59 Livy 9.14.1–9.
60 Gruen 1984, 96–101. Arbitration was a recognised means of settling disputes in the Greek world, but was not used by Rome before 200 BC. Pyrrhus offered to arbitrate in the dispute between Rome and the Italiotes but was refused.
61 Livy 9.14.1–9.
62 Cary 1920, 164–73; Giannelli 1974, 363; Brauer 1986, 121–35.
63 App. Samn. 7.1; Dio 39.4; Zon. 8.2.
64 App. Samn. 7.1; Wuilleumier 1939, 98–110; Garoufalias 1979, 300–12; Brauer 1986, 121–35.
65 Livy 7.25.3–4, 26.10–11, 26.13–15.
66 Diod. 10.104; Just. 12.2.1; Livy 10.2.1–3, 3.4–11. The appointment of *duoviri Navales* for the first time in 311 BC points to an increasing Roman

NOTES

interest in sea-power and a possible encroachment on Tarentine spheres of interest.
67 App. Samn. 7.1.
68 App. Samn. 7.1–2; Livy Per. 11; Plin. N.H. 34.32; Dion. Hal. 19.13, 20.4; Val. Max. 1.8.6.
69 App. Samn. 7.1–2.
70 Zon. 8.2.
71 Livy 24.2.8.
72 Plut. Pyrr. 13.5–6; Zon. 8.2; App. Samn. 7.2; Dion. Hal. 19.8.
73 For a discussion of sources, see Lévèque 1957, 18–79.
74 Lévèque 1957, 537–42.
75 Plut. Pyrr. 14.2–7; Just. 18.1.1; Dio 40.4; Zon. 8.2. Alexander of Epirus is said to have attempted to conquer an empire in emulation of Alexander the Great. Just. 12.2; Aul. Gell. NA 17.21.
76 Livy Per. 12–14; Plut. Pyrrh. 13.5–6; Strab. 6.3.5; App. Samn. 10.1; Lévèque 1957, 280, 303–7.
77 Pol. 1.7.1; App. Samn. 7.1, 9.1; Livy 31.31.6–8; Dion. Hal. 20.4; Livy Per. 12; Walbank 1957, 49–53.
78 Calderone 1976, 71–80; De Franciscis 1972, 75–84; E. Greco 1981, 88–94; Head 1911, 103–4.
79 Pol. 1.7.1; App. Samn. 9.1; Livy 31.31.6–8; Dion. Hal. 20.4; Livy Per. 12.
80 App. Samn. 9.1–3, 12.1; Front. Strat. 4.1.38; Livy 28.28.1–7, 31.31.6–8; Per.12, Per. 15; Pol. 1.6.8, 7.1; Dion. Hal. 20.4.1–5.5, 20.16; Dio 9.40.7–12.
81 App. Samn. 7.3; Zon. 8.368–9.
82 Salmon 1965, 265–70.
83 Càssola 1962.
84 Livy Per.12, 31.7.11; Zon. 8.368; Plut. Pyrr. 16; Dion. Hal. 19.9; Just. 18.1.1; Flor. 1.13.18.
85 Franke 1989, 463–6.
86 Paus. 1.12.1; Gruen 1991, 20; Lévèque 1957, 251–8.
87 Gruen 1984; n. 63 in this chapter.
88 Franke 1989, 468.
89 App. Samn. 9.1–3, 12.1; Front. Strat. 4.1.38; Livy 28.28.1–7, 31.31.6–8; Per. 12, Per. 15; Pol. 1.6.8, 7.1; Dion. Hal. 20.4.1–5.5, 20.16; Dio 9.40.7–12.
90 Plut. Pyrr. 16. For the chronology of the negotiations, see Lefkowitz 1959, 147–75.
91 Staveley 1959, 418–33.
92 De Franciscis 1972, 75–84.
93 Cic. Fin. 2.61; Tusc. 1.39; Plut. Pyrr. 21.5–10.
94 Plut. Pyrr. 22.1; Franke 1989, 473–81.
95 Zon. 8.377; Front. Strat. 3.6.4; App. Samn. 12.1–2.
96 Plut. Pyrr 25.5–26.5; Zon 8.378; Livy 29.18.1–9.
97 Plut. Pyrr. 26.1–2.
98 Livy Per. 15. Zonaras' 8.6 assertion that at Tarentum the walls were demolished and a tribute levied is unlikely.
99 Head 1911, 103–4.
100 App. Samn. 9.3; Dion. Hal. 20.5.5.
101 Salmon 1965, 288–92.

203

102 The setting up of the municipal laws of Heraklea at the League sanctuary argues that it was still of major significance in the first century BC. Crawford forthcoming.

3 THE PUNIC WARS

1 For a discussion of Livy's sources, cf. Walsh 1974, 20–54, 110–37.
2 See Introduction in this volume, pp. 13–17.
3 Von Fritz 1940, 60–1; De Sensi Sestito 1987, 92–4.
4 See Introduction in this volume, pp. 13–17.
5 Momigliano 1959.
6 Von Fritz 1940, 60–1; De Sensi Sestito 1987, 92–4; Livy 24.2.1–7 places emphasis on the occurrence of *stasis*. Cf. Walsh 1974, 37.
7 Livy 24.2.1–7.
8 App. Samn. 7.1.
9 Walsh 1974, 37.
10 Ciaceri 1932, 1–6; Pugliese Caratelli 1972, 37–54.
11 Livy 22.58.1–7; Pol. 3.77.2–7.
12 Sil. It. 12.63–81; Livy 24.13.6–7; Wuilleumier 1939, 70–5.
13 The Samnite League may not have been dissolved until 270, long after the conquest of most of the region. Salmon 1965, 291–2.
14 Gruen 1984, 55–95.
15 See Chapter 6 in this volume for a discussion of the evidence for connections between Magna Graecia and the Aegean.
16 Pol. 1.20.14; Walbank 1957, 74–5. For discussion of the naval contributions during the first Punic War see Thiel 1954, 64–76; Ciaceri 1931–2, 39–59.
17 Pol. 2.23.1–24.17.
18 Pol 3.75.4; Livy 25.10.1–3.
19 Livy 23.1.5–7, 14.5–9, 15.1–6, 35.3–38.3.
20 Livy 36.2.7, 35.23.5, 40.18.40; App. Syr. 15.
21 Livy Per. 14; Dio 11.43.1.
22 Livy 25.10.1–3.
23 Livy 22.58.1–9; Pol. 3.77.2–7.
24 Badian 1958, 141–5; Salmon 1980, 78–83.
25 Gruen 1984, 133–53.
26 Diod. 18.55.4, 19.61.3; Täubler 1913, 434–6; Gruen 1984, 133–53.
27 Pol. 4.84.4–5.
28 App. Samn. 10.1; Ined. Vat. 2; Pol. 1.7.10–13; Livy 29.27.1, 31.31.7; Gruen 1984, 143–4.
29 Sil. It. 9.1–27; Livy 22.61.10–12.
30 Livy 24.1.1–3.15, 25.11.1–13.10, 25.15.2–5; App. Hann. 6.32–5.
31 Livy 23.2.1–10.1.
32 Livy 23.1.5–7, 14.5–9, 15.1–6.
33 Livy 23.15.1.
34 Livy 23.35.1–36.10.
35 Livy 23.33.4, 23.38.8.
36 Livy 24.1.1–3.
37 Livy 23.30.8, 23.41.12.

NOTES

38 The importance of this sanctuary is indicated by Pol. 3.33.18, 56.4 and Livy
28.46.16. The continuing wealth of the sanctuary is mentioned by Livy
24.3.3–8. It had symbolic importance as it was traditionally a political and
religious centre for both the Italiotes and their Italian neighbours, and had
been the original headquarters of the Italiote League. Cf. De Sensi Sestito
1984, 41–50.
39 App. Hann. 9.57.
40 Livy 24.3.1–2.
41 Livy 29.6.1–7.17, 29.19.7–9, 27.35.3–4.
42 Livy 24.13.1–9, 24.20.9–16.
43 Livy 26.39.1–23, 25.11.1–13.10, 25.15.2–5, 25.22.14–16, 26.5.1; Pol.
8.32–33; App. Hann. 6.34; Zon. 9.5.
44 Livy 26.39.5.
45 App. Hann. 8.49; Plut. Fab. 22; Livy 27.15.9–16.16, 29.6.4–9.12.
46 App. Hann. 57–8; Livy 30.20.3–9.
47 Livy 8.14.10–11; Vell. Pat. 1.14.3; Fest. 126L.
48 Dion. Hal. 15.6.4; Vell. Pat. 1.4.2; Sil.It. 8.534; Diod. 12.76.4; Frederiksen
1984, 139, 143–4.
49 Strabo 5.4.7.
50 Livy 8.25.7–27.3; Dion. Hal. 15.5.2–8.
51 Livy 8.27.6; Ciaceri 1932, 19–21.
52 Plut. Marc. 10.1; Zon 9.2; Livy 23.14.5, 15.2.
53 Livy Per. 14; Vell. Pat. 1.14.7; Magaldi 1947, 199–202.
54 Livy 27.10.7–8.
55 Livy 26.39.5.
56 Livy 22.36.9.
57 Pugliese Caratelli 1972, 43–5; Pedley 1990, 97–112.
58 Val. Max. 1.1.1; Cic. Balb. 24.55; CIL 10.467; AE 1978.261.
59 Livy 26.39.5.
60 Wuilleumier 1939, 70–5; Ghinatti 1961, 117–33. Wuilleumier assumes
that Rhegium remained part of the League from 415 BC, but Ghinatti
suggests that the city did not rejoin following the expedition of Dionysios
and the assumption of hegemony by Tarentum.
61 Livy 28.28.1–2, 31.31.6–8; Dion. Hal. 20.4.3–5.5; Dio 9.40.11–12; App.
Samn. 9.3; Front. Strat. 4.1.38.
62 Livy 24.1.1–3, 26.40.16.18.
63 Livy 23.38.9.
64 Livy 24.3.14–15.
65 Livy 24.2.1–7.
66 Walsh 1974, 37, 69–70.
67 Sartori 1953, 128–42.
68 The sources for Tarentum indicate more explicitly that the source of the
disaffection was an aristocratic faction. Pol. 8.24.7; Livy 25.8.3–13. Livy
25.10.1–3 also implies a more general bad feeling between the inhabitants
of Tarentum and the Roman garrison.
69 Livy 24.1.4–13.
70 Livy 29.6.1–7.17.
71 Livy 23.30.6–8.
72 Livy 24.1.1–2.
73 Livy 24.2.1–7.

74 Livy 24.3.15.
75 Livy 22.12.3, 49.14, 27.12.7.
76 Livy 24.3.9–15.
77 Livy 25.25.11; Walsh 1974, 126.
78 App. Hann. 6.34.
79 Plin. N.H. 34.32; Dion. Hal. 20.4.2; App. Samn. 7.1–2; Livy Per. 11.
80 App. Hann 6.34.
81 Livy 26.39.14–20; App. Hann. 9.7.
82 App. Hann. 6.35.
83 Livy 25.11.10, 15.5–6; App. Hann. 4.33, 38.
84 Livy 26.39.14–20, 27.42.16, 43.1–3, 51.13.
85 Walsh 1974, 126.
86 Pol. 8.24.7.
87 Pol. 8.24.7.
88 Pol. 8.24.7; Livy 25.8.3–13.
89 Von Fritz 1940, 56–61.
90 Pol. 8.24.7.
91 Von Fritz 1940, 56–61; Frederiksen 1984, 148. Frederiksen's suggestion that the *nobiles iuvenes* were traditionally the group which formed the cavalry in both Greek and Oscan Campania is consistent with the interpretation of the group as aristocrats who were beneath the normal age for holding office.
92 Cic. Sen. 39 and 41; Powell 1988, 181–4; Brauer 1986, 195.
93 Pol. 8.24.7.
94 Livy 25.15.11.
95 Livy 26.20.7.
96 Livy 27.15.9–12.
97 Livy 27.15.9–16.9.
98 Livy 27.35.3–4.
99 Livy 27.15.9–12.
100 Livy 29.8.6–10.12.
101 Livy 29.19.7–9, 21.7–8.
102 Gruen 1984, 143–4.
103 Livy 27.21.8.
104 Livy 27.25.1–5.
105 Kahrstedt 1960, 108–21; Ghinatti 1977a, 147–60, and 1977b, 99–115.
106 Livy 30.37.1–13.

4 TREATIES AND DIPLOMACY: THE FORMALITIES OF RELATIONS WITH ROME 270–89 BC

1 Many of these are collected in Sherk 1969.
2 Sherwin-White 1939.
3 Dion. Hal. 6.95.2. The terms and language are very similar to some second-century treaties such as Pol. 21.32.1–15, IGRR 4.2, 4.1028, but Cicero (Balb. 53) claims that the text was still extant and available for consultation in his day, so it is not impossible that Dionysios' version is genuine.

NOTES

4 Dion. Hal. 6.95.2. '... βοηθείτωσάν τε τοῖς πολεμουμένοις ἁπάσῃ
   δυνάμει ...' ('... let them [the Romans and the Latins] help each other
   with all their forces, if attacked ...') Later treaties also leave the terms of
   military assistance vague. Cf. treaties with Maronea, Callatis, and As-
   typalaia (BCH 102 (1978), 724–6 and fig. 176; ILLRP 516; IGRR 4.2,
   4.1028), which all promise to 'βοεθειτω ὡς ἄν εὔκαιρον ἐκ τῶν
   συνθηκῶν καὶ ὁρκίων' ('give assistance in whatever way is appropriate
   under the treaty and the oaths').
5 Livy 8.26.6–7; Cic. Balb. 8.21.
6 Livy 22.32.4–9.
7 Badian 1958, 141–53.
8 Harris 1971, 94–5; Livy 7.38.1, 9.37–41, 10.37.4.
9 Crawford 1973b, 1–7.
10 Gruen 1984, 76–95.
11 Gruen 1984, 55–69.
12 Livy 8.14.11, Per. 14; Fest. 126L; Vell. Pat. 1.14.7.
13 Livy Per. 15. Zonaras 8.6 gives an alternative version, in which the
   Tarentines have all arms and ships confiscated, their city walls demolished
   and payment of tribute imposed, but this appears too drastic for 270 and
   may be a confusion with the sack of Tarentum in 209.
14 Livy Per. 15, 28.28.2–4; Dion. Hal. 20.16.1–2; Front. Strat. 4.1.38.
15 Plut. Pyrr. 16.4; Lefkowitz 1959, 147–75.
16 Livy 27.21.8, 29.21.8.
17 Gruen 1984, 143–4; App. Samn. 10.1; Ined. Vat. 2; Pol. 1.7.10–13; Livy
   29.27.1, 31.31.7.
18 Gruen 1984, 133–53; Diod. 18.55, 19.61.3; Täubler 1913, 434–6; Pol.
   4.84.4–5.
19 Livy 27.25.1–2.
20 Livy 27.25.1–5.
21 Livy 44.17.6 mentions a grant of land at Tarentum made in 169 BC, which
   was to be organised by the praetor, but it is not clear whether this was a
   praetor in Tarentum or in Rome.
22 Livy 36.2.7, 35.23.5, 40.18.40; App. Syr. 15.
23 Livy 31.29.9–10, 38.42.5–6, 39.39.8–10, 41.6–7; App. Syr. 15.
24 Plut. Gracch. 8.3–9.1; Vell. Pat. 1.14.7; Plin. N.H. 3.99; Tac. Ann. 14.27;
   Prob. Georg. 4.125.
25 Livy 29.8.1–9.12, 17.1–22.9.
26 Livy 29.8.
27 Livy 29.19.7. The wording of the declaration seems to echo the Greek
   formula 'ανδρας καλους και αγαθους και φιλους' which occurs in CIL
   1².588, but it is not clear whether this is a Hellenisation or not. Sherk 1969,
   13–14 suggests that the formulaic phrase 'ανδρα καλον και αγαθον
   παρα δημου καλου και αγαθου και φιλου προσαγορευσι', which
   occurs in many Greek translations of Roman decrees, is not a Greek
   phenomenon but a standard Roman translation of a Latin formula.
28 Matthaei 1907, 182–204; Marshall 1968, 39–55; Gruen 1984, 58–62,
   166–9.
29 IG 14.951 (=CIL 1².588); Marshall 1968, 39–55.
30 Livy 44.16.7.
31 Gruen 1984, 166–9, 179–80.

207

32 IG 14.12 (Syracuse), 256 (Gela), 258 (Segesta), 3.1.741, 745, 897 (Athens).
33 Gruen 1984, 143–4.
34 Mommsen 1888, 676–90; Ciaceri 1932, 101–30 and 1931–2, 39–59; Badian 1958, 28–30, 292. Cf. Horn 1930, 83–6, who disputes the lower status and military differences of the Italiote allies.
35 Milan 1973, 193–221.
36 Livy 9.38.2, 23.41.9, 31.17.3, 32.23.9–10, 32.34.10; Thiel 1954, 73-8.
37 Horn 1930, 83–7.
38 Pol. 2.23.1–24.13.
39 Pol. 1.20.14, 34.8.4, 35.16.3, 36.42.1, 42.48.7; Sil. It. 8.534; Livy 23.1.5–10, 26.40.17, 27.15.9; Horn 1930, 83–6. On the importance of Italiote and Campanian cavalry, see Frederiksen 1968, 3–31.
40 Livy 26.39.14–20, 27.10.7–10.
41 Livy 27.15.9.
42 Livy 23.15.1, 23.46.9.
43 Livy 29.6.1–17.
44 Strab. 5.4.13; Plin. N.H. 3.70; Fest. 28L; Aul. Gell. 10.3.17; App. Hann. 61; Brunt 1971, 279–80. For the possible loss of the Tarentine army, see Zon. 8.6.
45 App. BC 1.89.
46 Livy 34.8.4, 35.16.3, 36.42.1, 42.48.7.
47 Livy 34.8.4, 35.16.3, 36.42.1, 42.48.7.
48 Livy 26.39.14–20 (fifteen triremes), 34.8.4 (five ships), 36.42.1 (unspecified number of undecked ships), 42.48.7 (seven triremes).
49 Pol. 1.20.14; Livy 26.39.14–20.
50 Livy 22.32.4–9.
51 Sherwin-White 1939, 38–47.
52 Livy 22.36.9.
53 Livy 35.16.3–8.

5 DECLINE AND RECOVERY: MAGNA GRAECIA 200 BC–AD 14

1 Kahrstedt 1960, 108–21; Ghinatti 1977a, 147–60 and 1977b, 99–115.
2 Badian 1958, 141–53.
3 For instance, the request for arbitration in a land dispute between Naples and Nola. Cic. Offic. 1.33.
4 Livy 29.21.7. 'Locrensium . . . iis libertatem legesque suas populum Romanum senatumque restituere dixit'. Reparations were made for thefts from the temple of Persephone.
5 Livy 27.25.1–5; Plut. Flam. 1.4. The implication is that martial law was an interim measure and would be replaced by a proper settlement at a later date.
6 Livy 27.16.7–9; Plut. Fab. 21–3; Suet. Gramm. 18.1–3.
7 App. Hann. 8.49, 9.57; Livy 27.1.14.
8 No figures are available for Magna Graecia, but the complaints of the Latin colonies in 209 (Livy 27.9.1–10.10) indicate stress.
9 Brunt 1971, 269–77, 353–75; Ghinatti 1977a, 146–50.
10 Livy 31.29.9–10, 38.42.5–6, 39.39.8–10, 41.6–7; App. Syr. 15.

11 Gruen 1991, 39–78; Livy 39.8.3–9.1.
12 ILLRP 511; Livy 39.2.8–10, 41.6–7; App. Syr. 15.
13 Macrob. Sat. 1.18.9; Ciaceri 1927, 373; Peterson 1919, 194; Plut. Brutus 21–2; Napoli 1959, 153; IG 716, 717, 737; Brauer 1986, 89, 201.
14 Brunt 1971, 269–77, 353–75.
15 Kahrstedt 1960, 121–5; Toynbee 1965, 10–36; Ghinatti 1977a, 147–51.
16 Brunt 1971, 279–81.
17 Livy 34.45.4–5, 53.2; Vell. Pat. 1.15.4.
18 Livy 39.23.3–4; De Polignac and Gualtieri 1991.
19 Livy 39.53.2; Brunt 1971, 281.
20 De Polignac and Gualtieri 1991.
21 Plut. Gracch. 8; Vell. Pat. 1.14.7; Plin. N.H. 3.99.
22 The Lex Tarentina (CIL 1².590) refers to the city throughout as Tarentum, not as Neptunia.
23 Brunt 1971, 280–1; E. Greco 1981, 56–8, 163–5; CIL 1².638.
24 CIL 10.3703–4; Keppie 1983, 148–50; Sartori 1953, 38–42.
25 Tac. Ann. 14.27; Prob. Georg. 4.125; Gasperini 1968, 389–97 and 1971, 148; Mello and Voza 1968, nos. 36, 37, 86; Mello 1974, 119–25.
26 De Polignac and Gualtieri 1991.
27 Livy 40.42.13; Vetter 1953, nos. 108–13; Maiuri 1913a, 53–4; CIL 1².1011.
28 Pedley 1990, 113–25.
29 E. Greco 1981, 20–32; Pedley 1990, 114–19.
30 Pedley 1990, 119–25.
31 Plut. Aem. Paul. 39.1. D'Arms 1970, 171–232 gives a list of villa owners.
32 There is some evidence for villas at Velia, although it does not seem to have enjoyed as much popularity as the area further north. There was a brief period of prominence in the first century AD, when it became popular as a health resort following Augustus' much-publicised cold water cure. Hor. Epist. 1.15.1–2, 14–15.
33 Cic. Fam. 11.27; Att. 5.6.
34 Moretti 1971, 45–65.
35 Hatzfeld 1912, 130–4 and 1919, 1–8.
36 Cf. Chapter 6 in this volume.
37 Magaldi 1947, 202; Crawford 1985, 69–72.
38 Crawford 1985, 70–2.
39 Crawford 1973a, 87–110.
40 Crawford 1973a, 87–110 suggests, plausibly, that the function of the coinage was euergetic, not economic. However, see Crawford 1985, 69–72 for the possibility that the Greek administrative structure of cities like Paestum and Velia was responsible for the longer continuation of coinage.
41 Wiseman 1970, 130–3; Gell. 10.3.5; Plut. Cat. Mai. 14.
42 Wiseman 1970, 128–52.
43 Pedley 1990, 113–14.
44 Schiavone PECS, s.v. Bari; Mertens PECS, s.v. Herdonia.
45 App. BC 1.79.
46 Livy 36.42.1, 42.48.7.
47 Cic. Offic. 1.33.
48 Pugliese Carratelli 1972, 37–55.
49 Magaldi 1947, 169–78.
50 Cic. Balb. 21.

51 Sherwin-White 1939, 47; Cic. Balb. 28, Caec. 100.
52 Sherwin-White 1939, 138; Calderone 1976, 60–70.
53 Moretti 1971, 21–65; Lévêque 1970, 29–70.
54 Moretti 1971, 21–65, Lévêque 1970, 29–70.
55 The contacts between Tarentum and the Aegean are demonstrated by the presence of Spartan and Epirote mercenaries in the fourth century. For contacts between sanctuaries, see Bengtson 1953, 456–63.
56 See Chapter 6 in this volume.
57 Pedley 1990, 113–28; Napoli 1978, 341–406; Wuilleumier 1939, 253–468. The final erosion of Hellenised art forms in southern Italy took place in the second century, and there is little doubt that there was a flourishing artistic tradition comparable to that of other Hellenistic cities at least until 200 BC.
58 See Chapter 6 in this volume.
59 Strabo 6.1.2. For the concept of a unified Italy as Augustan propaganda, cf. Flor. 2.5.1; Res Gest. 25.
60 Crawford forthcoming.
61 Flor. 2.8.
62 App. BC 1.89.
63 D'Arms 1970; Arthur 1991, 61–87.
64 Cic. Fam. 11.27; Att. 5.5, 5.6; Flor. 2.8.
65 Cic. Att. 9.15; App. BC 2.40, 5.50; Plut. Ant. 35.1, 62.2; Dio 54.48.1.
66 App. BC 4.86. For the title Rhegium Iulium, see CIL 10.5.
67 Turano 1960, 65–75 and 1963, 76–82.
68 Suet. Aug. 64.
69 Gasperini 1968, 379–98 and 1971, 148; Prob. ad Verg. Georg. 4.125.
70 Res Gest. 25.2; Syme 1939, 276–93, 440–58.
71 On Augustan Hellenism, see Bowersock 1965.
72 Plin. N.H. 3.46; Salmon 1980, 153.
73 Plin. N.H. 3.62–3, 68–74, 99–106.

6 EAST/WEST RELATIONS: CONTACTS BETWEEN MAGNA GRAECIA AND THE EASTERN MEDITERRANEAN

1 The centrality of the region for contacts with the Eastern Mediterranean and the diffusion of Hellenism has been recently highlighted by Gruen 1991, 7–9, 79–92.
2 Strabo 5.4.4 comments on Hellenism at Cumae, but there is also evidence for Oscanisation. Vetter 1953, nos. 108–13; Livy 40.42.13.
3 Moretti 1957, nos. 128, 184, 225, 264, 305, 346, 358, 449, 479, 547, 679, 688, 745 (Croton); 294, 296, 315, 386 (Locri); 617 (Naples), 220 (Caulonia); 526 (Paestum); 54 (Rhegium); 559 (Sybaris); 767 (Terina); 109, 199 (Thurii); 62, 233, 355, 490, 621, 719, 725, 764 (Tarentum). The importance of athletic achievement in this aristocratic society is demon-strated by the so-called tombs of the Tarentine athletes – rich burials which contained strigils, oil flasks and other agonistic items. Pugliese Carratelli 1983, 706–8.
4 Diod. 12.9.5–6; Strab. 6.3.4.

5 Paus. 10.13.10; Williams 1989, 526–51. On the Delphic monuments, see Daux 1949, 151–3; Amandry 1949, 447–63.
6 SEG 33.328.
7 Plut. Them. 32.2–3; Herodot. 8.62.2.
8 See Chapter 1 in this volume; Raviola 1990, 34–41.
9 Diod. 12.54.4, 13.3.4–5; Thuc. 6.44–50, 7.1.
10 Musti 1966, 323–9; Von Fritz 1940.
11 Flacelière 1937, II.23a, 26a, 64b, 89a; FD III 4.414, 613; SEG 27.85, 115.
12 Pugliese Caratelli 1955, 1–7; Bengtson 1954/5, 456–63. On *asylia* and the Cos decree, see Gruen 1984, 71–2; Gauthier 1972, 226–30, 266–84. The dating of the Epidauros text (IG 4.1504) is disputed but must fall between 390 and 367 or 353 and 339.
13 Although no international contacts are known, the healing cult of Apollo Oulios at Velia was prominent until the first century AD. Hor. Epist. 1.15.1–2, 14–15; Ebner 1962, 125–136; Pugliese Caratelli 1963, 385–6 and 1970, 243–8; Nutton 1970, 211–25; Musitelli 1980, 240–55.
14 Ebner 1965, 306–9.
15 Pol. 8.4.1; Walbank 1957, 72, 415–16.
16 Pol. 8.4.1, 16.15.6; Walbank 1957, 72, 415–16, 497, 519–20.
17 Moschus ap. Athenaeus 14.634.
18 Pol. 13.4.1–5.6; Walbank 1957, 17–19; Fabricius, RE s.v. Herakleides (63). Herakleides also appears in IG 9.78, Livy 32.5.7 and Diod. 28.9 as a Macedonian general and diplomat.
19 Hatzfeld 1912, 42–3.
20 Livy 27.35.3–4.
21 IG 2/3.3779; Paus. 1.37.2; Athen. 13.603e; Diog. Laert. 7.13.
22 The evidence is collected by Hatzfeld in BCH 36 (1912), 5–218.
23 See Hatzfeld 1919, 257–65; Wilson 1966, 12–18.
24 For instance, Hermon of Velia, Herakleides Aristionos of Tarentum, Philostratos Philostratou of Naples, or Titos Satyrionos of Heraklea (Hatzfeld 1912, 11, 42–3, 67, 85–6).
25 Hatzfeld 1912, 52, 67.
26 For instance Herakleides Aristionos. Wilson 1966, 111–15 suggests that there was some degree of stable, resident population on Delos, but there is no firm evidence to support this.
27 For Philostratos Philostratou, see Hatzfeld 1912, 67; Deniaux 1980–1, 133–41; Mancinetti Santamaria 1982, 79–89 and 1983, 125–36.
28 Hatzfeld 1912, 11, 42, 78–9.
29 IG 7.416.
30 IG 7.540.
31 IG 11.108.
32 IG 7.3197; Vollgraff 1919, 252–8. The Argos inscription is assigned to the second or first century BC by Vollgraff on the basis of letter-forms. Gossage 1975, 115–34 gives some discussion of the two inscriptions. It is not unlikely that the Dorotheos of the Orchomenos inscription is the same person as the victor from Argos. As Gossage points out, the corpus of Boeotian inscriptions contains other examples of multiple victories. On Dorotheos see O'Connor 1908, 162–3; Ghiron-Bistagne 1976, 107, 176; Wuilleumier 1939, 713.

33 In particular, they appear more regularly on the victory lists of Boeotian festivals which rose to prominence in the first century, than on those of pan-Hellenic festivals. Cf. Moretti 1953, 57–62 and 1959 for lists of Italiote victors in major festivals.

34 Gossage 1975, 115–34.

35 SEG 27.1114.

36 Rawson 1985, 9–12.

37 IG 2.467, 470; Insc. Del. 1.2598; Hatzfeld 1912, 78.

38 IG 2.3042.

39 IG 2.3387.

40 IG 2/3.9116, 9117, 8483, 3779, 10413, 10412a, 10414.

41 Launey 1950, 600–1, 1260–1.

42 IG 7.342, 505.

43 A number of examples of proxeny decrees have been found in southern Italy, suggesting that Greek diplomatic practices continued at least until the first century BC, if not later. Cf. IG 14.612, from Rhegium, and Forni 1957–8, 61–70, from Velia. Deniaux 1980–1 suggests that this phenomenon represents the use of Greek terminology to camouflage Roman *amicita* and *clientela*, but it is possible that *proxenia* was genuinely perceived as an independent relationship. Proxeny in southern Italy is discussed further in Chapters 8 and 9. On the legal status of the *amicus populi Romani*, see Marshall 1968, 39–55. The device is very common in the Greek world. Gruen 1984, 116–19, 179–80.

44 Moretti 1971, 57–66.

45 The largest group represented are Tarentines, but there are substantial numbers of Velians and Neapolitans. Hatzfeld 1912 and 1919.

46 Livy 27.35.3–4.

47 Livy 29.6.1–7.17, 19.7–9, 21.7–8.

48 Launey 1950, 600–1, 1260–1.

49 Moretti 1965, 73–9.

50 App. Mith. 22.

51 Rawson 1985, 3–18.

52 Cic. Att. 5.21, 6.1–3.

53 Hatzfeld 1919, 178–89.

54 Sen. Epist. 86.4; Livy 38.52–3, 56.

55 Rawson 1985, 3–10, 23–5; D'Arms 1970, 40–61.

56 For example, Curio (Cic. Att. 10.1), Pompey (Cic. Att. 4.10), Varro (Cic. Fam. 9.5), Sulla (App. BC 1.104), Marius, Caesar (Sen. Ep. 51.11). For a full list, see D'Arms 1970, 171–232.

57 Cic. Att. 5.2. '*Habuimus in Cumano quasi pusillam Romam. Tanta erat in his locis multitudo . . .*'. Cicero is known to have had close connections with the Lucceii of Puteoli. Att. 1.17.11, 7.3.6, 9.1.3, 9.11.13, 16.5; Fam. 5.12; D'Arms 1970, 187–8.

58 Cic. Arch. 5, 10. Rawson 1985, 32–7 is inclined to take this gloomy view of southern Italy at face value, but this seems suspiciously close to the literary *topos* of decline discussed above (see Introduction in this volume, pp. 13–17).

59 Cic. Arch 5.

60 Cic. Arch 6.

61 Cic. Arch. 6; Deniaux 1980–1, 133–41.

62 Hatzfeld 1912, 67, 79, Deniaux 1980–1, 133–41; Mancinetti Santamaria 1982, 79–89; Cic. Fam. 13.30.
63 Strab. 5.4.7; IG 14.645.
64 Dio 55.10.9; Suet. Nero 20.2; Strab. 5.4.7; Buchner, Morelli and Nenci 1952; Geer 1935, 208–22; Arnold 1960, 241–51; Hardie 1983, 1–73. The games were modelled on the Olympic Games, although prize money was awarded. Some events were limited to Neapolitan citizens, and there were girls' races for daughters of *bouleutoi* (AE 1954, 186). Part of an inscription giving the regulations for the games has been found at Olympia (SEG 37.356), and Pausanias 1.16.2–4 makes reference to athletic events for women.
65 Gruen 1991, 14, 80–91. There was a guild of actors from Rhegium (IG 14.615). For the archaeological evidence for theatres and dramatic festivals, see Metzger 1967; Gigante 1967; Mitens 1988.
66 Strab. 5.4.7; Lycoph. Alex. 721–32; Timaeus ap. Schol. ad Lycoph. 72.
67 Arnold 1960, 241–51.
68 IG 14.737–9, 746–7; Moretti 1953.
69 Moretti 1953, 249–53; IG 14.615; Costabile 1979, 525–45.
70 IG 14.750–5; Colonna *NSc* 1890, 341–3; Civitelli *NSc* 1896, 1–82; Miranda 1990, 75–114.
71 IG 14.746.
72 Hardie 1983, 1–73; Rostagni 1952, 344–57.
73 Stat. Silv. 5.3.103–94.
74 Spawforth and Walker 1985, 78–104 and 1986, 88–106.
75 IG 5.1.37b, 12–17 (SEG 11.481). See also Spawforth and Walker 1986, 91; Gasperini 1984, 476.
76 Spawforth and Walker 1985, 78–104 and 1986, 88–106.

7 ECONOMIC DEVELOPMENT AND AGRARIAN PROBLEMS 200 bc–ad 200

1 Cic. Am. 13; Dio Chrysos. 33.25; Juv. Sat. 3.2–3.
2 Toynbee 1965; Frank 1940.
3 Dyson 1992, 27–45.
4 Kahrstedt 1960.
5 Strab. 6.1.1.
6 Hor. Epist. 1.15.1–2, 14–15; Nutton 1970.
7 Head 1911; G. Giannelli 1963.
8 Adamesteanu 1973.
9 Carter 1990, 405–44..
10 A. P. Greco 1979; Pedley 1990, 97–9.
11 Pedley 1990, 113–14.
12 Herring 1991a.
13 Herring 1991a.
14 Livy 24.13, 36; Pol. 1.56.10.
15 Toynbee 1965; Frank 1939.
16 Lepore 1983, 347–54.
17 Jongman 1988, 97–112.
18 Jongman 1988, 112–27.

19 Dyson 1992, 27–45.
20 App. Hann. 9.57; Plut. Fab. 22; Livy 27.15.9–16.16.
21 Livy 34.45.4–5, 53.2; Vell. Pat. 1.15.4.
22 De Polignac and Gualtieri 1991.
23 Small 1991.
24 D'Andria 1975; Carter 1981.
25 Hopkins 1978, 1–25.
26 App. BC 1.9.
27 Dyson 1992, 44–50.
28 Dyson 1992, 27–30.
29 Jongman 1988, 112–30; Arthur 1991.
30 Dyson 1992.
31 ILLRP 454.
32 '. . . *fecei ut de agro poplico | aratoribus cederent pastores | Forum aedisque poplicas heic fecei*' ('. . . I made the herdsmen give up the *ager publicus* to farmers, and I built a forum and public buildings there').
33 Gabba 1988, 134–41; Thompson 1988, 213–15; Gabba and Pasquinucci 1977, 79–91.
34 Livy 39.2.8–10.
35 Varr. R.R. 2.2.18.
36 Carter 1981, 167–78.
37 Ridgway 1989, 146–7; Carter 1984; Spadea 1984.
38 Dyson 1992, 27–55.
39 Guzzo 1981, 124–5.
40 Gualandi *et al.* 1981, 155–74.
41 Ridgway 1989, 146–7; Gasperini 1971.
42 Kahrstedt 1960; D'Andria 1975, 539–44.
43 Livy 24.13, 36; Pol. 1.56.10.
44 Plin. N.H. 3.60; Pol. 3.91; Arthur 1991.
45 Jongman 1988, 98–107.
46 Plin. N.H. 14.39, 69, 15.37, 55, 71, 90, 93–4; Athen. 1.26–7; Purcell 1985, 1–19.
47 D'Arms 1974; Hatzfeld 1912 and 1919.
48 Dyson 1992, 31–7; Small 1991; Wightman 1981.
49 Arthur 1991; Small 1991; Ridgway 1989.
50 Jongman 1988, 112–30.
51 Gasperini 1971; Orsi NSc 1912, 60–2.
52 Plin. N.H. 18.35; Plut. Tib. Gracc. 8.750.
53 Gabba 1988, 134–41; Gabba and Pasquinucci 1977, 79–91.
54 Varr. R.R. 2.9.6; Quintil. 7.8.4; Frayn 1984.
55 Gasperini 1971; Plin. N.H. 8.190; Varr. R.R. 2.2.18; Ed. Dioc. 21.2, 25.1.
56 Plin. N.H. 9.137; Ed. Dioc. 21.2, 25.1.
57 Morel 1978, 94–110.
58 Gabba 1988, 134–41; Gabba and Pasquinucci 1977, 79–91; Skydsgard 1974.

NOTES

8 RITUAL AND SOCIETY: CULTS AND CULTURAL TRANSITION

1 Geertz 1973, 87–125, 142–69; North 1976, 1–3.
2 North 1976, 1–12; Gordon 1990a, 194–8.
3 Gordon 1990b, 219–31.
4 Duthoy 1974, 134–54; Fishwick 1966, 139–202.
5 Liebeschuetz 1979, 63, 82–3.
6 Livy 29.10.4–11.8.
7 Gruen 1991, 77–8.
8 Beard 1990, 45.
9 Gasperini 1971, 160–3; Pedley 1990, 125.
10 Patterson 1987, 134–44.
11 Pugliese Carratelli 1952a, 420–6; Giannelli 1963 includes a full list of Greek cults from southern Italy.
12 IG 14.756; Correra 1904, 185; Ghinatti 1967, 98–100 and 1974, 6–7; Peterson 1919, 185–6; Napoli 1959, 139–40; Lepore 1967, 168–70. A possible Cumaean origin for the cult is indicated by Plut. De Mul. Virt. 262D.
13 Inscriptions from other parts of southern Italy record Terentia Paranome (IG 14.702), Sabina (CIL 10.1812) and Voconia Severa (AE 1978, 261, CIL 10.467) – also priestesses of this cult.
14 Dion. Hal. 6.17.2; Cic. Balb. 24.55; Ciaceri 1940, 372.
15 IG 14.645; Sartori 1967, 40–95 and 1980, 401–15; Lo Porto 1967, 181–92.
16 De Sensi Sestito 1984, 41–50; Nenci 1966, 128–31.
17 Seiler 1984, 231–42; Mertens 1983.
18 Cic. Inv. 2.1.1–3, Div. 1.24.48; Pol. 3.33.18, 3.56.4; Livy 42.3.1–11; Val. Max. 1.1.20. Livy emphasises the wealth of the sanctuary at 23.3.7.
19 The argument that this incident indicates the poverty and decline of the Greek element in the colony seems to be spurious. A lack of knowledge of sixth-century construction techniques in the second century BC does not seem to be a surprising phenomenon. Plut. Pomp. 24. For the wealth of the sanctuary, see also Strabo 6.1.1.
20 IG 14.645; Uguzzoni and Ghinatti 1968.
21 De Franciscis 1972, 75–84.
22 G. Giannelli 1963.
23 Cordano 1974, 86–90; Pugliese Carratelli 1962, 241–6.
24 Carter 1978.
25 Peterson 1919, 61–3; IG 14.744; AE 1914.306.
26 Ghinatti 1974, 1–6; Peterson 1919, 177; Pugliese Carratelli 1952a; Suet. fr. 203 Reifferscheid; Dion. Perieg. 357–9, Priscian. Perieg. 351–3; Suda s.v. Νεαπολις; Lycophr. Alex. 711–21; Strabo 1.213; Nicephoros Geog. 331. It is known that this cult had a gymnastic festival attached to it, and it may have been the forerunner of the Sebasta.
27 Miranda 1982, 163–74; Guarducci 1970, 252–61; Ghinatti 1967, 100–1, 592; IG 14.745; Galante, 1893–6, 5–24; Stat. Silv. II.2.76–82, III.1.147.
28 Livy 4.37.1, 44.12; Diod. 12.23.2, 76.4, 14.101–3; Front. Strat. 2.3.12; Polyaenus 2.10.2.
29 Aristox. ap. Athen. 16.632a.
30 Pugliese Carratelli 1972, 43–5.

215

31 IG 14.861.
32 Livy 27.23.2. The temple identified as that of Apollo is situated on a lower level and is both later in date and smaller in size. Vergil (Aen. 6.19, 41) gives a contradictory description, referring to two temples of Apollo situated on different levels. The issue is further confused by the difficulties of reconciling Vergil's description of Aeneas' descent from the temple of Apollo to the Sibyl's cave with the topography of the area. There is no good reason to accept Vergil's poetic account of the two temples of Apollo rather than the account of Livy, which clearly states that there was a temple of Zeus on the acropolis. Austin 1976, 55–7.
33 Vetter 1953, no. 108 (=Buck 1904, no. 25); Ribezzo 1924, 88. Although the dedication was to Jupiter, it was found near the temple of Apollo. A much larger number of these *iovilae* dedications were found at Capua, probably dating to the third century BC. Buck suggests that they were dedications made at festivals celebrated by collegia or by kinship groups. Frederiksen 1984, 148 suggests they are connected with an *ephebeia*. Cf. Buck no. 30 for a similar dedication *pro iuventute*. The epithet *Flagiui* is equated by Buck with the Latin epithet *Fulgurator*.
34 Peterson 1919, 71–4; Vetter 1953, no. 108.
35 Pedley 1990, 129–62; E. Greco 1981, 27–32, 108–10, 140–2.
36 CIL 10.472; Mello and Voza 1968.
37 Livy 39.8.1–18.9; CIL 1.196; Macrob. Sat. 1.18.9; Ciaceri 1940, 373; Peterson 1919, 194; Gruen 1991, 34–78.
38 Sogliano, *NSc* 1905, 377–80.
39 IG 14.716–17; Napoli 1959, 153. Dionysos at Naples has the epithet *Hebon*, which has no parallel elsewhere. It may indicate an association with the cult of Hebe, but the cult images represent Dionysos as an old man rather than a young one, as would be more appropriate. G. Giannelli 1963, 31–5.
40 *Napoli Antica*, 395–7.
41 Gruen 1991, 77–8.
42 Patterson 1987.
43 Stat. Silv. 4.8.47–9; Sil. It. 12.85–103; Paus. 8.24.5, 10.13.8; Schol. ad Lycoph. 1278; Verg. Aen. 6.42–156; IG 14.861; Peterson 1919, 50–61; D'Arms 1970, 80–1.
44 Peterson 1919, 55–61.
45 Peterson 1919, 74–9.
46 Ebner 1964, 72–6 and 1965, 306–9.
47 Ebner 1965, 306–9.
48 Ebner 1965, 306–9.
49 Ebner 1965, 308.
50 Ebner 1965, 308.
51 See Chapter 10 in this volume.
52 SEG 30.1175; Gigante 1980, 381–2; Lo Porto 1980, 282–8; Maddoli 1984.
53 Bengtson 1953, 456–63; CIL 10.1546.
54 Hor. Epist. 1.15.1–2, 14–15; Athen. 537e; *OGIS* 90.19, 26f.; Dio. 44.6.4; Suet. Aug. 70.1.
55 Ebner 1962, 125–36.
56 Ebner 1962, 125–36; Gigante 1964, 450–2; Pugliese Carratelli 1963, 385–6 and 1970, 243–8; Musitelli 1980, 240–55.

57 Nutton 1970, 211–25.
58 Suet. Aug. 59.
59 Ebner 1970, 262–6; Pugliese Carratelli 1970, 243–8. Cf. the form of the decree in honour of G. Julius Naso. Forni 1957–8, 61–100.
60 IG 14. 617–21; SEG 29.987–9; Costabile 1979, 525–45.
61 Paus. 5.25.2; Costabile 1979, 525–45.
62 For example, Sex. Numonius Sex. F. Maturus, Prytanis and Archon Pentaeterikos; C. Hortorius C.F. Balbillus and M. Pemponius M.F. Pulcher, Synprytaneis (IG 14.617).
63 Spawforth and Walker 1985, 78–104; Bowie 1974, 166–209.
64 Gordon 1990b, 219–31.
65 CIL 10.3685–8, 3697; Cic. Att. 1.17.11, 7.3.6, 9.1.3, 9.11.13, 16.5; Fam. 5.12; D'Arms 1970, 187–8.
66 Seiler 1984, 231–42; Mertens 1983; Orsi, AE 1922.102–6.
67 Hardie 1983, 3–11; Geer 1935; *Napoli Antica*, 390–2; Miranda 1990, 75–114.
68 IG 14.612; Ghinatti 1974, 13–14.
69 Gasperini 1984, 476–9.
70 Levi 1926, 378–402.
71 CIL 10.8342a.
72 Nisbet and Hubbard 1970, 34–6.
73 Ath. 537e; OGIS 90.19 and 26f.; Dio. 44.6.4; Suet. Aug. 70.1.
74 Duthoy 1974, 134–54; Ostrow 1985, 65–101.
75 ILS 6339; CIL 10.1, 10.3701.
76 Ostrow 1985, 65–101.
77 CIL 10.3698–700.
78 Gordon 1990a, 194–8.
79 IG 14.617–21; SEG 29.987–9.
80 IG 14.716–17, 745; ILS 6455.
81 Ebner 1962, 125–36; Pugliese Carratelli 1970, 243–8; Ebner 1970, 262–7.
82 Ebner 1970, 262–7, with reconstructions by Pugliese Carratelli 1970, 243–8.
83 '*Valerio G.F.* | *Rom. Caeoni* | *Aed. IIII i.d. Pholarc.* | *V.A. XLII* | *Valeria Caepilla* | *patri*'.

9 ADMINISTRATIVE STRUCTURES AND THE TRANSFORMATION OF POLITICAL LIFE

1 Sherwin-White 1939.
2 Sherwin-White 1939, 150–65.
3 Sherwin-White 1939, 150–73; Degrassi 1950, 281–344.
4 Sartori 1953, 17–27.
5 Laffi 1973, 37–54 and 1983, 59–74.
6 CIL 1².590.
7 Salmon 1980.
8 Sartori 1953, 15–28.
9 Sartori 1953, 46–7.
10 Strab. 5.4.7; ILS 6455; CIL 10.1478, 1492.
11 Livy 8.25.9.

12 Sartori 1953, 48–53.
13 Livy 8.25.5–26.5.
14 IG 14.737, 746, 758, 760; CIL 10.1489; AE 1954, 186.
15 Pol. 2.39.1–7; Von Fritz 1940.
16 Pol. 12.5.6–9, 16.10–11; Demosth. Timoc. 24; Sartori 1953, 128–9.
17 Walsh 1974.
18 Livy 24.1.7 ('. . . *levissimus quisque novas res novamque societatem mallent . . .*'), 2.8 ('. . . *senatus Romanis faveret, plebs ad Poenum rem traheret . . .*').
19 Livy 24.2.5–3.17. At Tarentum, the pro-Carthaginian party was oligarchic in nature and came to power by staging a *coup*. Livy 25.8.3.
20 Sartori 1953, 85–8; De Iuliis 1985, 17; Ghinatti 1980.
21 IG 14.645; SEG 30.1162–70.
22 Diog. Laert. 8.4.79, 82; Ael. Var. Hist. 7.14; Suda s.v. Αρχυτας (=Diels l.47 A 1); Wuilleumier 1939; Brauer 1986.
23 Thuc. 6.44.
24 Sherwin-White 1939, 159–73; Degrassi 1950, 281–344.
25 Sherwin-White 1939, 159–73.
26 Livy 32.29.2, 34.45.1–2, 34.53.2, Per. 14; Vell. Pat. 1.14.7–8, 15.3.
27 The division is reflected in the later constitution as represented in the Lex Tarentina, which had both quattuorvirs and duumvirs. Plut. G. Gracch. 8; Vell. Pat. 1.15.5; CIL 1².590.
28 Livy 8.14.10–12.
29 Sartori 1953, 165–71. The only extant example is Q. Herennius Rufus (ILS 910).
30 Livy 26.16.5–13.
31 Sartori 1953.
32 CIL 1².590.
33 Tac. Ann. 14.27; Gasperini 1971.
34 ILLRP 576; Cic. Ad Att. 10.13; Sartori 1953, 40–2.
35 ILLRP 576; Sartori 1953, 39–41.
36 Lib. Col. 232, Lachmann.
37 CIL 10.3698.
38 Sartori 1953, 39; Keppie 1983, 48–51.
39 CIL 10.3703, 3704. The fact that Pliny (N.H. 3.5.61) omits Cumae from his list of colonies cannot be regarded as proof that a colony did not exist.
40 Sartori 1953, 45–6.
41 NSc 1890, 220.
42 CIL 10.1492.
43 Lib. Col. 235; Ciaceri 1932, 243.
44 Stat. Silv. 3.7.78.
45 Sartori 1953, 46.
46 CIL 10.1491.
47 Sartori 1953, 36–42, 158–63.
48 Strabo 5.4.7.
49 Strabo 5.4.7, 6.1.2. The latest evidence for the demarchy is CIL 10.1492 (fourth century) and for the archonship NSc 1896, 103–4 (third century). These indicate that the Greek magistracies outlasted the Greek language, which seems to have disappeared from official use in the third century.
50 De Martino 1952, 335–43; Sartori 1953, 47–52.

51 It seems likely that a number of the offices listed on Neapolitan inscriptions were not civic magistracies but had religious or agonistic functions in connection with the *Sebasta*, such as the offices of *gymnasiarchos*, *agonothetes*, and possibly the *archon pentaeterikon*.
52 Cf. in particular Sartori 1953, 46–55; De Martino 1952, 335–43; Pinsent 1969, 368–72.
53 Mason 1974, s.v. αγοραvoμoς.
54 A. H. M. Jones 1940, 221–5.
55 CIL 10.1489, 1490 (=IG 14.758); MAL 1890, 555–72 (=ILS 6460).
56 Sogliano, NSc 1892; Spinazzola, NSc 1893; CIL 10.1483, 1484; ILS 5692
57 AE 1954.186.
58 De Martino 1952, 335–43; Sartori 1953, 47–52.
59 IG 14.745.
60 IG 14.716, 717, 737, 749; ILS 6455.
61 Strabo 5.4.6–7; Sartori 1953, 46–55.
62 Lepore 1967, 202–16.
63 Spart. Vit. Had. 1.9.1 is the latest literary reference to the demarchy, but the epigraphic evidence attests its continued existence as late as the fourth century (CIL 10.1492).
64 Spart. Vit. Had. 1.9.1.
65 IG 14.729; Spart. Vit. Had. 1.9.1.
66 CIL 4.2993, 3822, 10.901–2; Castren 1975, 61, 105.
67 Cf. also patronage of the phratries by Claudius; IG 14. 728.
68 IG 14.745.
69 IG 14.737, 758, 760; Correra 1904, 185; ILS 6460.
70 For the demarchy, see IG 14.741; CIL 10.1478, 1491; NSc 1890 (=ILS 6460). For archons at Naples, see IG 14.758, 760; CIL 10.1489. A. H. M. Jones 1940, 174 notes the increasing use of this title.
71 NSc 1896, 103–4.
72 NSc 1892; CIL 10.1491; EE 8.340.
73 ILS 6453 (=NSc 1896).
74 De Martino 1952, 335–43; Sartori 1953, 46–55.
75 Mason 1974, s.v. αvταρχωv.
76 Pinsent 1969, 368–72.
77 Sartori 1953, 105–7.
78 Mingazzini 1954.
79 Ebner 1966, no.18; CIL 10.426.
80 AE 1978, 260. For other examples cf. CIL 9.2353, 10.4210, 11.3260.
81 A. H. M. Jones 1940, 221–6.
82 IG 14.745, 616; SEG 1.418.
83 'Valerio G.F. | Rom. Caeoni | Aed. IIII i.d. Pholarc. | V.A. XLII | Valeria Caepilla | patri' (Ebner 1970, no. 18, with a slightly different reconstruction by Pugliese Carratelli 1970, 243).
84 CIL 10.7342b.
85 Forni 1957–8, 61–70; Ebner 1970.
86 Ebner 1970.
87 Forni 1957–8, 61–70.
88 This formula is found both in Hellenistic proxeny decrees, and in Roman decrees of amicitia. IG 7.342, 505; Livy 29.19.7.
89 Pliny Ep. 4.6, 6.6, 6.9; Burzachechi 1967, 125–34.

90 IG 14.612.
91 Cf the proxenia decrees of Pelops Dexiai of Naples, IG 7.505, 342, and Onomastos of Macedon, Livy 44.17.6.
92 For a list of references and main identifications, cf. Ghinatti 1974, 13–14.
93 IG 14.615; SEG 29.985.
94 SEG 1.418; IG 14.616.
95 Mingazzini 1954; Ebner 1966 and 1970; AE 1978.260; CIL 10.426.
96 Bowersock 1965, 81–4.
97 Sartori 1953, 141–2.
98 IG 14.617–21; SEG 29.987–9.
99 CIL 10.4.
100 Sartori 1953, 136–42; Costabile 1978, 537–42.
101 SEG 29.987.
102 Sartori 1953, 136–7.
103 IG 14.612.
104 Costabile 1978.
105 Camodeca 1982.
106 Veyne 1976, 5–18.
107 Jones 1940, 184, 220–2.
108 Bowie 1974, 166–209.
109 Bowersock 1965, 81–4.
110 Bowie 1974; Spawforth and Walker 1985, 78–104; Hardie 1983, 1–30.
111 Bowersock 1965, 81–4.
112 Kaimio 1979, 73–4.
113 Spinazzola, NSc 1893; CIL 10.1491, 10.6; AE 1978, 260; Mingazzini 1954, 50–2; Ebner 1970, no. 18; CIL 10.462.
114 CIL 10.3685–8; IG 14.861; CIL 10.482–3.
115 CIL 1².590, 26–31.
116 Camodeca 1982, 103–63; Wiseman 1971, 184–90.
117 Sartori 1976, 81–138.
118 CIL 10.110.
119 Camodeca 1982, 157–61.

10 URBAN SOCIETY IN MAGNA GRAECIA: ACCULTURATION AND CIVIC IDENTITY

1 Strab. 6.1.2. '. . . with the exception of Naples, Rhegium and Tarentum, it [Magna Graecia] has become barbarised, some parts having been taken and held by the Lucanians and Bruttians and some by the Campanians, in other words, by the Romans, since they have themselves become Romans'.
2 Wilkins and Whitehouse 1989, 102–26 give a résumé of some of the problems involved in studying Graeco-Oscan acculturation in southern Italy.
3 This is a common pattern throughout the Roman world. Macmullen 1982; Degrassi 1957.
4 Macmullen 1982, 238–9.
5 Mayer 1990.
6 Maiuri, NSc 1913, 53–4, 476; Buck 1904, no. 40; Vetter 1953, nos. 108–13.
7 Jeffrey 1961.

8 Duncan-Jones 1974, 127–31 discusses funerary and commemorative costs, many exceeding 10,000 sesterces, but these figures relate principally to the decurial class.
9 Veyne 1976, 10.
10 D'Arms 1970.
11 Duthoy 1974, 134–54; Ostrow 1985, 65–101.
12 CIL 10.109. The amounts are broadly comparable to those from other sportula inscriptions in Italy. Duncan Jones 1974.
13 For example, AE 1980, 241 (Cumae); CIL 10.13 (Rhegium), 22 (Locri), 496 (Paestum).
14 Gasperini 1971; Susini 1962, 59–63.
15 Gasperini 1971.
16 Gasperini 1968, 1971.
17 ILP 87, 112, 175–6. Also EE 8.282–3 (Velia), 8.443–4 (Cumae).
18 IG 14.766 (Antioche Alexandrou of Laodicea), 781 (Hermokles Euphemou of Alexandria), 785 (Heliodoros Alexandrou of Antioch). See also IG 14.750, 754, 771, 773, 805; Miranda 1990, 75–114.
19 CIL 10.7, 3699, 3700, 8339d.
20 CIL 10.3684; Waltzing 1895–1900.
21 IG 14.615; Livy 29.10.4–11.8, 14.5–14; Gruen 1991, 84.
22 IG 14.617–21.
23 Waltzing 1895–1900.
24 CIL 10.7.
25 Waltzing 1895–1900; CIL 10.3698–700.
26 CIL 10.3699–700.
27 Napoli 1959; Guarducci 1936; Suet. Claud. 11.2; Varr. L.L. 5.85; Strab. 5.4.7.
28 Maiuri 1913b, 21–36.
29 CIL 6.1.1851, 12.3232 and IG 14.743, 744 all record members of consular rank. Gifts include endowments of sportulae (IG 14.742; CIL 1.1491) and precious plate (IG 14.721, 722, 748). Jones 1940, 158–9, 171–2.
30 Veyne 1976, 5–18.
31 CIL 10.3704.
32 Jones 1940, 175.
33 CIL 10.3685–89; ILP 98–104.
34 Patterson 1990.
35 Patterson 1990.
36 E. Greco 1981; Pedley 1990, 113–124 indicates the problems arising out of the colonial rebuilding of an existing civic unit.
37 For instance, the repairs to the temple of Demeter at Cumae (CIL 10.3685–9) and the restoration of the baths at Tarentum (Lippolis 1984) and the temple of the Dioscuri at Naples dedicated by Ti. Julius Tarsus (IG 14.714).
38 CIL 10.109, 110.
39 For example, CIL 10.3703, honouring Sextia Kania. '. . . *quod ea munifica erga coloniam fuit*'.
40 Jones 1940.
41 CIL 10.6; AE 1978, 260; Mingazzini 1954, 21–55.
42 Duncan-Jones 1974, 286.
43 CIL 9.338.

44 Duncan-Jones 1974, 337 also points out that Regio I (Campania and Latium) is in any case the region with the highest density of both inscriptions and urbanism.
45 Gasperini 1971; Susini 1962, 60–2.
46 Camodeca 1982, 103–63; Wiseman 1971. For further details see Chapter 9 in this volume.
47 Jongman 1988, 196.
48 Patterson 1990.
49 D'Arms 1970; Hardie 1983, 1–20.
50 De Caro and Greco 1981, 76–90.
51 Miranda 1990, 75–114; IG 14.728.
52 IG 14.729 (=CIL 10.1481); NSc 1892, 220–1; Rend. Linc. 1912, 791–802.
53 Dio 55.13.4; Suet. Aug. 65. Turano 1963, 76–82 includes the epitaph of one of Julia's freedmen. Turano 1960, no. 5 suggests that Julia may also have had connections with Rhegium through her mother's family, the Scribonii.
54 Gasperini 1968 and 1971.
55 Veyne 1976, 102–3, 361–6.
56 The text simply states that he is honoured 'honoris causa'.
57 Forni 1957–8, 61–70; Pliny Ep. 4.6, 6.6, 6.9; Burzachechi 1967. For a similar example from Rhegium, see SEG 1.418.
58 Maiuri 1913b, 21–36; Guarducci 1936, no. 37.
59 CIL 10.4; Lippolis 1984, 119–53; Sogliano, NSc 1892, Spinazzola, NSc 1893.
60 By the second century AD, ancient authors placed great emphasis on buildings and physical structure in defining a city. Paus. 10.4.1.
61 Miranda 1990, 75–114.
62 Balsdon 1979, 146–60.
63 Conway 1897 includes a list of the supposed regional origins of nomina.
64 Gasperini 1971; Turano 1960.
65 On the problems of the Greek cognomen and its relation to servile origin, see Kajanto 1968.
66 Conway 1897.
67 Costabile 1978.
68 Strab. 5.4.7; IG 14.645.
69 Examples include IG 14.660 (Tertia Pakias tou Dionysiou); Levi 1926, 378-402 (Epilytos Bibiou, Trebios Epilytou, Pakia Epilytou); AE 1912, 218 (Trebios Zoilos Aristoboulos); Maiuri 1913a, 53–4 (Karis Brittiou).
70 Hopkins 1983, 31–119.
71 Kaimio 1979; Burke 1987, 79–94.
72 Kaimio 1979.
73 At Cumae, much of the Greek population fled in 421 BC. Liv. 4.44.12; Diod. 12.76.4; Dion. Hal. 15.6.4. For the alleged suppression of Greek language and customs at Paestum, see Athen. 16.632a.
74 Livy 40.42.13.
75 Livy 8.11.13–16, 14.11.
76 CIL 1².582; Vetter 1953, no. 2.
77 Vetter 1953, nos. 108–13.
78 IG 14.645; CIL 10.123, 125.
79 Mayer 1990.

80 For example, IG 14.624, 627, 789, 806, 870, 868.
81 Sherk 1970, 71–2.
82 Ebner 1970; Pugliese Carratelli 1970.
83 IG 14.617. *Prtyane/archon*: Sex. Numonius Sex. F. Maturus; *Synprytaneis*: K. Hortorius K.F. Balbillus, M. Pemponius M.F. Pulcher, M. Cornelius M.F. Martialis; *Hieroskopoi*: M. Cornelius Verus, G. Antonius Thytes; *Hierosalpistes*: G. Julius Reginus; *Hierokeryx*: G. Calpurnius Verus; *Hieroparektes*: K. Caecilius Reginus; *Tamias*: Melphthongos Matourou; *Spondaules*: Natalis; *Kapnauges*: Helikon Matourou.
84 Ebner 1962, 125–36; Pugliese Carratelli 1970, 243–8; Sartori 1953, 53; Macri Li Gotti 1977.
85 Forni 1957–8, 61–70; SEG 1.418; Ebner 1970, 262–70. For parallels, see IG 14.12 (Syracuse), 256 (Gela), 258 (Segesta), 3.1.741, 745, 897 (Athens). The decrees in honour of Pelops Dexiai of Naples (IG 7.342, 505) are more elaborate examples of the same genre.
86 MAMA 8.408, 409, 410; Hardie 1983, 2–14.
87 IG 14.760.
88 Cic. Balb. 24, 55; Dion. Hal. 6.17.2; Val. Max 1.1.1. For other Neapolitan priestesses of Demeter, see Correra 1904 (Cominia Plutogenia); IG 14.702 (Terentia Paranome); CIL 10.1812 (Sabina).
89 CIL 10.111 (. . . *Julia Grammae | uxori incomparabili* . . .), 10.108 (*Futiae | G. Fil | Lollianae | filiae piissimae* . . .), 10.1500 (. . . *coniugi op | timae* . . .), 10.489 (. . . *Aur. Olympiadi kastissi | mae femine* . . .).
90 EE 8.245–6, 10.1492.
91 CIL 10.482 (Paestum); CIL 10.1489, IG 14.758 (Naples); CIL 10.108 (Croton).
92 Sherk 1970, 63–7, 71–2.
93 Wallace-Hadrill 1990.
94 CIL 10.1489; IG 14.737, 746, 758; AE 1954, 186.
95 Galante 1893–6, 5–24.
96 Bowersock 1965.
97 Suet. Nero 12, 20–5.
98 Plut. Cat. Mai. 3.7.
99 D'Arms 1970, 55–61.
100 D'Arms 1970, 48–55.
101 Cic. Arch. 4–7.
102 Hardie 1983, 2–14.
103 Geer 1935, 208–21; Arnold 1960, 241–51.
104 For example, IG 14.729.
105 Strab. 5.4, 5.4.7.
106 Cartledge and Spawforth 1989, 105–19; Jones 1940, 158–9, 171–2.
107 Spawforth and Walker 1986, 100–1; Cartledge and Spawforth, 1989, 105–19.
108 Spawforth and Walker 1985, 78–90.
109 Bowie 1974, 188–90.
110 Spawforth and Walker 1985 and 1986.
111 Spawforth and Walker 1986, 88–96.
112 Bowie 1974, 197–9.
113 Philost. Vit. Soph. 1.22; Strab. 2.3.4; App. BC 5.50; Bowie 1974, 198–201.
114 CIL 9.239; Cic. Sen. 39; Powell 1988, 181–4.

115 Bowersock 1965.
116 Syme 1939, 276–7, 459–75.
117 Gruen 1991, 11–20.
118 Gellner 1983, 8–13.
119 Gasperini 1971; Susini 1962, 20.
120 Pensabene 1975, 264–97.
121 Pensabene 1975, 264–97.
122 Gasperini 1971; Lomas 1991, 233.
123 Degrassi 1957, 10–12 dates the emergence of the D[is] M[anibus] type of epitaph to the 50s AD, but it did not come into widespread use until the beginning of the second century. For the dating of the Sallentine H.S.E inscriptions, see Susini 1962, 66.
124 Susini 1962, 60–6.
125 Galante 1893–6, 5–24.
126 Ebner 1966, 337–41 and 1970, 262–6.
127 Frederiksen 1984, 285–318 (=PBSR 27, 1959).
128 Lomas 1991, 231–9.
129 Strab. 6.1.2

Bibliography

Adamesteanu, D. (1973) 'La suddivisione di terra di Metaponto', in M.I. Finley (ed.), *Problèmes de la terre en Grèce ancienne*, Paris.

Albore Livadie, C. (1975) 'Remarques sur un groupe de tombes de Cumes', *Contribution á l'étude de la société et de la colonisation eubéenes. Cahiers du Centre Jean Bérard* 2, 53–8.

Amandry, P. (1949) 'Le monument commémoratif de la victoire des Tarentins sur les Peucétians', *BCH* 73, 447–63.

Ampolo, C. (1980) 'La formazione della città nel Lazio', *DdA* 2, 2-234.

Arnold, I.R. (1960) 'Agonistic festivals in Italy and Sicily', *American Journal of Archaeology* 64, 241–51.

Arthur, P. (1991) *Romans in Northern Campania*, London.

Astin, A. (1978) *Cato the Censor*, Oxford.

Austin, R.G. (1976) *P. Vergili Maronis Aeneidos Lib. VI*, Oxford.

Badian, E. (1958) *Foreign Clientelae*, Oxford.

Balsdon, J.P.V.D. (1979) *Romans and Aliens*, London.

Barker, G. and Hodges, R. (eds) (1981) *Archaeology and Italian Society*, 2 vols, Oxford.

Barker, G. and Lloyd, J.A. (eds) (1991) *Roman Landscapes. Archaeological Survey in the Mediterranean Region*, London.

Beard, M. (1990) 'Priesthood in the Roman Republic', in M. Beard and J.A. North (eds), *Pagan Priests*, London.

Beard, M. and North, J.A. (eds) (1990) *Pagan Priests*, London

Beloch, K.J. (1890) *Campanien*, Breslau.

Bengtson, H. (1954/5) 'Randbemerkungen zu den Koinischen Asylierkunden', *Historia* 3, 456–63.

Bérard, J. (1941) *La colonisation grecque de l'Italie Méridionale et de la Sicile dans l'Antiquité. L'histoire et la légende*, Paris.

Boardman, J. (1980) *The Greeks Overseas*, 3rd edn, London.

Boersma, J. and Yntema, D. (1987) *Valesio: Storia di un insediamento Apulo*, Fasano.

Bowersock, G.W. (1965) *Augustus and the Greek World*, Oxford.

—— (1990) *Hellenism in Late Antiquity*, Cambridge.

Bowie, E.L. (1974) 'The Greeks and their past in the Second Sophistic', in M.I. Finley (ed.) *Studies in Ancient Society*, London.

Braccesi, L. (1974) 'Roma e Alessandro Il Molosso nella tradizione Liviana', *Rend. Ist. Lomb.* 108, 196–202.

Braccesi, V. (ed.) (1990) *Studi sulla grecità di occidente*, Venice.

Braudel, F. (1973) *The Mediterranean and the Mediterranean World in the Age of Philip II*, 2 vols, 2nd edn, London.

Brauer, G. (1986) *Taras: Its History and Coinage*, New York.

Breglia, L. (1947–8) 'Le "Campano-Tarentine" e la presunta lega monetale fra Taranto e Napoli', *RAAN* 23, 227–47.

Brunt, P.A. (1971) *Italian Manpower 225 BC–AD 14*, Oxford.

Bruun, P. (ed.) (1975) *Studies in the Romanisation of Etruria*, Rome.

Buck, C.D. (1904) *Grammar of Oscan and Umbrian*, Boston.

Buchner, G., Morelli, D. and Nenci, G. (1952) 'Fonti per la storia di Napoli antica', *PdP* 7, 370–419.

Burke, P. (1987) *The Historical Anthropology of Early Modern Italy*, Cambridge.

Burzachechi, M. (1967) 'Gli studi di epigrafia greca relativi alla Magna Grecia dal 1952 al 1967', *Acts of the 5th International Congress of Greek and Latin Epigraphy*, 125–34.

Calderone, S. (1955) "Η ἀρχαία 'Ιταλία', *Messana* 4, 77–124.

—— (1976) 'La Conquista Romana di Magna Grecia', *La Magna Grecia in Età Romana. Atti del 15° Convegno di Studi di Magna Grecia*, 30–81.

Camodeca, G. (1982) 'Ascesa al senato e rapporti con i territori d'origine Italia Regio I (Campania, esclusa di zona di Capua e Cales), Regio II (Apulia e Calabria), Regio III (Lucania e Bruttium)', in *Epigrafia e Ordine Senatorio*, Rome.

Cantarella, R. (1968) "Η Μεγαλη 'Ελλας', *La città e il suo territorio. Atti del 7° Conveeno di Studi di Magna Grecia*, 11–28.

Carter, J.C. (1978) *Ancient Crossroads: The Rural Population of Classical Italy*, Austin.

—— (1981) 'Rural settlement at Metaponto', in E. Barker and R. Hodges (eds), *Archaeology and Italian Society*, vol. 2, London.

—— (1984) 'Crotone', *Crotone. Atti di 23° Convegno sulla studi di Magna Grecia*, 169–77.

—— (1990) 'Metapontum – land, wealth and population', in J.P. Descoeudres (ed.), *Greek Colonists and Native Populations*, Canberra and Oxford.

Cartledge, P. and Spawforth, A.J.S. (1989) *Hellenistic and Roman Sparta. A Tale of Two Cities*, London.

Cary, M. (1920) 'The Early Roman treaties with Tarentum and Rhodes', *J. Phil.* 35, 164–73.

Càssola, F. (1962) *I gruppi politici romani nel III secolo a.C.*, Trieste.

—— (1986) 'Problemi di storia neapolitana', *Neapolis: Atti del 25° Convegno di Studi sulla Magna Grecia*, 37–82.

Castren, P. (1975) *Ordo Populusque Pompeianus. Polity and Society in Roman Pompeii*, Acta Inst. Romani Finlandiae, 8, Rome.

Cazzaniga, I. (1971) 'L'estensione alla Sicilia della espressione Magna Grecia in Strabone', *PdP* 26, 26–31.

Cébeillac-Gervasioni, M. (ed.) (1983) *Les 'bourgeoisies' municipales Italiennes aux IIᵉ et Iᵉʳ siècles av. J.-C.*, Paris and Naples.

Champion, T.C. (ed.) (1989) *Centre and Periphery. Comparative Studies in Archaeology*, London.

Ciaceri, E. (1926–40) *Storia della Magna Grecia*, 3 vols, 2nd edn, 1: 1926, 2: 1940, 3: 1932, Rome.

—— (1931–2) 'La cooperazione navale delle città Italiote alla vittoria Romana nella Prima Guerra Punica', *ARAN* 12, 39–59.

Coarelli, F., Musti, D. and Solin, H. (eds) (1982) *Delo e l'Italia*, Opuscula. Inst. Rom. Finlandiae, 11.

Conway, R.S. (1897) *The Italic Dialects*, 2 vols, Cambridge.

Cook, B.F. (1971) 'Two "Lost" Greek inscriptions', *Ant. Journ.* 51, 260–6.

Coppola, A. (1990) 'Diomede in età Augustea. Appunti su Iullo Antonio' in V. Braccesi (ed.), *Studi sulla grecità di occidente*, Venice.

Cordano, F. (1974) 'Il culto di Artemis a Rhegium', *PdP* 29, 86-90.

Correra, L. (1904) 'Miscellenea Epigrafica', *MDAI(R)* 19, 183–7.

Costabile, F. (1978) *Municipium Locrensium*, Naples.

—— (1979) 'Il culto di Apollo quale testimonianza delle tradizioni corali e religiose di Reggio e Messana', *MEFR* 91, 525–45.

Crawford, M.H. (1973a) 'Paestum and Rome: the form and function of a subsidiary coinage', in *La Monetazione di bronzo di Poseidonia-Paestum. Atti del III° Convegno del Centro Internazionale e Studi Numismatici*, Annali di Istituto Italiano di Numismatici, Suppl. 18–19, 47–110.

—— (1973b) 'Foedus and Sponsio', *PBSR* 28, 1–7.

—— (1985) *Coinage and Money under the Roman Republic*, London.

—— (ed.) (forthcoming) *Roman Statutes*, Oxford.

D'Agostino, B. (1968) 'Pontecagnano – Tombe orientalizzanti in contrada S Antonio', *NSc*, 78–205.

—— (1977) *Tombe 'principesche' dell'orientalizzante antico da Pontecagnano*, MAL, ser. misc. 2.

D'Andria, F. (1975) 'Metaponto Romana', *ACMG* 15, 539–44.

—— (1979) 'Salento arcaico: le nuove documentazione archeologica', in *Salento arcaico. Atti del colloquio internazionale, Lecce 1979*, Galantina, 15–28.

—— (1989) 'Il Salento e le sue radici indigene: le origini Messapiche', in S. Moscati (ed.), *Salento Porta d'Italia*, Lecce.

—— (1990) *Archeologia dei Messapici*, Bari.

D'Arms, J.H. (1970) *Romans on the Bay of Naples*, Harvard.

—— (1974) 'Puteoli in the second century', *JRS* 64, 104–24.

Daux, G. (1949) *Pausanias à Delphes*, Paris.

Davies, J.F.K. (1971) *Athenian Propertied Families*, Oxford.

De Caro, S. and Greco, A. (1981) *Campania*, Rome and Bari.

De Franciscis, A. (1972) *Stato e Società in Locri Epizefiri*, Naples.

De Iuliis, E. (1985) 'La ricerca archeologica in Puglia', *MG* 20 (1–2), 17.

De Martino, F. (1952) 'Le istituzioni di Napoli greco-romana', *PdP* 7, 335–43.

De Polignac, F. and Gualtieri, M. (1991) 'A rural landscape in western Lucania', in G. Barker and J.A. Lloyd (eds), *Roman Landscapes. Archaeological Survey in the Mediterranean Region*, London.

De Sensi Sestito, G. (1984) 'La funzione politica dell'Heraion del Lacinio al tempo delle lotte contro i Lucani e Dionisio I', in M. Sordi (ed.), *I Santuari e la Guerra nel Mondo Classico*, Milan.

—— (1987) 'Taranto post-Architea nel giudizio di Timeo. Nota a Strabo 6.3.4 C280', *11ᵃ Miscellenea Greca e Romana*, Rome, 84–113.

Degrassi, A. (1950) 'Quattuorviri in colonie Romane e in municipi retti da duoviri', *Mem. Linc.* 8.2, 281–344.

—— (1957) *L'epigrafia Latina in Italia nell'ultimo ventennio e i criteri del nuovo insegnamento*, Padua.

Delano Smith, C. (1979) *Western Mediterranean Europe. A Historical Geography of Italy, Spain and Southern France since the Neolithic*, London.

—— (1987) 'The Neolithic environment of the Tavoliere', in G.D.B. Jones (ed.), *Apulia*, vol. 1, London.

Deniaux, E. (1980–1) 'Civitate donati: Naples, Heraclée, Côme', *Ktema* 6, 133–41.

Descoeudres, J.-P. (ed.) (1990) *Greek Colonists and Native Populations*, Proceedings of the First Australian Congress of Classical Archaeology, Canberra and Oxford.

Duncan-Jones, R. (1974) *The Economy of the Roman Empire*, Cambridge.

Duthoy, R. (1974) 'La Fonction sociale de l'Augustalité', *Epigraphica* 36, 134–54.

Dyson, S.L. (1992) *Community and Society in Roman Italy*, Baltimore.

Ebner, P. (1962) 'Scuole di Medicina a Velia e a Salerno', *Apollo* 2, 125–136.

—— (1964) 'L'Athenaion, santuario estramurano di Velia', *PdP* 19, 72–6.

—— (1965) 'Atene in un iscrizione di Velia', *AC* 17, 306–9.

—— (1966) 'Nuove epigrafi di Velia', *PdP* 21, 337–41.

—— (1970) 'Nuove iscrizioni di Velia', *PdP* 25, 262-6.

Evans, A.J. (1889) 'The horsemen of Tarentum. A contribution towards the numismatic history of Greater Greece', *Num. Chron.*, 1–228.

Finley, M.I. (ed.) (1973) *Problèmes de la terre en Grèce ancienne*, Paris.

—— (ed.) (1974) *Studies in Ancient Society*, London.

—— (1975a) *Ancient History, Evidence and Models*, London.

—— (1975b), 'The Ancient Greeks and their nation', in *The Use and Abuse of History*, London.

Fishwick, D. (1966) 'The *Cannophori* and the March Festival of the Magna Mater', *TAPA* 9, 139–202.

Flacelière, R. (1937) *Les Aitoliens à Delphes*, Paris.

Forni, G. (1957–8) 'Intorno alle costituzioni di città greche in Italia e in Sicili', *Kokalos* 3, 61–100.

Frank, T. (1933) *An Economic Survey of Ancient Rome. Rome and Italy of the Republic*, vol. I, New York.

—— (1940) *An Economic Survey of Ancient Rome. Rome and Italy of the Empire*, vol. V, New York.

Franke, P.R. (1989) 'Pyrrhus', *Cambridge Ancient History* 7 (2), 2nd Edn, Cambridge, 456–85.

Fraschetti, A. (1981) 'Aristosseno, i romani e la "barbarizzazione" di Poseidonia', *AION* 3, 97–115.

Frayn, J.M. (1984) *Sheep Raising and the Wool Trade in Italy during the Roman Period*, Liverpool.

Frederiksen, M.W. (1959) 'Republican Capua: a social and economic study' *PBSR* 33, 189–306.

—— (1968) 'Campanian cavalry: a question of origins', *DdA* 2, 3–31.

—— (1984) *Campania*, ed. N. Purcell, London.

Gabba, E. (1988) 'La pastorizia nell'età tardo-imperiale in Italia', in C.R. Whittaker (ed.), *Pastoral Economies in Classical Antiquity*, Cambridge Philological Society, Suppl. 14.

Gabba, E. and Pasquinucci, M. (1977) *Strutture agrarie a allevamente trasumante nell'Italia romana (III–I sec. a.C.)*, Pisa.

Gabrici, E. (1913) 'Cuma', *MAL* 22.

Galante, G.A. (1893–6) 'Il sepolcro ritrovato in Napoli sotto il palazzo Di Donato in via Cristallini ai Vergini', *AAAN* 17, 5–24.

Garoufalias, E. (1979) *Pyrrhus*, London.

Gasperini, L. (1967) 'Note di Epigrafia Tarentina', *Acts of the 5th International Congress of Greek and Latin Epigraphy*, 135–40.

—— (1968) 'Su alcune epigrafia di Taranto Romana', *Seconda Miscellenea Greca e Romana*, Rome, 379–98.

—— (1971) 'Il Municipio Tarantino: Ricerche epigrafica', *Terza Miscellenea Greca e Romana*, Rome, 143–209.

—— (1980) 'Tarentina Epigraphica', *Settima Miscellenea Greca e Romana*, Rome.

—— (1984) 'Un buleuta Alessandrino a Taranto', in *Studi in onore di A. Adriani*, Rome.

Gauthier, P. (1972) *Symbola. Les étrangers et la justice dans les cités Grecques*, Nancy.

Geer, R.M. (1935) 'The Greek games at Naples', *TAPA* 66, 208–21.

Geertz, C. (1973) *The Interpretation of Cultures*, New York.

Gellner, E. (1983) *Nations and Nationalism*, Cambridge.

Ghinatti, F. (1961–2) 'Ricerche sulla Lega Italiota', *Atti Accad. Patav.* 74, 117–33.

—— (1967) 'Ricerche sui culti greci di Napoli in età Romana imperiale', *Atene e Roma* 12, 98–100.

—— (1974) 'Riti et Feste Della Magna Grecia', *Critica Storica* 2, 533–76.

—— (1977a) 'Magna Grecia Post-Annibalica', *QS* 5, 147–60.

—— (1977b) 'Magna Grecia Post-Annibalica', *QS* 6, 99–115.

—— (1980) 'Nuovi efori in epigrafi di Eraclea di Lucania', *In Forschungen und Funden, Festschrift Neutsch*, Innsbruck, 137–43.

Ghiron-Bistagne, P. (1976) *Recherches sur les Acteurs dans le Grèce Antique*, Paris.

Giannelli, C.A. (1969) 'L'Intervento di Archidamo e di Alessandro il Molosso in Magna Grecia', *CS* 8, 1–22.

—— (1974) 'Gli interventi di Cleonimo e di Agatocle in Magna Grecia', *CS* 13, 353–80.

Giannelli, G. (1963) *Culti e Miti della Magna Grecia*, Florence.

Giardina, A. and Schiavone, A. (eds) (1981) *Società romana e produzione schiavistica I. L'Italia: Insediamenti e forme economiche*, Rome and Bari.

Gigante, M. (1964) 'Parmenide Uliade', *PdP* 19, 450–2.

—— (1967) 'Teatro greco in Magna Grecia', *Annali Ist. Ital per gli Studi Storici* 1, 35–87.

—— (1980) 'Sulla *defixio* Metapontina', *PdP* 35, 381–2.

Gomme, E. (1970) *A Commentary on Thucydides*, Oxford.

Gordon, A. (1990a) 'From Republic to Principate: priesthood, religion and ideology', in M. Beard and J.A. North (eds), *Pagan Priests*, London.

—— (1990b) 'The veil of power: emperors, sacrificers and benefactors' in M. Beard and J.A. North (eds), *Pagan Priests*, London.

Gossage, A.G. (1975) 'The comparative chronology of inscriptions relating to the Boeotian festivals in the first half of the first century BC', *ABSA*, 115–34.

Graham, A.J. (1990) 'Pre-Colonial contacts: questions and problems', in J.-P. Descoeudres (ed.), *Greek Colonists and Native Populations*, Camberra and Oxford.

Greco, A.P. (1979) 'Segni di trasformazioni sociali a Poseidonia tra la fine del V e gli inizi del III sec. a.C.', *DdA* 1 (2), 27–50.

Greco, E. (1970) 'In margine a Strabone', *PdP* 25, 416–20.

—— (1981) *Magna Grecia*, Bari.

Gruen, E.S. (1984) *The Hellenistic World and the Coming of Rome*, Berkeley.

—— (1991) *Studies in Greek Culture and Roman Policy*, Leiden.

Gualandi, M.L., Palozzi, C. and Paoletti, M. (1981) 'La Lucania orientale', in A. Giardina and A. Schiavone (eds), *Società romana e produzione schiavistica I. L'Italia: Insediamenti e forme economiche*, Rome and Bari.

Guarducci, M. (1936) 'L'istituzione della fratria nella Grecia antica e nelle colonie Greche d'Italia', *Mem. Linc.*, 6.6.1.

—— (1970) 'Nuovi cippi di Velia', *PdP* 25, 252–61.

Guzzo, P.G. (1981) 'Il territorio dei Bruttii', in A. Giardina and A. Schiavone (eds.), *Società romana e produzione schiavistica I. L'Italia: Insediamenti e forme economiche*, Rome and Bari.

—— (1983) 'Lucanians, Bruttians and Italiote Greeks in the 4th and 3rd centuries BC', in T. Hackens, N.D. Holloway and R.R. Holloway (eds), *The Crossroads of the Mediterranean*, Louvain and Providence.

Hackens, T., Holloway, N.D. and Holloway, R.R. (eds) (1983) *The Crossroads of the Mediterranean*, Louvain and Providence.

Hardie, A. (1983) *Statius and the Silvae. Poets, Patrons and Epideixis in the Graeco-Roman World*, Liverpool.

Harris, W.V. (1971) *Rome in Etruria and Umbria*, Oxford.

Hatzfeld, J. (1912) 'Les Italiens Residants à Delos', *BCH* 36,5-218.

—— (1919) *Les Trafiquants Italiens dans l'Orient Hellénique*, Paris.

Head, B.V. (1911) *Historia Numorum*, 2nd edn, Oxford.

Herring, E. (1991a) 'Power relations in south-east Italy', in E. Herring, R. Whitehouse and J. Wilkins (eds), *The Archaeology of Power*, London.

—— (1991b) 'Socio-political change in the south Italian Iron Age and Classical Periods: an application of the Peer Polity Interaction Model', *Accordia Research Papers* 2, 33–54.

Herring, E., Whitehouse, R. and Wilkins, J. (eds) (1991) *The Archaeology of Power. Proceedings of the 4th International Conference of Italian Archaeology*, London.

Hopkins, K. (1978) *Conquerors and Slaves*, Cambridge.

—— (1983) *Death and Renewal*, Cambridge.

Horn, H. (1930) *Foederatae*, Frankfurt.

Jacoby, F. (1923-58) *Die Fragmente der Griechischen Historiker*, Berlin and Leiden.

Jeffery, L.H. (1961) *The Local Scripts of Archaic Greece*, Oxford.

Jones, A.H.M. (1940) *The Greek City*, Oxford.

Jones, G.D.B. (ed.) (1987) *Apulia*, vol. 1, London.

Jongman, W. (1988) *The Economy and Society of Pompeii*, Amsterdam.

Kahrstedt, U. (1960) *Der Wirtschaftsliche Lage Grossgriechenlands unter der Kaiserzeit*, Historia einzelschriften 4.

Kaimio, J. (1975) 'The ousting of Etruscan by Latin in Etruria', in P. Bruun (ed.), *Studies in the Romanisation of Etruria*, Rome.

—— (1979) *The Romans and the Greek Language*, Helsinki.

Kajanto, I. (1968) 'The significance of non-Latin cognomina', *Latomus* 27, 517–34.

Keppie, L.J.F. (1983) *Colonisation and Veteran Settlement in Italy, 14–47 BC*, London.

Kilian, K. (1990) 'Mycenaean colonisation: norm and variety', in J.P. Descoeudres (ed.), *Greek Colonists and Native Populations*, Canberra and Oxford.

Laffi, U. (1973) 'Sull'organizzazione amministrative dell'Italia dopo la guerra sociale', *Akten des VI Internationalen Kongress für Griechische und Lateinische Epigraphik. München 1972*, 37–54.

—— (1983) 'I senati locali nell'Italia repubblicana', in M. Cébeillac-Gervasioni (ed.), *Les 'bourgeoisies' municipales Italiennes aux IIᵉ et Iᵉʳ siècles av. J.-C.*, Paris and Naples.

La Genière, J. de (1979) 'The Iron Age in southern Italy', in D. Ridgway and F.R. Ridgway (eds), *Italy Before the Romans*, London.

Larsen, J.A.O. (1968) *Greek Federal States. Their Institutions and History*, Oxford.

Launey, M. (1950) *Recherches sur les Armées Héllenistiques*, Paris.

Lefkowitz, M.R. (1959) 'Pyrrhus' negotiations with the Romans, 280–278 BC', *HSCP* 64, 147–77.

Lepore, E. (1967) 'La Vita Politica e Sociale', in *Storia di Napoli*, vol. I, Naples, 139–372.

—— (1983) 'Roma e le città greche o ellenizzati nell'Italia meridionale', in M. Cébeillac-Gervasioni, *Les 'bourgeoisies' municipales Italiennes aux IIᵉ et Iᵉʳ siècles av. J.-C.*, Paris and Naples.

Lévèque, P. (1957) *Pyrrhos*, Paris.

—— (1970) 'Problèmes Historiques de l'époque Héllenistique en Grand Grèce', *La Magna Grecia nel mondo ellenistico. Atti di 9ᵉ Convegno sulla studi di Magna Grecia*, 29–70.

Levi, A. (1926) 'Camere sepolcrali scoperte in Napoli durante i lavori della direttissima Roma-Napoli', *MAL* 31, 378–402.

Liebeschuetz, J.H.W.G. (1979) *Continuity and Change in Roman Religion*, Oxford.

Lippolis, G. (1984) 'Le terme pentascinenses di Taranto', *Taras* 4, 119–53.

Lomas, K. (1991) 'Local identity and cultural imperialism. Epigraphy and the diffusion of Romanisation in Italy', in E. Herring, R. Whitehouse and J. Wilkins (eds), *The Archaeology of Power*, London.

Lo Porto, F. (1967) 'Stipe del culto di Demetra Heraclea di Lucania', in B. Neutsch (ed.), *Archaeologisches Forschungen in Lukanien. Herakleiastudien*, *MDAI(R)*, Suppl. 11.

—— (1980) 'Medici Pitagorici in una *defixio* greca da Metaponto', *PdP* 35, 282–8.

—— (1986) *Napoli Antica*, Naples.

Macmullen, R. (1982) 'The epigraphic habit in the Roman Empire', *AJP* 103, 233–46.

Macri Li Gotti, M.V. (1977) 'Greco λαυκελαρχευω, etrusco *lucairce*, miceneo *rawaketa*', *Rend. Ist. Lomb.* 111, 273–84.

Maddoli, G. (1982) 'Il concetto di Magna Grecia: Gennesi di un realtà storico-politiche', *Megale Hellas: Nome e immagine. Atti di 21° Convegno sulla studi di Magna Grecia*, 9–30.

—— (1984) 'I Culti di Crotone', *Crotone. Atti di 23° Convegno sulla studi di Magna Grecia*, 313–43.

Magaldi, E. (1947) *Lucania Romana*. Rome.

Maiuri, A. (1913a) 'Cuma – Altra stele sepolcrale con iscrizione Osca', *Notizie degli Scavi*, 53–4.

—— (1913b) 'La nuova iscrizione della fratria Napoletana degli Artemisi', *SR* 1, 21–36.

Mancinetti Santamaria, G. (1982) 'Filostrato di Ascalona, banchiere in Delo', in F. Coarelli, D. Musti and H. Solin (eds), *Delo e l'Italia*, Opuscula. Inst. Rom. Finlandiae, 11.

—— (1983) 'La concessione della cittadinanza a greci e orientali', in M. Cébeillac-Gervasioni (ed.), *Les 'bourgeoisies' municipales Italiennes aux IIe et Ier siècles av. J.-C.*, Paris and Naples.

Manni, E. (1962) 'Alessandro Il Molosso e la sua spedizione in Italia', *Studi Sallentini* 14, 344–52.

Marchese, R. (ed.) (1983) *Aspects of Graeco-Roman Urbanism: Essays on the Classical City*, British Archaeological Report 188, Oxford.

Marshall, B.M. (1968) 'Friends of the Roman people', *AJP* 89, 39-55.

Mason, H.J. (1974) *Greek Terms for Roman Institutions: A Lexicon and Analysis*, Toronto.

Matthaei, L. (1907) 'On the classification of Roman Allies', *CQ* 1, 182–204.

Mayer, E.A. (1990) 'Explaining the epigraphic habit in the Roman Empire: the evidence of epitaphs', *JRS* 80, 74–96.

Mello, M. (1974) *Paestum Romana*, Rome.

Mello, M. and Voza, G. (1968) *Le Iscrizioni Latine di Paestum*, Naples.

Meloni, P. (1950) 'L'Intervento di Cleonimo in Magna Grecia', *Giornale Italiano di Filologia* 3, 103–21.

Mertens, D. (1983) 'Aspetti dell'archittetura a Crotone', *Crotone. Atti di 23° Convegno sulla studi di Magna Grecia*, 189–231.

Metzger, H. (1967) 'L'Imagerie de Grand Grèce et les textes littéraires à l'époque classique', *Litteratura e arte figurata nella Magna Grecia. Atti di 6° Convegno sulla studi di Magna Grecia*, 151–81.

Milan, A. (1973) 'I "Socii Navales"', *Critica Storica* 10, 193–221.

Mingazzini, P. (1954) 'Velia. Scavi 1927. Fornace di mattoni ed antichità varie. Elenco di bolli laterizi statali', *ASMG* 1, 1–55.

Miranda, E. (1982) 'Nuove iscrizioni sacre a Velia', *MEFR* 94, 163–74.

—— (1990) *Iscrizioni greche di Napoli*, Rome.

Mitens, K. (1988) *Teatri greci e teatri ispirati all'architettura greca in Sicilia e nell'Italia meridionale c. 350–50 a.C.: Un catalogo*, Rome.

Momigliano, A. (1929) ''Η Μεγάλη 'Ελλάς', *Boll. Filol. Class.* 36, 47–9.

—— (1959) 'Atene nel III secolo a.C. e la scoperta di Roma nella storie di Timeo di Tauromenio', *RSI* 71, 529–56.

Mommsen, T. (1888) *Römisches Staatsrecht*, vol. III.I, Leipzig.

Morel, J.P. (1978) 'La Laine de Tarente', *Ktema* 3–4, 94–110.

BIBLIOGRAPHY

—— (1983) 'Greek colonisation in Italy and the West', in T. Hackens, N.D. Holloway and R.R. Holloway (eds), *The Crossroads of the Mediterranean*, Louvain and Providence.

Moretti, L. (1953) *Iscrizioni agonistiche greche*, Rome.

—— (1957) 'Olympionikai: I vincitori negli antiche agone Olympici', *Mem. Linc.* 8.8, 55–200.

—— (1965) 'Epigraphica', *RFIC* 93, 73–9.

—— (1971) 'Problemi di storia tarantina', *Taranto nella civiltà della Magna Grecia. Atti di 10° Convegno sulla studi di Magna Grecia*, 21–66.

Moscati, S. (ed.) (1989) *Salento Porta d'Italia*, Lecce.

Musitelli, S. (1980) 'Ancora su φωλαρχοι di Velia', *PdP* 35, 240–55.

Musti, D. (1966) 'Fonti per la storia di Velia', *PdP* 21, 318–35.

—— (1985a) 'Strutture cittadine e funzione del santuario', in D. Musti (ed.), *Le Tavole di Locri. Atti del colloquio sugli aspetti politici, economici, cultuali e linguistici dei testi dell'archivio locrese*, Naples.

—— (ed.) (1985b) *Le Tavole di Locri. Atti del colloquio sugli aspetti politici, economici, cultuali e linguistici dei testi dell'archivio locrese*, Naples.

—— (1988) *Strabone e Magna Grecia*, Padua.

Napoli, M. (1959) *Napoli Greco-Romana*, Naples.

—— (1978) *Civiltà di Magna Grecia*, Naples.

Nava, M. (1990) 'Greek and Adriatic influences in Daunia in the Early Iron Age', in J.P. Descoeudres (ed.), *Greek Colonists and Native Populations*, Canberra and Oxford.

Nenci, G. (1966) 'L'Heraion di Metaponto (Plinio N.H. 14.2.9)', *PdP* 21, 128–31.

Neutsch, B. (ed.) *Archaeologisches Forschungen in Lukanien. Heraklciastudien, MDAI(R)*, Suppl. 11.

Nisbet, R.G.M. and Hubbard, M. (1970) *A Commentary on Horace: Odes 1*, Oxford.

North, J.A. (1976) 'Conservation and change in Roman religion', *PBSR* 44, 1–12.

Nutton, V. (1970) 'The medical school of Velia', *PdP* 25, 211–25.

O'Connor, J.B. (1908) *Chapters in the History of Actors and Acting in Ancient Greece*, Chicago.

Ogilvie, R.M. (1965) *A Commentary on Livy Books 1–5*, Oxford.

Orr, D.G. (1983) 'The Roman city: a philosophical and cultural summa', in R. Marchese (ed.) *Aspects of Graeco-Roman Urbanism: Essays on the Classical City*, British Archaeological Report 188, Oxford.

Ostrow, S. (1985) '*Augustales* along the Bay of Naples: a case for their growth', *Historia* 34–5, 65–101.

Paget, J. (1968) 'The ancient port of Cumae', *JRS* 58, 152–69.

Pallottino, M. (1991) *A History of Earliest Italy*, London.

Paratore, E. (1977), 'Virgilio e Cuma', in *I Campi Flegrei nell'archeologia e nell'Arte*, Atti di Convegno dei Lincei 33, Rome, 9–39.

Parlangèli, O. (1960) *Studi Messapici*, Milan.

Patterson, J.R. (1987) 'Crisis: what crisis? Rural change and development in imperial Appennine Italy', *PBSR* 55, 115–46.

—— (1990) 'Settlement, city and élite in Samnium and Lycia', in J. Rich and A.F. Wallace-Hadrill (eds), *City and Country in the Ancient World*, London.

233

Pearson, L. (1987) *The Greek Historians of the West: Timaeus and his Predecessors*, Atlanta.

Pedley, J.G. (1990) *Paestum. Greeks and Romans in Southern Italy*, London.

Pellegrini, G. (1903) 'Tombe greche arcaiche e tomba greco-sannitica a *tholos* della necropoli di Cuma', *MAL* 13, 204–94.

Pensabene, P. (1975) 'Cippi funerari di Taranto', *MDAI(R)* 82, 264–97.

—— (1990) 'Il tempio ellenistico di S Leucio di Canosa', in M. Torelli (ed.), *Italici in Magna grecia. Lingua, insediamenti e strutture*, Venosa.

Peroni, R. (1983) 'Presenze Micenee e forme socio-economiche nell'Italia protostorica', *La Magna Grecia e il mondo miceneo. Atti di 21° Convegno sulla studi di Magna Grecia*, 211–83.

Peter, H. (1914) *Historicorum Romanorum Reliquiae*, Leipzig.

Peterson, R.M. (1919) *The Cults of Campania*, Rome.

Petrochilos, N. (1974) *Roman Attitudes to the Greeks*, Athens.

Pinsent, J. (1969) 'The magistracy at Naples', *PdP* 24, 368–72.

Powell, J.G.F. (1988) *Cicero Cato Maior de Senectute*, Cambridge.

Pugliese Carratelli, G. (1952a) 'Sul culto delle Sirene nel golfo di Napoli', *PdP* 7, 420–6.

—— (1952b) 'Napoli Antica', *PdP* 7, 243–68.

—— (1955) 'Un decreto di Velia del sec. III a.C.', *ASCL* 24, 1–7.

—— (1962) 'Santuari estramurani in Magna Grecia', *PdP* 17, 241–6.

—— (1963) 'φωλαρχος', *PdP* 18, 385–6.

—— (1969) 'Lazio, Roma, e Magna Grecia prima del sec. IV a.c.', *La Magna Grecia e Roma nell'età arcaica. Atti di 8° Convegno sulla studi di Magna Grecia*, 49–82.

—— (1970) 'Ancora su φωλαρχος', *PdP* 25, 243–8.

—— (1972) 'Sanniti, Lucani, Bruttii e Italioti dal secolo IV a.C.', *Le genti non greche della Magna Grecia. Atti di 11° Convegno sulla studi di Magna Grecia*, 37–54.

—— (ed.) (1983) *Megale Hellas. Storia e civiltà della Magna Grecia*, Milan.

Pulgram, E. (1958) *The Tongues of Italy*, Cambridge, Mass.

Purcell, N. (1985) 'Wine and wealth in Ancient Italy', *JRS* 75, 1-19.

Raviola, F. (1990) 'La tradizione letteraria su Parthenope', in V. Braccesi (ed.) *Studi sulla grecità di occidente*, Venice.

Rawson, E.D. (1985) *Intellectual Life in the Late Roman Republic*, London.

Ribezzo, F. (1924) 'Studi e scoperte di epigrafia osco-lucano nell'ultima decennio', *RIGI* 8, 83–100.

Rich, J. and Wallace-Hadrill, A.F. (eds) (1990) *City and Country in the Ancient World*, London.

Ridgway, D. (1989) 'Archaeology in Sardinia and southern Italy', *Archaeological Reports*, 130–47.

Ridgway, D. and Ridgway, F.R. (eds) (1979) *Italy before the Romans*, London.

Rostagni, A. (1952) 'La cultura letteraria di Napoli antica', *PdP* 7, 344–57.

Rowland, R.J. (1983), 'Rome's earliest imperialism', *Latomus* 42, 749–62.

Rutter, N.K. (1979) *Campanian Coinages 475–380 BC*, Edinburgh.

Salmon, E.T. (1965) *Samnium and the Samnites*, Cambridge.

—— (1980) *The Making of Roman Italy*, London.

Sartori, F. (1953) *Problemi di Storia Costituzionale Italiota*, Rome.

—— (1967) 'Eraclea di Lucania: Profilo storico', in B. Neutsch (ed.), *Archaeologisches Forschungen in Lukanien. Herakleiastudien, MDAI(R)*, Suppl. 11.

BIBLIOGRAPHY

—— (1976) 'Magna Grecia dopo la Conquista Romana', *La Magna Grecia in Età Romana. Atti di 15° Convegno sulla studi di Magna Grecia*, 81–138.

—— (1980) 'Dediche a Demetra in Eraclea Lucana', in *Forschungen und Funden, Festschrift Neutsch*, Innsbruck, 401–15.

Scherillo, A. (1977) 'Vulcanismo e bradisismo nei Campo Flegrei', in *I Campi Flegrei nell'archeologia e nell'Arte*, Atti di Convegno dei Lincei 33, Rome, 81–116.

Schoder, R.V. (1963) 'Ancient Cumae. History, topography and monuments', *Scientific American* 209 (6.12.63), 109–18.

Seiler, F. (1984) 'Un Complesso di Edifici Pubblici nel Lacinio a Capo Colonna', *Crotone. Atti di 23° Convegno sulla studi di Magna Grecia*, 231–42.

Sherk, R.K. (1969) *Rome and the Greek East to the Death of Augustus*, Baltimore.

—— (1970) *The Municipal Decrees of the Roman West*, Buffalo.

Sherwin-White, A.N. (1939) *The Roman Citizenship*, Oxford.

Skydsgaard, J.E. (1974) 'Transhumance in Ancient Italy', *ARID* 7 Suppl., 7–36.

Small, A. (1991) 'Late Roman rural settlement in Basilicata and western Apulia', in G. Barker and J. A. Lloyd (eds), *Roman Landscapes. Archaeological Survey in the Mediterranean Region*, London.

Spadea, R. (1984) 'La topografia', *Crotone. Atti di 23° Convegno sulla studi di Magna Grecia*, 119–61.

Spawforth, A.J.S. and Walker, S. (1985) 'The world of the Panhellenion I', *JRS* 75, 78–104.

—— (1986) 'The world of the Panhellenion II', *JRS* 76, 88–106.

Staveley, E.S. (1959) 'The political aims of Appius Claudius Caecus', *Historia* 4, 418–33.

Susini, G. (1962) *Fonti per la storia Greca e Romana del Salento*, Bologna.

Syme, R. (1939) *The Roman Revolution*, Oxford.

Täubler, E. (1913) *Imperium Romanum*, Leipzig.

Thiel, J.H. (1954) *A History of Roman Sea-Power Before the Second Punic War*, Amsterdam.

Thompson, J. (1988) 'Pastoralism and transhumance in Roman Italy', in C.R. Whittaker (ed.), *Pastoral Economies in Classical Antiquity*, Cambridge Philological Society, Suppl. 14.

Torelli, M. (ed.) (1990) *Italici in Magna grecia. Lingua, insediamenti e strutture*, Venosa.

Toynbee, A.J. (1965) *Hannibal's Legacy*, 2 vols, Oxford.

Tsopanakis, A.G. (1984) 'Postilla su l'εϰβεβαϱβαϱωσθαι di Strabone', *PdP* 39, 139–43.

Turano, C. (1960) 'Note di Epigrafia Classica', *Klearchos* 2, 65-75.

—— (1963) 'Note di Epigrafia Classica', *Klearchos* 5, 76–82.

Uguzzoni, A. and Ghinatti, F. (1968) *Le Tavole Greche Di Eraclea*, Rome.

Vattuone, R. (1976-7) 'Scambi di beni tra ricchi e poveri nel IV sec. a.C. Note sul Archita di Taranto', *RSA* 6–7, 285–300.

Verbrugghe, G.T. (1973) 'The *elogium* from Polla and the First Slave War', *CP* 68, 25–35.

Vetter, E. (1953) *Handbuch der Italischen Dialekte*, Heidelberg.

Veyne, P. (1976) *Bread and Circuses. Historical Sociology and Political Pluralism*, trans. O. Murray 1990, London.

Vollgraff, W. (1919) 'Novae Inscriptiones Argivae', *Mnemosyne* N.S. 47, 252–8.

Von Fritz, K. (1940) *Pythagorean Politics in Southern Italy*, New York.

Walbank, F.W. (1957) *A Historical Commentary on Polybius*, vols 1–3, Oxford.

Wallace-Hadrill, A.F. (1990) 'Roman arches and Greek honours: the language of power at Rome', *PCPS* 36, 143–81.

Walsh, P.G. (1974) *Livy: His Historical Aims and Methods*, Oxford.

Waltzing, J.P. (1895–1900) *Etude sur les Corporations Professionelles Romaines*, Louvain.

Whitehouse, R.D. and Wilkins, J.B. (1989) 'Greeks and natives in south-east Italy: approaches to the archaeological evidence', in T.C. Champion, (ed.), *Centre and Periphery. Comparative Studies in Archaeology*, London.

Wightman, E. (1981) 'The Lower Liri valley: problems, trends and peculiarities', in G. Barker and R. Hodges (eds), *Archaeology and Italian Society*, vol. 2.

Williams, D. (1989) 'Knight Rider. The Piot bronze', *Arch. Anz.*, 529–53.

Wilson, A.J.N. (1966) *Emigration from Italy in the Republican Age of Rome*, Manchester.

Wiseman, T.P. (1970) 'Roman Republican road building', *PBSR* 28, 122–35.

—— (1971) *New Men in the Roman Senate 139 BC–AD 14*, Oxford.

Wuilleumier, P. (1939) *Tarente*, Paris.

Yntema, D. (1982) 'Some notes on Iapygian pottery from the Otranto excavations: a preliminary report', *Studi di Antichità* 3, 62-82.

Zancani Montuoro, P., Stoop, M.W. and Maaskant Kleibrink, M. (1972) 'Francavilla Marittima: Varia', *ASMG* 11–12, 9–82.

Index